# Twentieth-Century Music
# Theory and Practice

# Twentieth-Century Music Theory and Practice

*Edward Pearsall*

Routledge
Taylor & Francis Group

NEW YORK AND LONDON

First published 2012
by Routledge
711 Third Avenue, New York, NY 10017

Simultaneously published in the UK
by Routledge
2 Park Square, Milton Park, Abingdon, Oxon OX14 4RN

*Routledge is an imprint of the Taylor & Francis Group, an informa business*

© 2012 Taylor & Francis

*Library of Congress Cataloging in Publication Data*
Pearsall, Edward, 1954–
   Twentieth-century music theory and practice/Edward Pearsall.
   p. cm.
   1. Music theory—History—20th century. I. Title.
   MT90.P34 2012
   781.09′04—dc23
   2011022241

ISBN: 978–0–415–88895–0 (hbk)
ISBN: 978–0–415–88896–7 (pbk)

Typeset in Caslon by
Florence Production Ltd, Stoodleigh, Devon
Printed and bound in the United States of America on acid-free paper
by Sheridan Books, Inc.

# Table of Contents

## Aural Skills Supplement 254

## Appendices

# Preface

As its title states, this book addresses twentieth-century music theory and practice. It may be surprising to learn, then, that the discussion extends to music that is over a hundred years old as well as music written by living composers. Such a broad span of musical history is included because the aesthetic ideas that emerged in the late nineteenth century are still resonating in the world today. Indeed, many of these ideas arose long before the nineteenth century; J. S. Bach, for example, subjected melodic motifs to inversion, retrogression, and retrograde inversion, important operations in Schoenberg's twelve-tone method.

What we can learn from this is that compositional practice over the last 100 years or so is not so different from that of the more distant past. To be sure, not all music is cut from the same cloth. Western music written before 1890, for example, is primarily tonal, based on functional triadic harmony and drawn from the diatonic collection. Much of the music written after 1890 is not. But this does not mean that music, whether tonal or "post-tonal," does not also incorporate deep principles of organization common to music in general. Instead, it appears that there are a number of musical constants involving motives, textures, instrumentation, and the like that pervade the music of many periods.

*Twentieth-Century Music Theory and Practice* introduces a number of analytical tools for analyzing a wide range of twentieth-century musical styles and genres. Admittedly, these tools have been devised primarily to provide insight into the music of the Second Viennese School and its progeny. To the extent that they express fundamental musical principles, however, they have a much richer applicability. In this text, we will capitalize on this idea by using the theoretical devices most commonly associated with atonality to explore music inclusive of a large number of schools and "isms." Hence, we will encounter composers representing an assortment of twentieth-century trends, including, but not limited to, Paul Hindemith, George Crumb, Ellen Taaffe Zwilich, Steve Reich, Michael Torke, Philip Glass, Alexander Scriabin, Ernest Bloch, Ruth Crawford, Igor Stravinsky, Béla Bartók, Sergei Prokofiev, Arnold Schoenberg, Maurice Ravel, Claude Debussy, Aaron Copland, Lukas Foss, Alfred Schnittke, Leonard Bernstein, and Witold Lutoslawski.

## A Word about Tonality

Since many of the musical examples in this text are drawn from works composed in the tonal tradition and have key signatures, a word about the definition of tonality may be in order here. Tonality is sometimes cast in very broad terms to refer to music that highlights a central tone or tonic, a definition that applies to an exceptionally wide range of musical styles. Many post-tonal works also revolve around centric tones. Such a definition of tonal parameters, then, does not allow for a very nuanced description of musical styles and periods. Unlike most tonal music written before 1890, twentieth-century tonal music often downplays goal-directed harmony based on dominant/tonic polarity. What remains are merely the trappings of tonal music: diatonic collections, triadic harmony, lyrical melodies, etc. In addition to its "tonal" features, such music often incorporates processes associated with post-tonal music such as inversional symmetry, non-tertian harmony, and twelve-tone operations. Works composed under these circumstances are just as accessible to the tools used to analyze post-tonal music as those that have a more modernistic exterior and may even be considered to be a species of post-tonal literature themselves. It is for this reason, and because they too are an integral part of the twentieth-century milieu, that these examples have been included.

## Aims

Most college and university music programs now offer standalone theory courses on twentieth-century music. These courses are divided into two main camps: those devoted to stylistic and historical studies and those devoted to theory and analysis. This text fits most clearly in the latter category, although it will also include some coverage of stylistic principles; in my view, *theories need contextualization* in order to be fully understood.

The text is primarily intended for classes on post-tonal, twentieth-century, contemporary, or atonal music theory, but is also suitable for the general graduate student population. By providing comprehensive coverage of a large number of theoretical concepts, the text may introduce topics that are outside the purview of some courses. These topics can be left out at the discretion of the instructor.

Among the specific aims of the textbook are:

1) to investigate twentieth-century music theory and practice without retreating from the technical language that is fundamental to twentieth-century theories of music;
2) to show the intrinsic musical relevance of the traditional analytical tools for twentieth-century music;
3) to show how these tools can provide important analytical insight into a broad array of musical styles stretching from the late nineteenth century to the present day; and
4) to show how twentieth-century music reflects its time and place in history.

## Organization

Post-tonal theories and concepts are often separated into isolated categories. The present textbook takes a more integrated approach and unfolds in a progressive manner. This allows many pertinent aspects of the musical examples to be considered in addition to the specific analytical concept under investigation. The harmonies and scales discussed in Chapter 1, for example, are referred to throughout the text and become the springboard for the study of interval cycles in Chapter 2. Similarly, the four interval types described in Chapter 2 are used to support the discussions of ordered and unordered sets in Chapters 3, 4, 5, and 6. The discussions of motive in Chapter 6 and contour and rhythm in Chapter 7 have a direct bearing on the analyses of row compositions in Chapter 8. An Introduction has been included to provide the historical context needed to more fully understand the musical innovations of the twentieth century. The study of textural features described in Chapter 9 rounds out the discussion by establishing categories that can be used to identify links between the diverse styles encountered in the previous chapters. The discussion of "coloristic" music, silence, and conceptual music at the end of Chapter 9 brings us full circle by expanding on topics already introduced in the Introduction.

Despite the progressive unfolding of the text, the chapters may also be reordered to fit various curricular needs. Since resurrected material is generally accompanied by a brief description, such reordering of the material should not be inordinately disruptive. The same is true for material that is left out of the discussion.

As the chapter titles suggest, the text is broadly organized around sets. This is done to highlight the differences between pitch and pc constructions and to help students keep track of these differences. The various types of intervals associated with sets receive at least as much attention as the sets themselves. Other important analytical and historical topics, including atonality, set theory, and the twelve-tone method, are emphasized within this framework.

## Pedagogical Features

Owing to their abstract nature and emphasis on mathematical principles, the theories described in this text can themselves easily become the focus of attention rather than the music they are meant to embellish. For the most part, however, these theories engage or build on musical ideas that have been in place for centuries. As much as possible, then, theories are presented in a way that emphasizes their fundamental musicality, while building on musical principles with which the student is already familiar. There are also a number of new pedagogical tools for analyzing pitch and rhythm. These include ordered pitch interval motives (a.k.a. shape/interval motives) and ordered and unordered duration classes.

Twentieth-century music theory incorporates an abundance of terms and concepts. In recognition of this fact, each chapter begins with a list of terms and topics to help organize class discussions. While the text may center on theoretical terms and concepts, however, these are always illustrated with examples from the literature. In addition, there are many detailed visual aids showing how theoretical tools are grounded in logical music/analytical principles. Footnotes have been included to provide additional insight as well as to help contextualize and legitimize the discussion. The endnotes and boxed material may also be used as a point of departure for deeper explorations of the topics under discussion in upper division seminars and graduate courses.

## Exercises and Aural Skills Supplement

This textbook provides a number of analytical exercises in addition to compositional and written exercises. The exercises are organized by chapter and address the material in the same order as the chapter they pertain to. The chapters and exercises can therefore easily be divided into more digestible units at the discretion of the instructor.

The textbook also includes an aural skills supplement with an aural skills trainer available on the companion website: www.motivichearing.com.

The inclusion of the aural skills supplement stems from my fruitful association with John Wm. Schaffer at the University of Wisconsin, but also from the assumption that the theories we use to describe recent music are essentially musical phenomena that can best be accessed through listening. The supplement provides brief explanations of the exercises found in the online computer program, *Motivic Hearing*, and how they relate to the material covered in the textbook. The supplement also suggests strategies that can be used to complete the exercises successfully.

The exercises themselves are divided into three streams. **Stream 1** focuses on interval identification, **Stream 2** on TTOs (P, I, R, and RI), and **Stream 3** on developing greater facility using the skills learned in Streams 1 and 2. The exercises also provide practice in identifying trichord prime forms by ear. Instructions on how to access and use the program are included.

Given the fact that among the most distinguishing characteristics of twentieth-century music is its variety and innovation, it is not possible to provide a comprehensive account of all of its diverse styles and episodes in a single text. Although there is some discussion of non-pitch-based music, most of the examples in this text come from compositions whose pitch material is drawn from the twelve tones of the equal tempered scale. Jazz, another genre that came to fruition during the twentieth century, has its own rich theoretical tradition and has largely been left out of the discussion along with other forms of commercial music. In general, music based on microtones, divisions smaller than a semitone, requires a different theoretical approach than the one taken here and is not included. Even without these exceptions, we are left with an ample amount of music to analyze, and it is this repertoire we will explore in this text.

Edward Pearsall
April 2011

# Acknowledgments

The ideas in this book are rooted in so much lore and tradition that it is difficult to precisely identify their origins. I am fortunate indeed to have been able to come into contact with so many formidable scholars, both in writing and conversation, and I am deeply indebted to them all. Of the many people cited in this text, Robert Morris, John Rahn, Milton Babbitt, Allen Forte, George Perle, and Elliot Antokoletz deserve special mention. This book could not have been written without the pioneering efforts of these theorists. Among those I would like to thank personally are Guy Capuzzo, Byron Almén, Michael Berry, Matthew Santa, and Eric Drott for providing timely advice and encouragement when it was most needed. I am especially indebted to John Wm. Schaffer, whose influence is felt throughout the text. Finally, I would like to express my deep gratitude to Ludim Pedroza, not only for her patience throughout the long process of writing this book, but also for her many thoughtful comments, literal contributions, and help in editing the manuscript.

# Introduction

## Modernism in Music

Every generation experiences its time as *modern*, up to date, contemporary. The late nineteenth and early twentieth centuries, on the other hand, witnessed the burgeoning of an unusually protracted and self-conscious interest in things new and unprecedented. This was owing in part to the global influence of industrialization, which caused many to question the relevance of traditional political, cultural, and social ideologies. As composers, artists, authors, and architects searched for a contemporary aesthetic response to their changing world, they began to reject the artistic values of the past, turning instead to more abstract forms of expression. The term most often used to identify this radical turn of the twentieth-century trend in art and literature is **modernism**. Late nineteenth- and early twentieth-century modernism is rooted in a particular kind of modern experience, one whose innovative spirit, while difficult to pin down, is exceptionally earnest and trenchant.

Modernism is often associated with a radical break from the past and the artistic values and traditions it entails. The modernist perspective is far more complex than this, however. As Paul Childs observes, "modernity is an imprecise and contested term" and involves a number of "paradoxical if not opposed trends toward revolutionary and reactionary positions, fear of the new and delight at the disappearance of the old, nihilism and fanatical enthusiasm, creativity and despair."[1] In music, these paradoxical trends eventually led to the breakdown of musical style into a plethora of styles and "isms," including atonality, serialism, aleatory composition, neo-classicism, primitivism, expressionism, and impressionism, to name just a few. Yet, despite the departure from the norms and conventions of the past, many of these trends are rooted in age-old practice. Let us, then, embark on an investigation of this exhilarating and complex episode in history in order to come to a better understanding of its richness and artistic vitality.

Arnold Schoenberg, one of early modernism's most recognizable figures and senior member of what has become known as the **Second Viennese School** of composition, was himself no enemy of the past. Indeed, Schoenberg purposefully set out to provide what he saw as the inevitable next step in the evolution of Western music. Born in 1874, Schoenberg grew up in a society that divided the cultural landscape into high and low art forms. It should come as no surprise, then, that music history for Schoenberg—as well as many others of his generation—was epitomized by a long line of master composers, primarily German, each of whom introduced innovations that, in their view, took music further down the path toward greater refinement. There is, perhaps, no better description of this view than that expressed by Schoenberg himself:

As everybody knows, while Bach still was living a new musical style came into being out of which there later grew the style of the Viennese Classicists, the style of homophonic-melodic composition, or, as I call it, the style of Developing Variation.[2]

Schoenberg viewed his own efforts in a similar light, noting that "composition with twelve tones and what many erroneously call 'atonal music' is not the end of an old period, but the beginning of a new one."[3]

As these statements reveal, Schoenberg did not have his eye set on the avoidance or destruction of past conventions. On the contrary, he consistently cast his ideas in a positive light. One of his best known axioms is the "emancipation of dissonance," a principle that led him to count such traditionally dissonant intervals as seconds, sevenths, and tritones among the harmonic intervals along with thirds, fifths, sixths, and octaves.[4] Schoenberg's characterization of dissonance as an enslaved entity suggests that he did not consider the incorporation of traditionally dissonant intervals to be an act of rebellion or an *attack* on music, but rather a benevolent act of inclusion. In a similar vein, Schoenberg expressed dislike for the term **atonal** along with its negative connotations, preferring instead the term *pantonal*.[5]

To see how the materials and techniques of the past emerge in new guises in Schoenberg's music, let us briefly examine the fifth movement of his first **twelve-tone composition**, the *Suite for Piano*, Op. 25.[6] One of the first things we notice about this movement is its form, Menuett and Trio. The menuett and trio (or minuet and trio), of course, is the stock form for one of the middle movements of instrumental works written during the eighteenth and early nineteenth centuries, including sonatas, string quartets, and symphonies. Other aspects of the work that recall historical practices are the use of imitative counterpoint and the inverted response in the Trio.

While the *Suite for Piano* resembles the music of Schoenberg's predecessors in some ways, it departs significantly from them in others. Example 0.1 contains the first few measures of the Trio. Notice that the melody here is angular, full of leaps, rather than primarily smooth as in Bach's fugal themes. Notice also that the right-hand part is not a *tonal*, but a *real* response.[7] This is because the piece does not remain in a single key. Instead, each statement of the theme articulates all twelve tones in the octave, making the twelve tones of the chromatic octave the basis for the piece rather than a major or minor scale.

**EX. I.1**—Arnold Schoenberg, *Suite for Piano*, Op. 25, Trio, mm. 1–3 (Excerpt with Mixed Old and New Techniques)

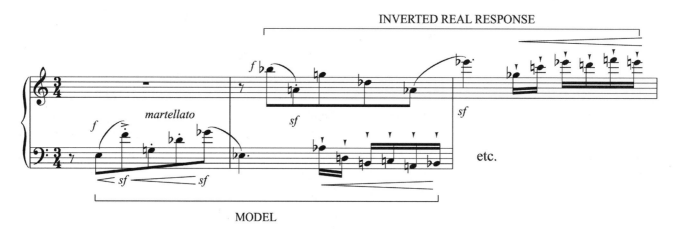

Not all European composers at the turn of the twentieth century shared Schoenberg's views. One important example is Claude Debussy. Debussy believed that the hegemony of German music overshadowed the musical traditions of his native France. As a result, he made a conscious effort to move away from compositional practices he associated with Germanic tradition.

> We have, however, a purely French tradition in the works of Rameau. They combine a charming and delicate tenderness with precise tones and strict declamation in the recitatives—none of the affected German pomp, nor the need to emphasize everything with extravagant gestures or out-of-breath explanations . . .[8]

The compositional ramifications of Debussy's perceived excesses in German musical practice are manifested primarily in his approach to harmony and form. Example 0.2 shows an excerpt from Debussy's Prelude, "La Cathédrale engloutie" (The Sunken Cathedral). Unlike the excerpt from Schoenberg's Op. 25, this excerpt incorporates familiar scales and triads. These are used, however, in unconventional ways; note the parallel octaves and fifths (largely forbidden in traditional tonal contexts), the subversion of the leading-tone function through the arrival of B♭ in m. 33, and the absence of functional harmony. While not apparent from this excerpt alone, the piece is also less formally conventional than Schoenberg's Op. 25 Menuett and Trio. While the main theme re-emerges at the end of the movement, for example, there is no recapitulation in the traditional sense. Instead, as Figure 0.1 illustrates, themes are recycled in an ad hoc manner, imparting an improvisational character to the piece.

EX. I.2—Claude Debussy, Preludes, Book 1, No. 10, "La Cathédrale engloutie," mm. 28–34 (Conventional and Non-Conventional Features in Debussy)

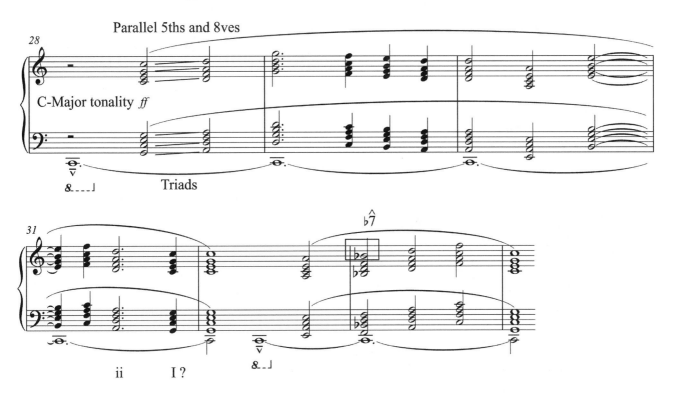

Measures:   1    7    14              28    47    72    84

Themes:   A . . . B . . . A + Expansion . . . C . . . B . . . C . . . A

**FIGURE I.1** Themes in "La Cathédrale engloutie"

Debussy was not the only *fin de siècle* French composer to have remarked on the differences between French and German perspectives. Maurice Ravel, for example, also alluded to what he called the distinctive "national consciousness" of German and French composers.[9] **Nationalism** in general came to have broad appeal in the early twentieth century as composers on both sides of the Atlantic began to take a stronger interest in their aesthetic and cultural heritages. Manifested by the incorporation of folk tunes into concert music, this trend may be observed in the music of Béla Bartók (Hungary), Leoš Janàček (Czechoslavakia), *les six* (France), the Russian Five, and Charles Ives (United States). Their interest in national identity, on the other hand, did not prevent composers from using the indigenous music of countries other than their own as the basis for composition. Antonín Dvořák's *New World Symphony*, for example, was influenced by his exposure to Native American music and Afro-American Spirituals during his visit to the United States from 1892 to 1895, and both Ravel and Debussy were inspired by American Jazz.[10]

Although Schoenberg and Debussy engaged with the past in different ways, neither rejected it entirely and their music incorporated important elements linking it to the traditions each composer valued most. Later in the century, composers would adopt a more contentious view of the past. Where Schoenberg attempted to link dissonance with consonance, for example, Charles Seeger inverted them.[11] Seeger advocated a compositional model based on **dissonant counterpoint** rather than traditional sixteenth- and eighteenth-century contrapuntal models. In dissonant counterpoint, dissonant intervals are substituted for consonant ones; consonance, that is, "resolves" to dissonance, not the other way around. Seeger's ideas were adopted by a number of important **American experimentalists**, including Ruth Crawford, Henry Cowell, and Carl Ruggles. While the music written by American experimentalists may resemble that of Schoenberg in some ways, it has entirely different origins. As we shall see, this is a theme that resonates throughout the twentieth century.

In the post-World War II era, composers became even more resolute and outspoken in their stance against past practices. One particularly vocal proponent of a radical break with the past was Pierre Boulez. In a famous article, Boulez scolds Schoenberg for holding on too strongly to traditional forms.[12]

> What then was his [Schoenberg's] main ambition once a chromatic synthesis—or safety net— had been established by serialism? To create works of the same nature as those of the old sound-world which he had only just abandoned[?] . . . It certainly does not show much faith in serial organization to deprive it of its own modes of development in favour [sic] of others that seem safer . . .[13]

In Boulez's view, Anton Webern and Claude Debussy—despite the differences in their musical vocabularies—came closer to recognizing the potential for novelty to stand on its own merits because they reacted "against all inherited rhetoric."[14] Building on this foundation, Boulez and his associates (e.g., Luigi Nono, Luciano Berio, and Karlheinz Stockhausen) adopted an approach to composition in which Schoenberg's practice of serializing pitch was applied to other musical parameters, including register, duration, articulation, and dynamics.

While Boulez attempted to introduce strict control over every aspect of his music, others just as vigorously shunned such control. Principal among these is **avant-garde** composer John Cage. Cage, a one-time student of Schoenberg, challenged the very definition of music by incorporating noises and environmental sounds into his compositions. Even more famous is his **aleatory music** in which chance techniques are used to make compositional decisions. It is interesting that, despite the sharp contrast in their compositional approaches, music written by both Boulez and Cage often evokes remarkably similar aural effects. Boulez himself acknowledged such a connection when he noted that, "[t]he tendency of these experiments by John Cage is too close to my own for me to fail to mention them."[15] What these pieces have in common are their **pointillistic** textures—with a profusion of wide leaps—and rhythmic complexity, and it is these modernistic characteristics that link them despite the divergent motivations of the two composers.

Whether they embrace or repudiate it, history and its traditions loom large in the consciousness of modernist composers. The past they dwell on, however, is a narrowly defined past, one whose heroes—the canonized masters of the tonal tradition—are few and far between. Given this view of history, one can easily understand how some composers may have felt the need to work as much *against* the old as *for* the new in order to carve out a space for their own creative expression and to ensure their place in history alongside their famous predecessors.[16]

## Other Trends

While the Second Viennese, Darmstadt, and American Experimental schools pushed music toward greater abstraction, other early and mid twentieth-century composers continued to make use of the tonal vocabulary, albeit in ways that often departed sharply from their nineteenth-century predecessors. Prokofiev, Shostakovich, Stravinsky, Poulenc, Satie, Bloch, Copland, McDowell, all relied to some extent on the accoutrements of tonal music (e.g., triads, seventh chords, major and minor keys, etc.). Beyond the use of lyrical melodies and triadic harmony, however, much of this music has little in common with pre-modernist practices. Traditional rules regarding the treatment of dissonance, for example, rarely apply and the dominant function is mostly absent.

It is also important to recognize that composers themselves did not always adhere to one school or another. Both Copland and Stravinsky, for example, experimented with Schoenberg's twelve-tone technique. Prokofiev's early works reflect the influence of such modernist composers as Stravinsky and Schoenberg while his later works, those written following his return to Russia in 1923 after living in Paris and the United States, incorporate lyrical melodies, folk material, and lush tertian harmonies, stylistic features that are more in line with **Socialist Realism**.[17] Stravinsky was an especially versatile composer and at various times in his career wrote primitivistic, neo-classical, and even serial works.

Innovation began to take on an added demeanor in the latter half of the twentieth century. During this period, many composers and artists became less intensely reactionary toward the past and, at the same time, more interested in popular culture. As a result, the distinction between high and low art forms began to blur and the culture of *L'art pour l'art* (art for art's sake), so pervasive during the nineteenth and early twentieth centuries, grew to occupy only one niche domain among many. Soon, styles that were more inclusive of popular and non-Western music in addition to classical traditions began to emerge amidst the insular schools and "isms" of the modernist camp.

These developments bespeak a new tradition, one that operates under the rubric of **postmodernism**. Despite its apparent indifference toward the past, postmodernism is nevertheless dependent on the legacy of modernist ideals, for it is from these ideals that its disparate trends emerged.[18] One of the most prevalent features of postmodernism is, as Charles Jencks observes, its "intense commitment to pluralism."[19] **Pluralism** is manifested, among other things, through genre mixing and an interest in non-Western, popular, and folk materials. Postmodernism thus gives the impression of operating outside of modernism's narrow definitions of the world or even of being somehow beyond it. But by using, again in Charles Jencks's words, "very modernist tactics against the Modernists," postmodernists continue to engage modernism's contentious relation with the past and are essentially defined in terms of it.[20] While the term postmodern itself appears to consign modernism to the past, moreover, the influences of modernism may still be felt. Composers such as John Corigliano and George Crumb, for example, have used twelve-tone rows in their compositions, albeit without subjecting them to the twelve-tone method prescribed by Schoenberg. Hence, we can see that modernism and postmodernism continue to engage each other in an ongoing and mutually interdependent dialogue.

Pluralism in music gives rise to at least two disparate trends. The first of these is the emergence of a niche mentality, which tends to place all genres on an equal playing field rather than arranging them into a hierarchy of high and low value. Under these circumstances, the listener's preferences appear to take precedence over social and cultural demands. Even so, the niche mentality engenders its own form of rejection, for it sees as "other" that which is not of itself.

The second trend is a more "composerly" one and centers around the juxtaposition of contrasting styles. An example of this may be found in the Sting song, "Russians." Sting, a classically trained musician, places a theme borrowed from Sergei Prokofiev's classically conceived orchestral score for *Lieutenant Kijé*, a Soviet film released in 1934, in a popular music setting with guitars and synthesizers to make a statement about cold war politics.

Self-proclaimed postmodernist George Crumb also incorporates material from multiple sources.[21] Crumb acknowledges influences ranging from Debussy, Bartók, and Mahler to the folk music of his native West Virginia. Hence, one finds folk instruments such as the banjo and musical saw alongside traditional classical instruments in his scores in addition to a variety of source material. This blending of popular, folk, and classical archetypes is an important and pervasive aspect of postmodern music and art.

While the novelty of postmodern music is sometimes downplayed, most likely in reaction to what has often been viewed as the excesses of modernism, the creative spirit prevails and there is a freshness to postmodern music that is, in many ways, as inventive as that of many modernist composers. Modernism and postmodernism alike are steeped in contradiction and paradox; a deep reverence for monolithic figures of the past vs. the renunciation of past practice, the emancipation of dissonance vs. the exclusion of consonance, novelty vs. tradition, greater structural control vs. through-composed forms and chance procedures, the individualistic imperative vs. absolutism, abstraction vs. expression, high art vs. low art . . . More important for the purposes of this text is the fact that much pitch-based music written since 1890—whether modern or postmodern, abstract or folkloristic, tonal or atonal—is grounded in common musical principals with deep historical roots.[22] Focusing on such principles allows us to view pieces that incorporate widely varying strategies, compositional philosophies, and content from a similar vantage point. Keeping this idea in mind, let us now proceed to the theories themselves . . .

# Chapter 1

# Scales, Harmony, and Referential Collections

| | |
|---|---|
| Tertian harmony | Modal scales |
| Added note chords | Synthetic (a.k.a. exotic or artificial) scales |
| Polymodal chord | Referential collections |
| Polytriads | Diatonic modes |
| PLR transformations | Pitch centricity |
| Parsimonious voice leading | Lydian-Mixolydian scale (a.k.a. acoustic scale) |
| Secundal harmony | Tertiary heptatonic scale |
| Quartal harmony | Melodic-minor ascending scale |
| Quintal harmony | Pentatonic scale |
| Tone clusters | Whole-tone scale |
| Tristan chord | Hexatonic scale |
| Mystic chord | Octatonic scale |
| Petrushka chord | Modes of limited transposition |

## Tertian Harmony

In a series of lectures he delivered to a small group of dilettantes at a private Vienna residence in 1932–33, Anton Webern expressed the view that harmony is derived primarily from the *harmonic series*.[1] This line of reasoning gave him the foundation he needed on which to build a theory of contemporary harmony:

> we must understand that consonance and dissonance are not essentially different—that there is no essential difference between them, only one of degree. Dissonance is only another step up the scale [harmonic series], which goes on developing further.[2]

Whether or not harmony is grounded in the acoustical properties of the harmonic series, as Webern suggests, it is true that the definition of consonance and dissonance has changed over time, and in a way that for the most part has moved progressively up the harmonic series. Early Christian church music, for example, was saturated by perfect consonances (fifths, fourths, and octaves), intervals that occur at the bottom of the harmonic series.[3] (See Figure 1.1.) In Western music written during the seventeenth to nineteenth centuries, thirds, along with the dominant seventh chord, played a central role in the harmonic texture. These occur higher up in the series. Chords in music written since 1890 are often more complex and can incorporate a wide variety of intervals, including traditionally dissonant intervals such as seconds and tritones. In this chapter we will focus on two types of chords, those built up from a single diatonic interval (seconds, thirds, fourths, and fifths) and those identified with a particular composer or work. Chords containing a mix of consonant and dissonant intervals will be discussed in Chapters 4 and 5.

Dominant 7th
Perfect 4th
Perfect 5th
Perfect Octave

**FIGURE 1.1** Harmonic Series

Although music written since 1890 may contain a variety of harmonic intervals, **tertian harmony** (harmony consisting of thirds) continues to play an important role. Tertian chords include triads and sevenths but do not always function according to tonal protocol and may appear in the company of non-tertian chords. Neither one of the seventh chords in Example 1.1, for instance, commonly occurs in eighteenth- and nineteenth-century tonal music.[4] Yet, both are made up of thirds. Notice too that the two chords are inversions of each other; that is, the major and minor thirds in the first chord are projected in the opposite direction in the second.[5]

**EX. 1.1**—Schoenberg, *Three Piano Pieces*, Op. 11, No. 1, mm. 14 and 58 (Nontraditional Seventh Chords)

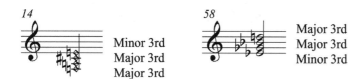

Augmented major 7th          Minor major 7th

The passage in Example 1.2 contains a succession of tertian chords. These chords are mostly seventh and ninth chords, but do not adhere to conventional voice leading principles or tonal function.

**EX. 1.2**—Maurice Ravel, *Valses Nobles et Sentimentales*, I, mm. 47–52 (Non-functional Tertian Texture)

In some cases, chords that are otherwise tertian may contain non-chord tones. The non-triadic tone in these **added note chords** imparts richness to the chord without detracting from its triadic origins.[6] The B♮ in the left-hand part of Henri Duparc's *Le manoir de Rosemonde* shown in Example 1.3 could be treated as the root of a half-diminished chord. The sustained D minor chord in the right-hand part along with the key signature and left-hand ascending scale pattern, however, suggest that D minor is the prevailing harmony here. Understood in this way, B takes on the guise of an added sixth.[7]

EX. **1.3**—Henri Duparc, *Le manoir de Rosemonde*, mm. 3–6 (Added Note Chord)

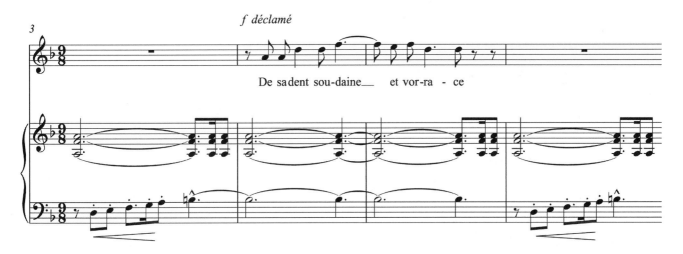

A **polymodal chord** is a particularly interesting kind of added note chord in which the major and minor forms of a triad are combined. In Example 1.4, E major is combined with E minor.

EX. **1.4**—Francis Poulenc, *Napoli suite pour le piano*, "Caprice Italien," mm. 128–32 (Polymodal EMaj/min Chord)

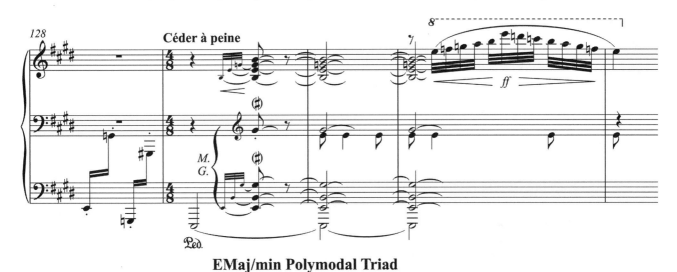

**EMaj/min Polymodal Triad**

Composers have also made use of **polytriads**, harmonies consisting of more than one triad. Polytriads can sometimes be analyzed as a single extended chord. The chord in m. 8 of Example 1.5, for instance, could be analyzed as a C#$^{11}$ chord. This analysis, while technically correct, does not take into account the independence of the left- and right-hand parts. Notice too the enharmonically spelled polymodal triad in m. 3.

**EX. 1.5**—Benjamin Britten, *Winter Words*, 1, "At Day-Close in November," mm. 1–9 (Polytriads)

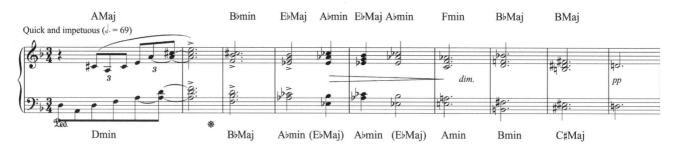

## PLR Transformations and Voice Leading Parsimony

In the absence of functional harmony, triads may form successions based on other criteria. Chief among these are the **PLR transformations** in Figure 1.2.[8] Two of these transformations, P (parallel) and R (relative), will already be familiar. P and R relations are traditionally associated with keys, but can also be used to identify relations between triads; P changes the mode of the chord while R replaces it with the tonic of its relative major or minor. In both instances, the chords share two common tones; P-related chords share a fifth, R-related chords share a major third. The only other relation that produces triads with two common tones is the leading-tone exchange or L.[9] L replaces the root of a major triad with its leading-tone, the note a semitone below it. When the chord is minor, L replaces the fifth of the chord with the note a semitone above it, producing a major chord. L-related chords share a minor third.

**FIGURE 1.2** PLR Transformations

PLR transformations may be combined to produce triadic streams with **parsimonious voice leading**. In parsimonious voice leading, voices move as efficiently (or as smoothly) as possible.[10] In each of the parsimonious PLR cycles shown in Figure 1.3, for example, each pair of chords share two common tones while the remaining tone moves by step. Each cycle, moreover, eventually leads back to the starting point. The LR cycle requires twenty-four chords to complete itself while the PL (six), and PR (eight) cycles are much shorter. Notice that each cycle produces a series of alternating major and minor triads with root movement by third. The cycles may begin with either member of the pairing. (Be sure to play the cycles both forward and backward to familiarize yourself with their unique non-functional characteristics.)

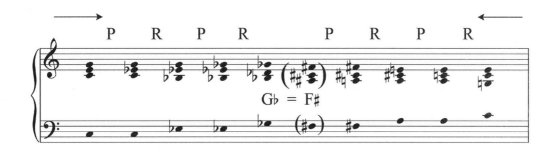

FIGURE 1.3 PL, PR, and LR Cycles

PLR transformations may be invoked without parsimony. Each of the RL cycles in Example 1.6, for instance, contains some voice leading parsimony, but also includes leaps and a gradual thickening of the texture. Notice that PLR transformations have to do with how we get from one chord to the next. Hence, the labels are placed between chords rather than beneath the chords themselves.

**EX. 1.6**—Johannes Brahms, *Rhapsody*, Op. 119, No. 4, mm. 21–39 (RL Cycles)

## Non-Tertian Harmony

Other chords routinely derived from stacked intervals include those consisting of major and minor seconds (**secundal harmony**), perfect fourths (**quartal harmony**), and perfect fifths (**quintal harmony**). Example 1.7 contains an excerpt with secundal harmony doubled at the octave.

**EX. 1.7**—Maurice Ravel, *Miroirs*, I, "Noctuelles," mm. 8–9 (Secundal Harmony consisting only of Major and Minor Seconds)

Chords in which seconds are inverted and/or transposed, as in Example 1.8, may also be analyzed as secundal chords.

**EX. 1.8**—Bartók, *Mikrokosmos* Vol. 6, No. 144, "Minor Seconds, Major Sevenths," mm. 3–4 (Inverted Secundal Chords)

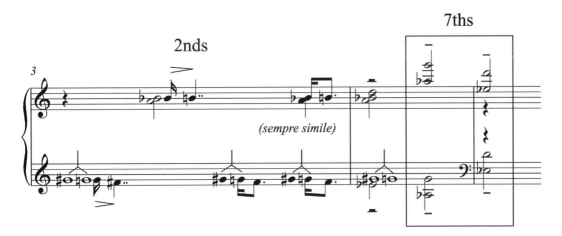

Very dense secundal chords are sometimes referred to as **tone clusters**. Tone clusters constitute a type of musical effect rather than a harmonic sonority per se. The excerpt in Example 1.9 provides a particularly dramatic illustration of this idea.

**EX. 1.9**—Charles Ives, *Majority*, mm. 1–3 (Tone Clusters)

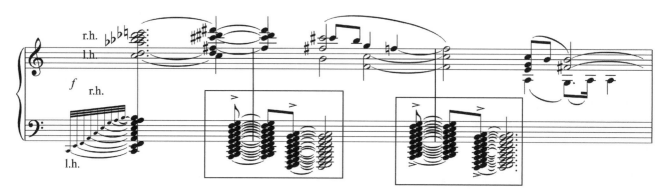

The accompaniment to the vocal part in Example 1.10 consists primarily of *quartal* chords. In some cases the vocal part either extends the chord or doubles a chord tone. Notice that there are also a number of non-chord tones in both the vocal and piano parts.

**EX. 1.10**—Charles Ives, *Majority*, mm. 18–20 (Quartal Chords)

Example 1.11 contains a series of three-note arpeggiated *quintal chords*. These chords serve as an accompaniment for the non-quintal oboe and clarinet parts.

**EX. 1.11**—Leoš Janàček, *Sinfonietta*, II, mm. 173–81 (Quintal Chords)

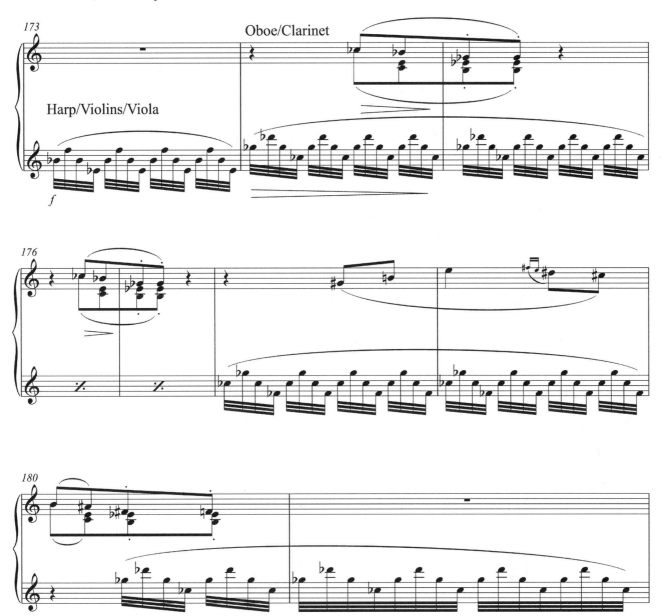

Because fifths and fourths are inversions of each other, it can sometimes be difficult to distinguish between *quintal* and *quartal* harmony. The chords in Example 1.12, for instance, contain both fifths and fourths. In such cases, the initiating events may provide insight into the harmonic organization of the passage. The intervals at the bottom of the texture are perfect fifths. It would probably be best, then, to think of all the chords as fundamentally quintal in character with the perfect fourths in the passage arising from octave doublings in the horn and viola parts.

**EX. 1.12**—Claude Debussy, *"Images" pour orchestre*, No. 2, "Iberia," III, mm. 102–3 (Quintal Harmony with Octave Doubling)

The passage in Example 1.13 contains what might at first glance appear to be a loosely organized collection of quintal, secundal, and added-note tertian chords. Although technically correct, this assessment does not express the overall coherence of the passage. Once again, the initiating event, in this case a quintal chord, provides a clue for analyzing the passage more efficiently. Notice that the initial chord continues to sound throughout mm. 22–23 and that its two pitches occur in every chord that follows it. The added notes in each chord, moreover, gradually build up in a circle of fifths fashion. Although the chords incorporate seconds and thirds, then, all appear to have quintal origins.

EX. 1.13—Claude Debussy, Preludes, Book 1, No. 10, "La Cathédrale engloutie," mm. 22–25 (Inverted and Transposed Quintal Chords)

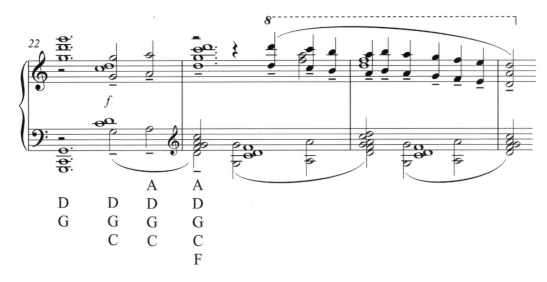

## Other Well-Known Chords

There are a few chords that have come to be associated with a particular composer or work. These include the Tristan chord, the mystic chord, and the Petrushka chord. Each of these chords has ties to one of the types of harmonies we have already discussed. The Tristan chord, for example, may be described as a tertian chord, the mystic chord a quartal chord, and the Petrushka chord a polytriad. These particular chords have been singled out because of their idiosyncratic features and settings.

The **Tristan chord**, so named because of its numerous appearances in the prelude to the first act of Richard Wagner's music drama *Tristan und Isolde*, is one of the first enigmatic chords to have become associated with a particular work. Marked with arrows in Example 1.14, the Tristan chord appears on the downbeats of mm. 2, 6, 10, 12, and 19. Of these, the chord in m. 19 is the easiest to explain because it is spelled, and behaves, like a vii°⁷, moving to D⁷, which arrives on the second eighth note of the measure, before resolving as expected to G.

The chords in mm. 2 and 6 are not hard to account for if we take into consideration the augmented sixths that occur in each chord. In both cases, the augmented sixth follows tonal protocol; the bass note descends by step and the upper note slips down to the seventh of the ensuing dominant seventh chord.[11] Just as important in these cautious first steps of the prelude are the voice exchanges that occur in mm. 2–3 and 6–7.

In m. 10 the augmented sixth is inverted and respelled as a major second or inverted "minor seventh" (C/D), breaking the pattern of the first seven measures. The "seventh" in the bass ultimately descends by semitone to the root of the B[7] chord, which arrives in m. 11. Meanwhile, both D and F move to E, forming an augmented triad with the as yet unresolved C in the bass. The linear motions in mm. 10–11, while different than those that precede them, make sense in light of the goal of the passage, a root position B[7] whose notes occur in precisely the same order bottom-to-top as the dominant sevenths in mm. 3 and 7 (root–third–seventh–fifth).

Overall, the first eleven measures of the prelude outline a root progression of thirds; the gesture in mm. 1–3 comes to rest on E[7], the one in mm. 4–7 on G[7], and the final gesture in mm. 10–11 (repeated in mm. 12–13) on B[7]. The arrival of D[7] in m. 19 continues the ascending root progression by thirds and pushes the music forward toward the less restrained section that follows it.

Although this music tests the limits of tonality, dissonant intervals retain their voice-leading tendencies. The tonic of the work, however, is less certain. If it is not wholly non-tonal, then, Wagner's *Tristan* does explore the fringes of tonality and in the process glimpses, however briefly, into the not too distant future of music.

**EX. 1.14**—Richard Wagner, *Tristan und Isolde*, Prelude to Act 1, mm. 1–21 (Tristan Chords)

The **mystic chord** is the invention of Alexander Scriabin who used it both as a chord and as a scale. Sometimes called the "Prometheus chord," owing to its important role in Scriabin's symphonic tone poem *Prometheus*, the mystic chord is traditionally spelled in fourths as illustrated in Figure 1.4. Unlike the quartal chords we have already discussed, however, the mystic chord includes not only perfect fourths, but also two augmented fourths and a diminished fourth.

**FIGURE 1.4** The Mystic Chord

Most theorists agree that, functionally, the mystic chord has dominant origins, although it generally does not incorporate strong voice leading tendencies. Indeed, it is frequently sustained over several measures, as in Example 1.15, producing a sense of arrested motion. Incomplete versions of the chord, like those in mm. 122–25, are also common.

**EX. 1.15**—Alexander Scriabin, Piano Sonata No. 5, Op. 53, mm. 122–27 (Transposed Mystic Chords)

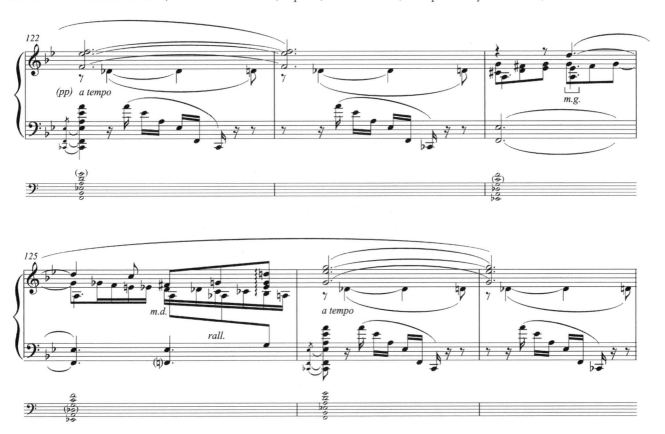

The **Petrushka chord** is associated with Igor Stravinsky's ballet of the same name, which premiered in 1913. This chord, which appears in Figure 1.5, may be described as a polytriad consisting of two triads whose roots are a tritone apart. The chord also appears to have a preferred position with the lower triad in first inversion and the higher triad in root position.

**FIGURE 1.5** The Petrushka Chord

Although there is some controversy over the origins of the Petrushka chord, it appears to have close ties to the octatonic collection and consists entirely of notes found in the octatonic scale.[12] Stravinsky's primary teacher, Nicolai Rimsky-Korsakov, moreover, was strongly drawn to the octatonic collection and both Rimsky-Korsakov and Stravinsky professed a deep admiration for Franz Liszt who made some excursions into octatonic territory.[13] In fact, the Petrushka chord itself appears in Liszt's *Malediction Concerto* as shown in Example 1.16.

**EX 1.16**—Franz Liszt, *Malediction*, mm. 10–11 (An Early Appearance of the Petrushka Chord)

An excerpt from the second tableau of *Petrushka* appears in Example 1.17. Note that Stravinsky here makes reference to *maledictions*, providing a semantic link to Liszt's concerto.

**EX. 1.17**—Igor Stravinsky, *Petrushka*, Second Tableau, mm. 33–34 (Petrushka Chord in Stravinsky's Ballet)

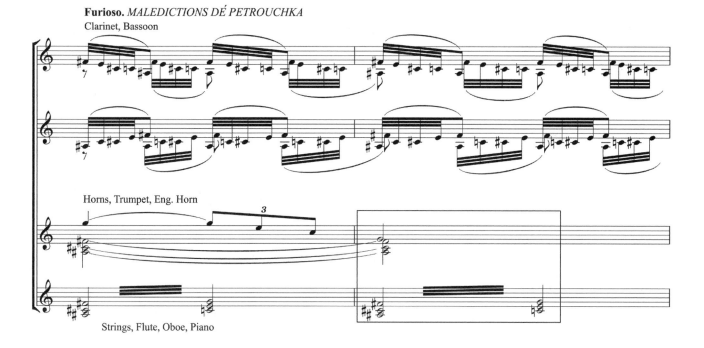

## Scales and Referential Collections

Like earlier music, music written since 1890 is sometimes based on scales. Here, we will focus our attention mainly on two types of scales, **modal** and **synthetic** (a.k.a. **exotic** or **artificial**) **scales**. Scales treated as the accumulated assortment of notes from which melodies and harmonies are drawn in a composition are referred to as **referential collections**.

Among the scales used by composers in modern times are those that correspond to the eight church modes. These are given Greek names and contain only the notes of the major and natural minor scales. It is for this reason that they are sometimes referred to collectively as the **diatonic modes**.

The eight diatonic modes appear in two different forms in Figure 1.6. The scales on the right illustrate how each mode—along with its particular arrangement of whole-tones and semitones—can be created by starting on a different major scale degree and then playing the remaining notes of the scale in ascending order. The left-hand column presents the scales as derivatives of the major and natural minor scales.

The different identities of the scales emerge most clearly when those in the left-hand column are played. The Lydian and Mixolydian scales, like the Ionian, have a major orientation because the first three scale steps outline a major third. The others, those denoted with filled-in noteheads, begin with a minor third and thus are minor in character. In addition to its major or minor orientation, each scale has a unique set of intervallic traits that contributes to its peculiar temperament. The Lydian mode, for example, may be thought of as a major scale with a raised $\hat{4}$ and the Mixolydian as a major scale with a flat $\hat{7}$. The Dorian mode also has a flat $\hat{7}$ but is minor. The Locrian mode differs from Phrygian mode only by the inclusion of flat $\hat{5}$. Both begin with a semitone ascent to flat $\hat{2}$.

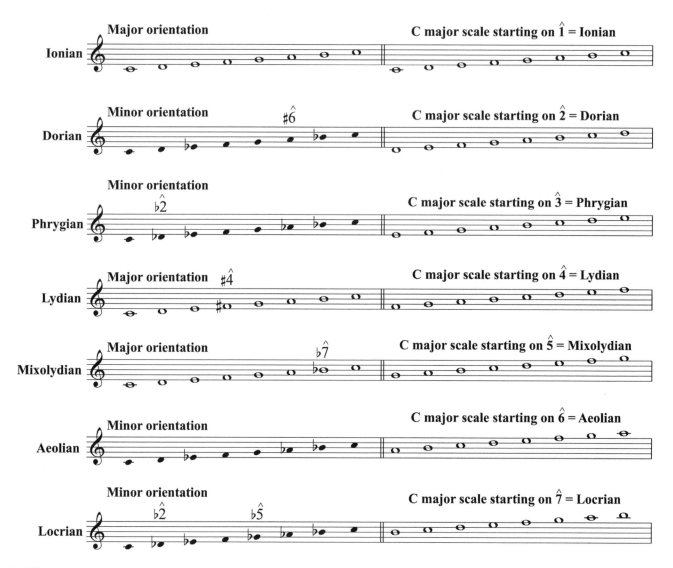

**FIGURE 1.6** Diatonic Modes

The church modes correspond to the earlier Greek *tonoi*, which were given names associated with various ethnic groups in the ancient world. The *tonoi* were thought by some to produce specific attitudes and behaviors—some virtuous, some less so—in those who listened to them. In the sixth century, the Roman scholar Boethius Latinized the Greek *tonoi*, but read them upside down, thus naming them incorrectly. Although they do not correspond to the original *tonoi*, Boethius's labels are the ones most commonly in use today.

In tonal music, the tonic is defined as much by goal-directed harmony as by its actual appearance in the texture. Tonal function, on the other hand, does not always play a central role in modal music, in part because most modes contain flat $\hat{7}$ rather than a leading-tone. For this reason, we will rely on **pitch centricity**, the use of a single pitch as a linchpin, to identify tonal centers. Centric pitches may be emphasized by means of repetition as well as agogic and metrical accents. In addition, centric tones often occur at registral boundaries or at the end of a piece or passage.

The chart in Figure 1.7 shows the steps for determining modes under three different conditions. As the chart indicates, modes can be determined using key signatures to identify the scale-degree that corresponds to the centric pitch (following the right column in Figure 1.6) or to identify scale-degree inflections (following the left column). When there is no key signature, a signature can sometimes, but not always, be manufactured using the accidentals in the music.

---

a) Key Signature—No additional accidentals

   1) Identify the centric pitch.

   2) Identify the major scale represented by the key signature.

   3) Determine the mode based on the scale degree that corresponds to the centric pitch (Figure 1.6, right column) or by identifying scale-degree inflections (Figure 1.6, left column).

b) Key Signature—With additional accidentals

   1) Identify the centric pitch.

   2) Add the accidentals found in the music to the key signature (NOTE: naturals may cancel accidentals in the key signature).

   3) Identify the major scale represented by the fabricated key signature.

   4) Determine the mode based on the scale degree that corresponds to the centric pitch (Figure 1.6, right column) or by identifying scale-degree inflections (Figure 1.6, left column).

c) No Key Signature

   1) Identify the centric pitch.

   2) Arrange the accidentals found in the music to form a recognizable key signature.

   3) Identify the major scale represented by the fabricated key signature.

   4) Determine the mode based on the scale degree that corresponds to the centric pitch (Figure 1.6, right column) or by identifying scale-degree inflections (Figure 1.6, left column).

---

**FIGURE 1.7** Steps for Identifying Modes

Let us now look at several examples. The tonal center in the excerpt from Stravinsky's *Rite of Spring* shown in Example 1.18 is E♭; it is the lowest note in the texture and occurs on the downbeat of every measure. The key signature has five flats and there are no added accidentals. We can therefore use the steps in **Condition a** to determine the mode. E♭ is $\hat{2}$ in D♭ major, so the mode is Dorian. The Dorian mode's distinctive character is imparted by its minor mode orientation and the presence of sharp $\hat{6}$ and flat $\hat{7}$ as indicated in the left column of Figure 1.6.

**EX. 1.18**—Igor Stravinsky, *The Rite of Spring*, Part II, "Spring Roundelays," mm. 15–19 (E♭ Dorian with Key Signature)

In Example 1.19, all the Es are flat despite the fact that there is no E♭ in the written key signature. Adding E♭ to the written key signature produces the virtual key signature for B♭ major (**Condition b**). The excerpt itself is F centric because F occurs at the beginning of each of the four phrases and because it is the final resting pitch of the excerpt. F is $\hat{5}$ in B♭ major and E♭ is flat $\hat{7}$ in the key of F major so the mode is Mixolydian.

**EX. 1.19**—Ralph Vaughan Williams, *The Wasps*, mm. 355–69 (D Mixolydian with Key Signature and Added Accidentals)

The passage from Poulenc's *Valse* in C major in Example 1.20 has no key signature. Because all the Fs in the passage are sharp, however, we can invoke **Condition c** by manufacturing the key signature for G major. C is $\hat{4}$ in G major, leading us to conclude that the mode is Lydian. F♯, of course, is sharp $\hat{4}$ in the key of C major, which leads to the same result.

**EX. 1.20**—Frances Poulenc, *Valse*, mm. 1–9 (C Lydian with No Key Signature)

As we have already observed, the Phrygian and Locrian modes are similar because both begin with a semitone ascent to flat $\hat{2}$. Of the two, the Phrygian mode appears more often. There are, however, a few important works that incorporate the Locrian mode. One such piece is Alexander Scriabin's Piano Sonata No. 5 shown in Example 1.21.

**EX. 1.21**—Alexander Scriabin, Piano Sonata No. 5, Op. 53, mm. 3–8 (Locrian Mode)

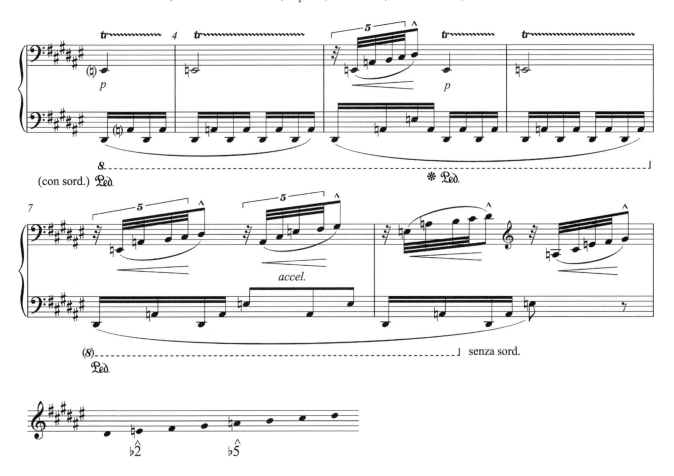

An example of the Phrygian mode appears in Example 1.22. Most of the Fs in this example are natural. The sole F♯ in m. 2 forms part of a French augmented sixth chord that functions as an embellishing chord for G minor. Additional notes do not necessarily undermine the principal referential collection in a passage. Here, the essence of the Phrygian mode is preserved owing to the motion from A♭ (flat $\hat{2}$) to G in the cello part.

**EX. 1.22**—Claude Debussy, String Quartet in G Minor, I, mm. 1–3 (Phrygian Mode)

The Ionian and Aeolian modes are the most commonly used modes in tonal contexts, including popular and folk idioms. Music with no chromatically altered tones, on the other hand, is rare. Example 1.23 contains two excerpts based on "pure" Ionian (a) and Aeolian (b) collections. Notice that neither excerpt contains an authentic cadence. The C♭ in m. 13 of Example 1.23b alters the mode of the underlying chord without affecting the overall Aeolian orientation of the passage.

**EX. 1.23a**—Sergei Prokofiev, *Alexander Nevsky*, No. 7, "Alexander's Entry into Pskov," mm. 1–10 (Ionian Mode)

**EX. 1.23b**—Sergei Prokofiev, *Alexander Nevsky*, No. 6, "Field of the Dead," mm. 11–14 (Aeolian Mode)

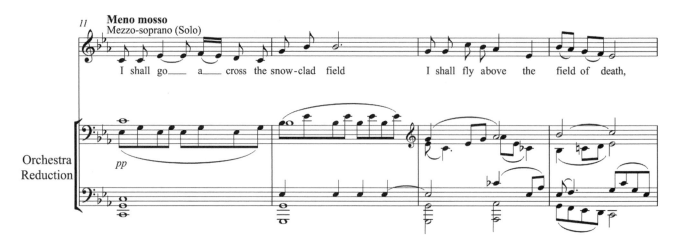

In addition to the seven diatonic modes, there are two non-diatonic seven-note scales with two semitones. These are shown in Figure 1.8. The first combines sharp $\hat{4}$ from the Lydian scale with flat $\hat{7}$ from the Mixolydian to form a **Lydian–Mixolydian scale** (a.k.a. the **acoustic scale**). The second is a **tertiary heptatonic scale**. The two semitones in tertiary heptatonic scales occur next to each other.[14] Both of these scales have twelve potential modes of their own. Playing the Lydian–Mixolydian scale beginning on $\hat{5}$, for example, produces a **melodic-minor ascending scale**.

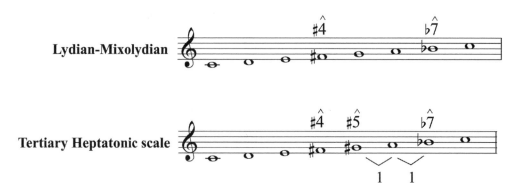

**FIGURE 1.8** *Remaining Seven-note Scales with Two Semitones*

Because the scales in Figure 1.8 contain non-diatonic pitches, they cannot be identified using the key signature method. To help identify non-diatonic collections, then, we may add a fourth condition to those in Figure 1.7. This condition appears in Figure 1.9.

---

d)  Unidentifiable Key Signature
    1)  Identify the centric pitch.
    2)  Notate the notes of the scale in ascending order.
    2)  Use the interval series and/or raised and lowered scale-degrees to determine the *non-diatonic* collection.

---

**FIGURE 1.9**  Condition d

Example 1.24 shows the beginning of Bartók's *Mikrokosmos*, Vol. 2, No. 41, "Melody with Accompaniment." At the top of the page, Bartók provides a notated version of the scale along with an unusual key signature, suggesting that **Condition d** may be in play here. The music is G centric, major, and includes both sharp $\hat{4}$ (C♯) and flat $\hat{7}$ (F♮). The scale is therefore Lydian–Mixolydian.

**EX. 1.24**—Béla Bartók, *Mikrokosmos*, Vol. 2, No. 41, "Melody with Accompaniment," mm. 1–7 (Lydian–Mixolydian

Example 1.25 shows a rare appearance of the tertiary heptatonic scale. In this example the two semitones are separated and occur at the bottom and top of the collection.

**EX. 1.25**—Béla Bartók, *Music for String Instruments, Percussion, and Celesta,* III, mm. 35–36 (Tertiary Heptatonic Scale)

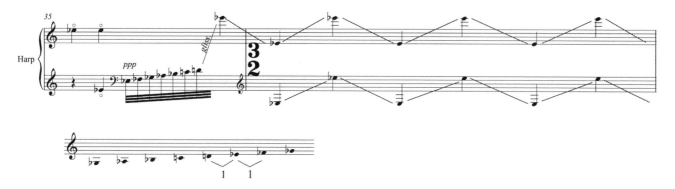

There are several other scales commonly found in recent music that do not consist of seven tones. These "synthetic" scales include the **pentatonic scale** (five notes), the **whole-tone scale** (six notes), the **hexatonic scale** (six notes), and the **octatonic scale** (eight notes). Like the diatonic modes, the individual character of these scales stems from their interval content.

Pentatonic scales are associated with various folk traditions and come in a variety of forms. The pentatonic scale most often used in Western music is the *anhemitonic* or *tonal* pentatonic scale.[15] This scale, which appears in Figure 1.10, consists only of whole-tones and minor thirds. Notice that intervals are expressed as whole numbers representing the number of semitones in the interval; this is a common way to express intervals when discussing twentieth-century music.

**FIGURE 1.10** Pentatonic Scale

The black keys on the piano constitute one version of the anhemitonic pentatonic scale. Example 1.26 contains two overlapping pentatonic scales: a white-key and a black-key version.

**EX. 1.26**—Béla Bartók, *Music for String Instruments, Percussion, and Celesta*, III mm. 35–36 ("White-key" and "Black-key" Pentatonic Scales)

There are only two unique whole-tone collections. These are shown in Figure 1.11. As the figure indicates, the scales are labeled Whole-tone$_0$ and Whole-tone$_1$. The integers 0 and 1 refer to pitches. In the integer system 0 = C, 1 = C♯, 2 = D, 3 = E♭, 4 = E♮, and so on. (Integer notation has a number of important advantages and will be covered more thoroughly in Chapter 2.)

**FIGURE 1.11** Whole-tone Scales

Whole-tone scales divide the octave evenly into six whole-tones. This allows the notes of each scale to fit neatly between those of the other. Playing the scale using any one of its members as the starting point, moreover, always generates the same collection. This means that each whole-tone scale has multiple potential tonal centers. Both of the excerpts in Example 1.27, for instance, incorporate the same whole-tone collection. The first excerpt, however, is D centric while the second is B♭ centric. The key signature in Example 1.27b suggests E major even though the excerpt itself articulates a whole-tone collection. This brings up an important point: not all music with a key signature is diatonic.

**EX. 1.27a**—Claude Debussy, Preludes, Book 2, No. 12, "Feux d'artifice," mm. 53–56 (D Whole-tone Scale)

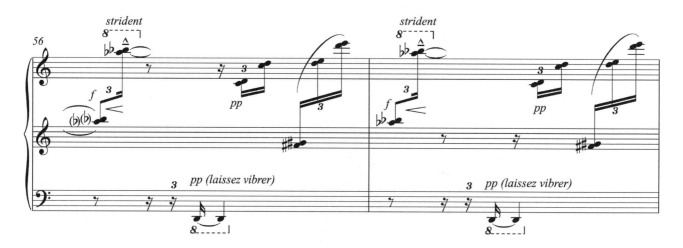

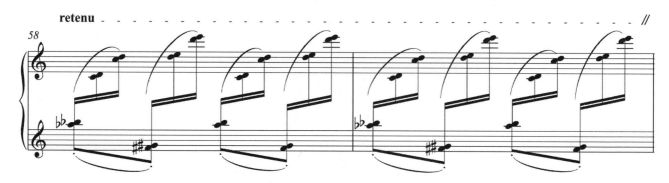

**EX. 1.27b**—Maurice Ravel, *Jeux d'eau*, m. 6 (B♭ Whole-tone Scale)

The hexatonic scale contains six notes and consists of alternating semitones and minor thirds. The four distinct hexatonic scales are shown in Figure 1.12. All other transpositions of the scale duplicate one of these four collections. The hexatonic$_{4,5}$ and hexatonic$_{8,9}$ scales in Figure 1.13, for example, are merely rotations of the hexatonic$_{0,1}$ scale. Any of the scale's six notes may function as a tonal center. Three of the scales built on these tones will begin with a minor second (cf. Figure 1.13). The other three will begin with a minor third.

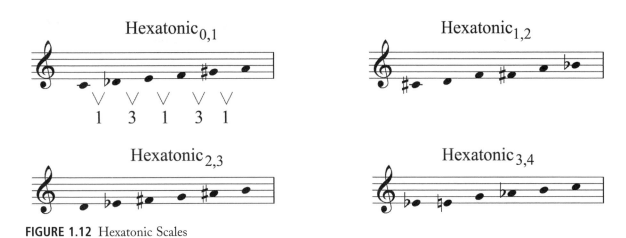

**FIGURE 1.12** Hexatonic Scales

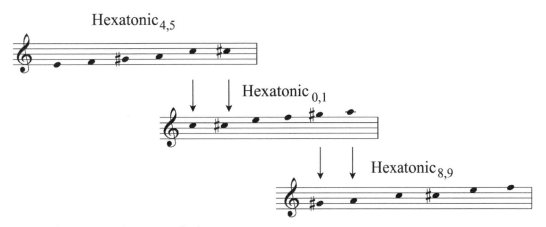

**FIGURE 1.13** Overlapping Hexatonic Scales

The hexatonic scale has a number of interesting features and relations to other collections. As Figure 1.14 illustrates, for example, hexatonic scales are generated spontaneously by PL cycles, in this case, the hexatonic$_{3,4}$ scale. Triads connected by dashed lines are called *hexatonic poles*. Hexatonic poles have no notes in common, but together form a complete hexatonic scale. Each hexatonic scale shares its notes with two other hexatonic collections. Scale-degrees 1, 3, and 5 of the Hexatonic$_{0,1}$ scale, for example, also occur in Hexatonic$_{3,4}$, while scale-degrees 2, 4, and 6 occur in Hexatonic$_{1,2}$.

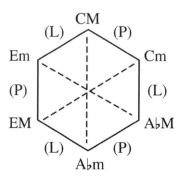

**FIGURE 1.14** PL Cycle with Hexatonic Poles

Webern's Concerto for Nine Instruments begins with the two hexatonic collections shown in Example 1.28. Together, these scales form the basis for the twelve-tone row on which the piece is based and are one of only two pairs of hexatonic collections that share no common tones.

**EX. 1.28**—Anton Webern, Concerto for Nine Instruments, Op. 24, I, mm. 1–3 (Non-overlapping Hexatonic Scales)

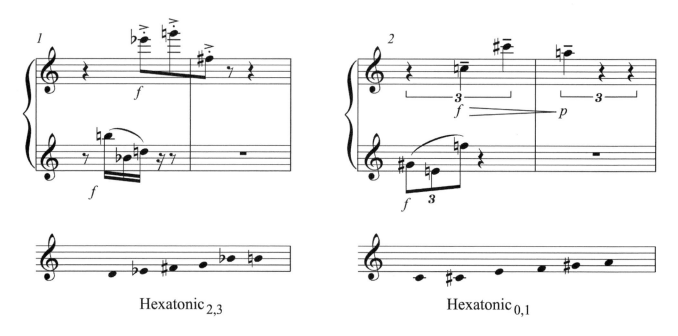

Another scale with an alternating interval sequence is the octatonic scale. In this case, the scale alternates between semitones and whole-tones.[16] There are three distinct octatonic scales: octatonic$_{0,1}$, octatonic$_{1,2}$, and octatonic$_{2,3}$. These are shown in Figure 1.15.

**Figure 1.15** Octatonic Scales

Owing to their redundant series of semitones and whole-tones, octatonic scales, like whole-tone and hexatonic scales, have multiple tonal centers. Example 1.29 is based on the octatonic$_{0,1}$ collection even though its centric pitch is B♭. Notice too that in this case, the scale begins with a whole-tone rather than a semitone.

**EX. 1.29**—Olivier Messiaen, *Quartet for the End of Time*, 7, "Fouillis d'arcs-en-ciel, pour l'Ange qui annonce la fin du Temps," mm. 1–2 (Octatonic Exerpt)

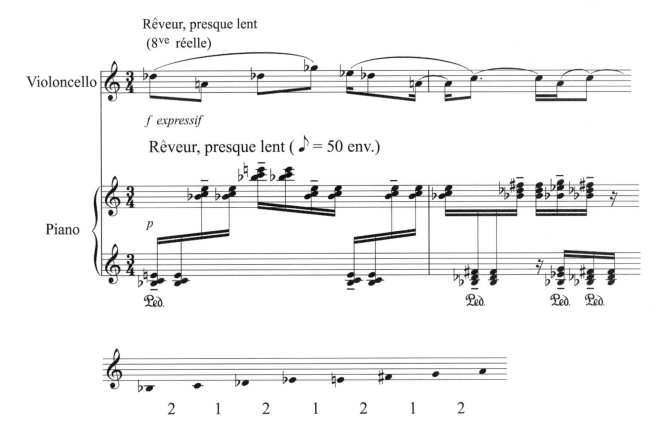

Among the most idiosyncratic scales to arise in the twentieth century are Olivier Messiaen's **modes of limited transposition**. Transposing each mode of limited transposition produces fewer than twelve unique collections. We have just encountered two such scales, the whole-tone scale, which generates only two collections under transposition, and the octatonic scale, which generates three.

The modes of limited transposition also entail a reduced number of modes. The whole-tone scale, for example, has only one mode consisting of six equal divisions of the octave. The octatonic scale has two modes, one beginning with a semitone and the other beginning with a whole-tone as illustrated in Figure 1.16. (See also Example 1.29.) The seven modes of limited transposition, along with the numbers assigned to them by Olivier Messiaen, appear in Appendix A.[17]

**FIGURE 1.16** The Two Octatonic Modes

The discussion of harmony and scale material in this chapter accounts for some of the main trends in recent music but is by no means comprehensive. Composers are imaginative individuals whose creativity can lead in many different directions. Here, we have concerned ourselves with materials drawn from the traditional twelve tones of the chromatic octave. Twentieth-century composers have also used microtones, notes that are less than a semitone apart. Of these, the quartertone is probably the most common. There are also a number of possible note combinations that fall outside the purview of traditional scales and chords built up from a single diatonic interval. In Chapter 4, we will outline a method for analyzing pitch collections that takes into account this broader array of possibilities.

## Chapter 1 Exercises

1) Fill in the blanks with the term that best describes the harmony.

a)

Ernest Bloch, *Schelomo*, mm. 149–150

**Piu animato (** ♩. = ♩ **del c )**

b)

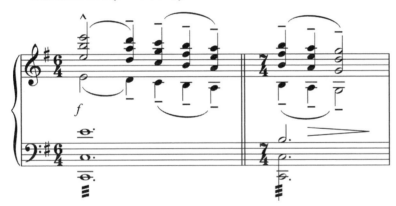

Ernest Bloch, *Schelomo*, m. 50

c)

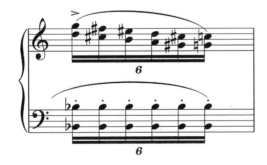

Sergei Prokofiev, *Alexander Nevsky*, No. 4, mm. 1–2

d)

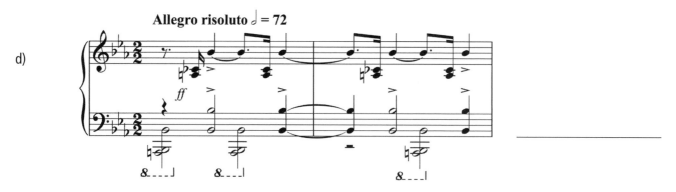

2) Complete the following for the excerpt below.

   a) Find the two polytriads and label them (e.g., D♭/A♭).

   b) Find and label the polymodal triad (e.g., BMaj/min).

   c) Find and label the two added note chords (e.g., G^(add 6)).

   d) Now label the remaining chords in the excerpt using letter names and Arabic numerals (e.g., A^M9).

   e) What term (secundal, tertian, quartal, quintal) best describes the harmonic texture overall?

3) The chords in the passage below incorporate a number of different intervals. Upon closer inspection, however, it can be seen that all the chords are derived from the same basic chord prototype built on a single interval. Name this chord type (e.g., secundal, tertian, quartal, or quintal) and explain how you arrived at your answer.

Darius Milhaud, *Les Choéphores*, VI, "La justice et la lumiére," mm. 1–4

4) Compose a short keyboard piece using at least four of the chord types discussed in Chapter 1.

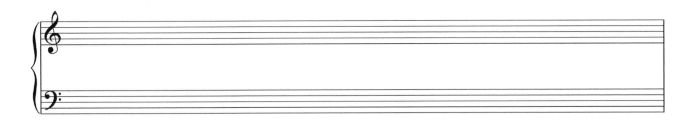

5)  Name the centric tone and modal or synthetic scale used in each of the following.

a) Claude Debussy, Preludes, Book 1, No. 5, "Les collines d'Anacapri," mm. 16–20

_____

b) Claude Debussy, Preludes, Book 1, No. 11, "La danse de Puck," mm. 1–5

_____

c) Darius Milhaud, Sonata No. 1 for Piano, II, mm. 1–10

_____

d) Alexander Scriabin, Prelude, Op. 74, No. 3, mm. 21–24

_____

e) Nicolai Rimsky-Korsakov, *Cappriccio Espagñol*, IV, mm. 70–73

f) Claude Debussy, *"Image" pour orchestre*, No. 2, "Iberia," III, mm. 17–18

g) Maurice Ravel, Trio in A Minor, III, "Passacaille," mm. 1–5

h) Heiter Villa-Lobos, *Carnaval das Criancas*, No. 6, "The Coquette's Mischievousness," mm. 30–33

i) Heiter Villa-Lobos, *Carnaval das Criancas*, No. 4, "The Little Domino's Jingle Bells," mm. 19–23

6) While the following excerpt could be analyzed using Roman numerals, a PLR analysis of the passage accounts better for the cyclical nature of the root movement by thirds and alternating major/minor orientation of successive triads. Identify the principal chords in the passage by letter name and quality along with their PLR transformations.

Nicolai Rimsky-Korsakov, *Sadko*, Scene 4, Nezhata's Song, "Kak na ozere na Il'mene," mm. 22–34 (Orchestra part only)

# Chapter 2

# Pitch and Interval

---

| | |
|---|---|
| Integer notation | Unordered pitch interval |
| Octave equivalence (generalization) | Ordered pitch-class interval |
| Pitch | Unordered pitch-class intervals |
| Pitch-class (pc) | Interval classes (ics) |
| Pitch-space | Contour inversion |
| Pc-space | Total interval-class content (interval-class |
| Modulo arithmetic | content) |
| Mod 12 | Interval cycle |
| Inversion | Aggregate |
| Complement | Compound interval cycles |
| Axis of inversion | Multi-aggregate cycle |
| Pc inversion | Cell x |
| Mirror symmetry | Cell y |
| Index | Cell z |
| Ordered pitch interval | Transpositional combination |

## Integer Notation

The first movement of Paul Hindemith's String Quartet in E-flat begins with the melodic theme shown on the upper staff in Example 2.1. This melody moves from E♭, the main key of the quartet, to its dominant, B♭, in m. 4. The melody itself, however, incorporates a number of pitches not usually associated with the key of E♭ including B♮, C♯, D♯, and F♯. The second excerpt is an octave transposition of the first in which several of the notes have been respelled. These respelled notes change the diatonic intervals in the passage, but do not affect our recognition of the theme. Spelling is therefore of little consequence because the tendencies usually associated with tonal harmony are downplayed.

**EX. 2.1**—Paul Hindemith, String Quartet No. 5 in E-flat, II, mm. 1–4 and 18–21 (Theme with Enharmonic Spellings)

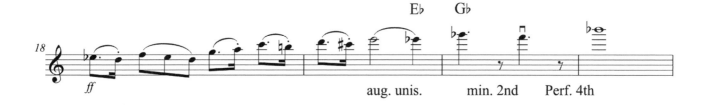

In cases like this, a simplified form of notation, such as **integer notation**, may be used to represent our perceptions more accurately. Integers have long played an important role in music; intervals, figured bass, chord inversions, beats, all are typically expressed with integers. As we learned in Chapter 1, integers can also be used to identify pitches. When using integer notation, 0 is usually assigned to C. Integers are added in semitone increments until we arrive back on C, at which point the series begins again, just as it does when using letter names. The complete collection, consisting of the integers 0 through 11, appears in Figure 2.1. The integers 10 and 11 are assigned the letters "T" and "E" so that each note can be identified with a single character.[1] This procedure lessens the chance for confusion when integers are used in a series. A 10, for example, might be misread as a 1 followed by a 0 and an 11 as two 1s. The integer system fully assimilates enharmonic spellings by assigning one label for each white or black key on the piano. Expressed as integers, for example, the last four notes of both excerpts in Example 2.1 are 3, 6, 5, and T. These integers remain the same regardless of octave or spelling.

**FIGURE 2.1** Integer Labels for Pitches in a One-octave Chromatic Scale

In the integer system, intervals are measured in semitones. The interval between C (0) and G (7), a perfect fifth, is seven semitones. Because the distance between the notes of any given interval remains constant under transposition, we may infer that all perfect fifths will span seven semitones. Hence, the distance from D♭ to A♭ is the same as that from C to G, seven semitones. A complete list of the integer names for intervals in a one-octave chromatic span appears in Table 2.1.

**TABLE 2.1** Integer Labels for Intervals

| | | |
|---|---|---|
| 0 | = | unison |
| 1 | = | minor second, augmented unison |
| 2 | = | major second, diminished third |
| 3 | = | minor third, augmented second |
| 4 | = | major third, diminished fourth |
| 5 | = | perfect fourth, augmented third |
| 6 | = | diminished fifth, augmented fourth, tritone |
| 7 | = | perfect fifth, diminished sixth |
| 8 | = | minor sixth, augmented fifth |
| 9 | = | major sixth, diminished seventh |
| 10 | = | minor seventh, augmented sixth |
| 11 | = | major seventh, diminished octave |
| 12 | = | octave |

Counting semitones, of course, is not a very efficient way to identify intervals. The intervals in the above list should therefore be committed to memory before continuing. To simplify this process, use a logical approach. Except for the unison, the semitone is the smallest possible interval in the equal-tempered system and is denoted by a 1. The whole-tone is one step larger or 2. Next to the octave, the largest interval is 11, a major seventh, and 10, a minor seventh, is one semitone smaller. The integer for a minor third, 3, corresponds to its ordinal number in tonal theory and the major third is one step larger or 4. Intervals are vital to the study of music and will be explored in more detail later in the chapter.

We should remember, of course, that many instruments are not limited to fixed pitches the way keyboard instruments are. Musicians trained in the subtleties of tonal harmony may perform enharmonically equivalent intervals differently depending on the demands of the local context. Even pianos and other keyboard instruments have not always been tuned according to the equal-tempered system. As little as a hundred years ago, pianos were tuned so that the intervals in keys with fewer accidentals remained purer (closer to their natural form) than their counterparts in keys with more accidentals.* Enharmonic substitutions, of course, were not uncommon in the tonal era and composers such as Franz Schubert, Robert Schumann, and Ludwig van Beethoven routinely used them for a variety of reasons, including, most conspicuously, modulations to distantly related keys. In music that contains a high degree of chromaticism, spelling can become almost completely arbitrary, subject only to the whims of the composer and matters of orchestration.

* For more in-depth discussions of tuning systems and their history see Stuart Isacoff, *Temperament: How Music Became a Battleground for the Great Minds of Western Civilization* (New York: Vintage Books, 2001) and Ross W. Duffin, *How Equal Temperament Ruined Harmony (and Why You Should Care)* (New York: W. W. Norton & Company, 2007).

So far, we have been speaking about pitches as though there were only twelve of them. In fact, there are many more, as the reader will be able to corroborate from experience. Reducing the full range of pitches to only twelve reflects a certain way of thinking about pitch, one based on the affinity pitches separated by one or more octaves have for one another. This phenomenon is known as **octave equivalence**. (Cognitive theorists use another term, **octave generalization**, to refer specifically to the perception of octave equivalence.) Under certain circumstances (e.g., when analyzing tonal harmony), such a conceptualization may be quite useful. At other times, the specific register of pitches needs to be taken into account (e.g., the study of counterpoint). We will therefore continue to acknowledge both perspectives, using the terms **pitch** and **pitch-class** (**pc**) to distinguish between them.

A pitch may be defined as a musical tone of some approximate frequency. (The notion of approximation in this definition accounts for the impurities that invariably arise when playing acoustical instruments as well as adjustments in intonation made in response to individual contexts.) A pitch-class, on the other hand, is a *family* of musical tones consisting of a pitch and all of its octave transpositions regardless of spelling. From time to time, it will also be necessary to refer to the spaces occupied by pitches and pitch-classes; we will use the term **pitch-space** to refer to a span filled by pitches and **pc-space** for a span filled by pcs.

To accommodate pitches, the integer system may be extended up and down from 0 as illustrated in Figure 2.2. In this example, 0 is assigned to middle C.[2] Negative numbers represent pitches below middle C and positive numbers represent pitches above middle C. One of the advantages of the integer system is that only one integer is needed to specify enharmonic pitches. As we shall see, it also allows intervals to be easily calculated through subtraction.

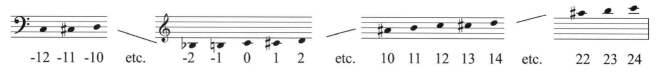

**FIGURE 2.2** Pitch Integers

Despite their advantages, the integers used to represent pitches can sometimes become unwieldy. To avoid this problem we may identify pitches by letter name and register using the method outlined by the Acoustical Society of America. In this system, C4 is middle C, C5 an octave above middle C, C3 an octave below middle C, and so on. The lowest three pitches on the piano are A0, B♭0, and B♮0 and the highest pitch C8. Since an octave spans twelve semitones, we can quickly determine the number of semitones in large intervals by counting octaves. The interval between D4 and G6, for example, is two octaves (twenty-four semitones) plus a perfect fourth (five semitones) or 29. In this text, we will use the nomenclature that most clearly illuminates the topic under discussion, letter names, integers, or both.

## Mod 12 Arithmetic

When discussing music that incorporates the twelve tones of the chromatic octave, it can be useful to express relations using **modulo** (a.k.a. "modular") **arithmetic**. In modulo arithmetic, two numbers are considered to be equivalent if their difference is exactly divisible by the modulo. Modulo arithmetic is useful for describing cyclical systems—calendars, seasons, clocks, etc. The chromatic collection is a **mod 12** system; it continuously cycles from 0 through 11 (twelve pcs in all) and back again. The cyclicity of the chromatic scale may be modeled using a clock-face diagram as in Figure 2.3. In this diagram, the twelve integers of the chromatic octave line up precisely with the numbers on a twelve-hour clock, the sole exception being 0, which occupies the twelve o'clock position. Octave-equivalent *pitches* always occur at the same position on the clock-face. Hence, C♯5 (13) lines up with the one o'clock hour, D5 (14) with the two o'clock hour, and so on.[3] Pitches below 0 in pitch-space are denoted by negative numbers.

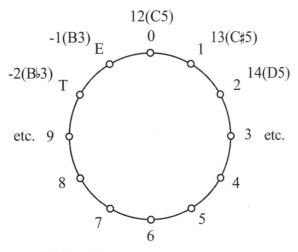

**FIGURE 2.3** Clock-face Diagram of Mod 12 Pc-Space

## Inversion

One of the most common operations used to analyze pcs and pitches is **inversion**. Not to be confused with chord inversion, inversion, as the term is used most often in this text, replaces intervals, pitches, or pcs with their complements. A **complement** is the element or group of elements that together with another forms a balanced or complete set. Complementary pcs are defined in reference to the center of the collection, which is known as the **axis of inversion** or simply the "axis" of the collection. The axis in Figure 2.4 is 0. (The actual axis, represented by a dotted line, cuts through both 0 and 6.) Notice that in **pc inversion** complementary pairs of pcs—we may call them *inversionally equivalent* pcs—produce **mirror symmetry**; each pc is the "reflection" of its inversion and thus equidistant from the center. For example, E, one step to the left of 0 is the inversion (or complement) of 1, which is one step to the right of 0, and so on. Notice also that inversionally equivalent pairs of pcs always sum to 0 mod 12; 0 + 0 = 0, 1 + 11 = 0, 2 + 10 = 0, 6 + 6 = 0, etc. This sum is called the **index** of the collection.

The mod 12 equivalent of a negative number is the inversion of its absolute value mod 12. The mod 12 equivalent for –1 is 11, the inversion of 1. To express this equivalence mathematically, add 12 (12 + (–1) = 11).

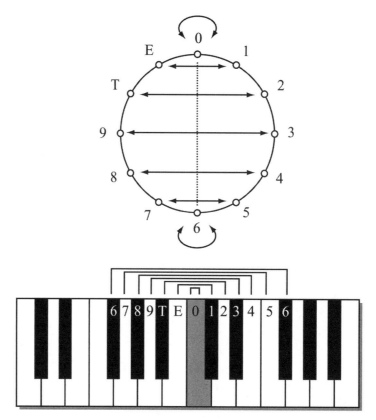

**FIGURE 2.4** Clock-face Diagram and Keyboard showing Inversional Symmetry

Other axes of inversion may also be encountered. Figures 2.5a and b show two possibilities. In every case, the sum of inversionally equivalent pcs will be the index. When the axis passes *between* two pcs, as in Figure 2.5a, inversionally equivalent pcs will always sum to an odd number, in this case 5. When the axis passes *through* a pc, as in Figure 2.5b, the sum is even.

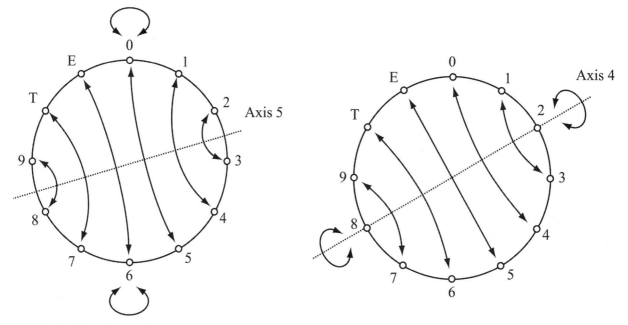

**FIGURE 2.5** Other Axes in Pc-Space

The excerpt in Example 2.2 contains two inversionally equivalent melodies, one in the right-hand part and the other in the left-hand part. Here, the index is 8; inversionally equivalent pairs of pcs sum to 8 and are mirror symmetrical around the 4/T axis. (See Figure 2.6.)

**EX. 2.2**—Béla Bartók, *Mikrokosmos*, Vol. 6, No. 141, "Subject and Reflection," mm. 1–3 (Inversionally Equivalent Melodies and their Contours)

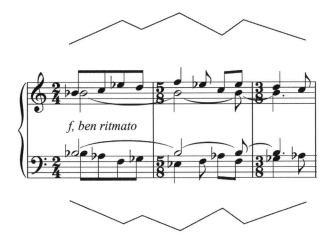

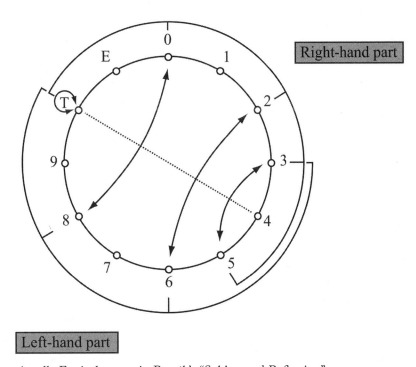

**FIGURE 2.6** Inversionally Equivalent pcs in Bartók's "Subject and Reflection"

In addition to their inversional symmetry in pc-space, the two collections in Example 2.2 are symmetrical in pitch-space. Figure 2.7 shows the first five pitches of both parts. Notice that inversionally equivalent pitches are equidistant above and below the pitch axis, E4. The right- and left-hand parts also move in synchrony with each other, but in opposite directions, creating mirror contours as indicated by the line drawings above and below the grand staff in Example 2.2.

**FIGURE 2.7** Pitch Symmetry in Bartók's "Subject and Reflection"

## Intervals

As we have already seen, intervals in pitch-space can differ from those in pc-space. In addition, intervals may be either *ordered* or *unordered*. Ordered intervals are essentially the same as *melodic* intervals, those whose notes follow each other in a particular chronological succession. The notes of unordered intervals may occur in any order or simultaneously. Unordered intervals are useful for analyzing *harmonic* intervals, although they may also be used to identify melodic intervals if chronological succession is not a crucial concern. The interval between two pitches or pcs is equal to their difference and may be determined through subtraction.

In this text, we will concentrate on four different kinds of intervals:

1) *ordered pitch intervals*
2) *unordered pitch intervals*
3) *ordered pitch-class intervals*
4) *unordered pitch-class intervals*.

One of the consequences of presenting pitches in a particular order is that it produces shape or contour. Building on this idea, we may define an **ordered pitch interval** as the distance measured in semitones between two pitches *with direction specified*. A (+) sign added to the interval denotes an ascending motion in pitch-space while a (−) sign denotes a descending motion. Plus signs are sometimes left out in which case the interval is understood to be ascending. In contrast, an **unordered pitch interval** is the distance measured in semitones between two pitches in which direction is *not* specified. Figure 2.8 illustrates these two types of intervals. In both cases the integers match, but the ordered pitch intervals are accompanied by (+) and (−) signs indicating the direction traveled from one pitch to the next. (Notice that the signs for ordered pitch intervals emerge spontaneously when the integer name of the first pitch is subtracted from the second; e.g., 3 (E♭4) − 7 (G4) = −4 while 17 (F5) − 3 (E♭4) = (+)14.) To identify unordered pitch intervals, convert them to their absolute values by removing all signs.

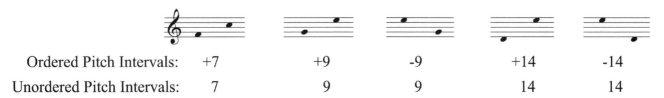

| Ordered Pitch Intervals: | +7 | +9 | -9 | +14 | -14 |
| Unordered Pitch Intervals: | 7 | 9 | 9 | 14 | 14 |

**FIGURE 2.8** Ordered and Unordered Pitch Intervals

Pcs too may occur in succession. Register, on the other hand, is irrelevant where pcs are concerned since pcs may occur in any octave without changing position on the clock-face. The motion from pc 2 to pc 1, for example, may be notated in a number of ways including those shown in Figure 2.9.

**FIGURE 2.9** Alternate Notation for Pcs

Notice that whether we descend one semitone (Figure 2.9a) or ascend eleven semitones (Figure 2.9b) in pitch-space we reach the same pc. Negative moves, of course, register as positive numbers in mod 12 pc-space and correspond to the inversions of their absolute values (−1 = 11, −2 = 10, and so on). One way to determine an **ordered pitch-class interval**, then, is to convert all ascents and descents in pitch-space to their mod 12 equivalents, remembering to replace negative numbers with their inversions mod 12. This method ensures that the ordered pitch-class interval between consecutive pcs will always be the same regardless of the direction traveled (up or down) in pitch-space. The ordered pitch-class interval from D to C♯, for example, is 11 whether pc 1 is approached from above or below. *Plus and minus signs are unnecessary and should not be used.* To calculate ordered pitch-class intervals mathematically, simply subtract the first pc from the second using mod 12 arithmetic (e.g., 1 − 2 = −1 = 12 + (− 1) = 11).

> Another way to calculate ordered pitch-class intervals is to treat them as clockwise moves from one pc to the next; 7 to 1, 5 to 0, and so on. No matter how they are determined, ordered pitch-class intervals take into account the order of the pcs in a melodic sequence, which comes first, which comes second, etc.

**Unordered pitch-class intervals** are indifferent to succession and may be defined as the shortest distance between two pcs. Integers larger than 6 should be replaced by their inversions mod 12. The inversion of an unordered pc interval is the same as in tonal theory. The inversion of a minor second (1), for example, is a major seventh (11). To figure inversions mathematically, subtract from 12 (e.g., 12 − 1 = 11).

Figure 2.10 recasts the intervals in Figure 2.8 as ordered and unordered pitch-class intervals. Notice that, in many cases, each type of interval conveys different information about the relations between the pitches.

| | | | | |
|---|---|---|---|---|
| Ordered Pitch Intervals: +7 | +9 | −9 | +14 | −14 |
| Unordered Pitch Intervals: 7 | 9 | 9 | 14 | 14 |
| Ordered Pitch-class Intervals: 7 | 9 | 3 | 2 | 10 |
| Unordered Pitch-class Intervals: 5 | 3 | 3 | 2 | 2 |

**FIGURE 2.10** Ordered and Unordered Pitch and Pitch-class Intervals

The alert reader may have already deduced that there are only seven possible unordered pitch-class intervals. This is because pcs that are more than six hours apart on the clock-face can be reached via a smaller interval (the inversion) by moving in the opposite direction. Figure 2.11 provides a graphic illustration of this idea; it takes seven steps to move clockwise from 1 to 8, but only five steps if we move counter-clockwise. The seven unordered pitch-class intervals are most often referred to as **interval classes** (**ics**). As illustrated in Table 2.2, each ic subsumes both itself and its inversion.

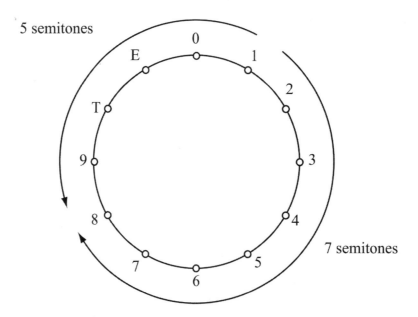

**FIGURE 2.11** Two Ways to Get from Pc 1 to Pc 8

**TABLE 2.2** Interval-Classes (ics)

| ics | Ordered Pitch-class Intervals |
|---|---|
| 0 | 0 |
| 1 | 1 & 11 |
| 2 | 2 & 10 |
| 3 | 3 & 9 |
| 4 | 4 & 8 |
| 5 | 5 & 7 |
| 6 | 6 |

As we have seen, ordered pitch intervals convey both contour and interval information. All of the bracketed figures in mm. 1–2 of Example 2.3, for instance, have the same ordered pitch interval content, −1/+3. While other interval types could be used to express the relations between these figures, ordered pitch intervals are the most discriminating. The melodic fragment in Figure 2.12, for example, has the same *unordered* pitch interval content as the figures in Example 2.3, but does not follow the same contour. The ordered pitch intervals explicitly convey the differences in contour between the figures in Example 2.3 and Figure 2.12 whereas the unordered pitch intervals do not.

**EX. 2.3**—Paul Hindemith, String Quartet No. 5 in E-flat, II, mm. 1–4 (−1/+3 Figures)

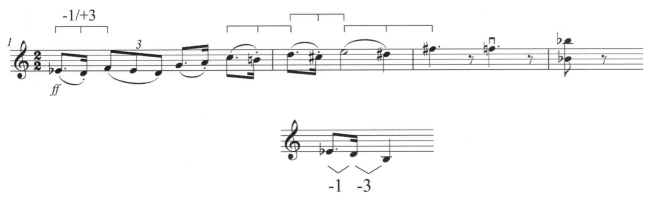

**FIGURE 2.12** −1/−3 Figure

Other ways of conceptualizing intervals may lead to important insights when contours do not match. The first three measures of George Crumb's "Verte desnuda es recordar la tierra" from his first book of *Madrigals* contains a number of three-note gestures—offset by rests and distinguished by their instrumental or vocal timbres—whose intervallic relations are less obvious than those in Example 2.3. These gestures are enclosed in boxes and labeled with the letters (a) through (f) in Example 2.4.

**EX. 2.4**—George Crumb, *Madrigals*, Book 1, No. 1, "Verte desnuda es recordar la tierra," mm. 1–3 (Melodic Gestures)

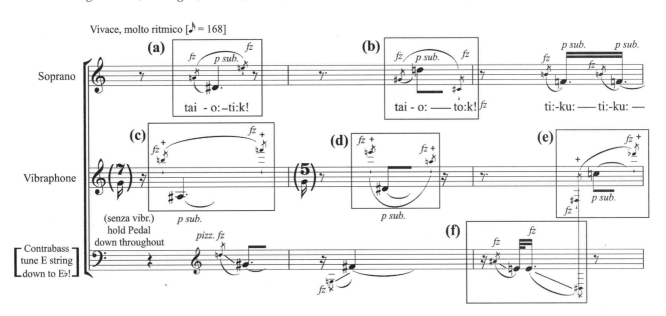

This piece typifies Crumb's "coloristic" approach to composition in which dynamics and articulation contribute to the expressive aspects of the work as much as the pitch content. In this excerpt, the voice too is treated like an instrument; its dynamics and articulations imitate those of the vibraphone and contrabass and the nonsense syllables, with their hard "t"s and "k"s, are more percussive than discursive.

The contours of the melodic gestures in this excerpt—we may call them motives—vary widely, yet there are also important similarities. As Example 2.5 illustrates, motives (a), (b), and (f) contain the same sequence of unordered pitch intervals. Motive (b), moreover, constitutes a **contour inversion** of motive (a)—ascents and descents are swapped—while motive (f) inverts only the second shape of motive (a); the +13 in motive (a) becomes −13 in motive (f).

**EX. 2.5**—(Melodic Gestures with Shared Unordered Pitch Interval Content)

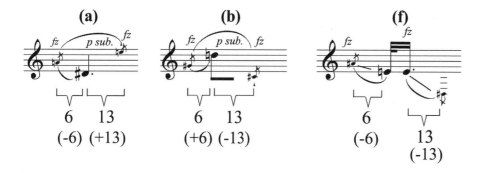

Motive (d) can be brought into closer contact with motives (b) and (f) using ordered pitch-class intervals. As Example 2.6 shows, all three motives articulate ordered pitch-class intervals 11 and 6.

**EX. 2.6**—(Melodic Gestures with Shared Ordered Pitch-class Interval Content)

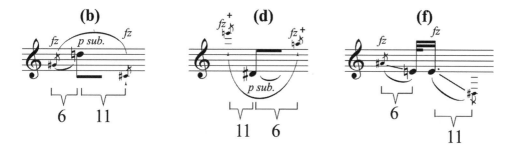

Motive (d) presents the pitches of motive (a) in reverse order with two of the pitches, A and E, shifted an octave higher. In fact, this *reordering* is precisely why the *ordered* pitch-class intervals of the motives do not match even though the two motives share the same pcs!

All of the motives encountered so far—along with motive (e) shown in Example 2.7—incorporate unordered pitch-class intervals 1 and 6.

**EX. 2.7**—(Unordered Pitch-class Interval Content of Motive (e))

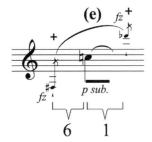

The contrabass part in m. 1 and the soprano part in m. 3 articulate these same intervals in isolation. (See Example 2.8.)

**EX. 2.8**—(Melodic Gestures with Shared Unordered Pitch Interval Content)

That the beginning of Crumb's madrigal is based primarily on ics 1 and 6 would appear to be undeniable were it not for motive (c), which occurs in the first measure of the vibraphone part. The succession of unordered pitch-class intervals in this motive is 1/5. Admittedly, this is a small difference; only one of the intervals is altered and by only one semitone at that. Motive (c), however, has an even stronger connection to the other motives in the passage than the analysis of its interval succession reveals. This connection comes to light when we examine the **total interval-class content** of the motives in the passage.[4] To determine the total interval-class content, tally the intervals between each pc and every other pc in the motive as illustrated in Example 2.9. In three-note groupings, this process brings a third interval into play, that between the first and third pitches. The total interval-class content for motive (c) is 1/5/6. As it happens, these intervals also occur in the other three-note groupings in the excerpt. Viewed in this way, all the groupings appear to spring from the same intervallic antecedents.

**EX. 2.9**—(Total Interval-class Content of Motive (c))

The interval analysis of Crumb's "Verte desnuda es recordar la tierra" reveals strong connections between the gestures that occur at the beginning of the piece. It also suggests that while there are many ways one might interpret a given event, the event itself may provide the best clue as to which approach will lead to the most fruitful insights. Analytical tools not only provide a way to hear and interpret music, they also provide a glimpse into the complexities of musical structure. Composers have an intimate familiarity with the materials of music and may often make forays into uncharted territory. Analytical tools can help reveal the inherent rationality of such explorations and can lead to greater understanding on the part of listeners and performers alike.

## Motivic Hearing

Having learned about intervals, the student may now begin working on the **Stream 1** Exercises in the online *Motivic Hearing* program introduced in the "Aural Skills Supplement." For now, simply identify the unordered pitch intervals in the exercises. Prime forms and TTOs will be discussed in Chapters 3, 4 and 6.

## Interval Cycles

An **interval cycle** may be thought of as a particular kind of scale, one that has a repeating interval series.[5] We have already encountered scales of this kind. The whole-tone scale, for example, is a 2/10 cycle; it can be generated by playing either a series of whole-steps (2s) or a series of minor sevenths (10s). (cf. Figure 1.11 in Chapter 1.) Figure 2.13 lists all six interval cycles and their transpositions. Only the 1/11 and 5/7 cycles produce the complete **aggregate** (the collection of all twelve pcs). Because 6 is its own inversion, 6 cycles have only 2 members. Each 3/9 cycle produces the four notes of a diminished seventh chord, while each 4/8 cycle produces three tones, forming an augmented triad.

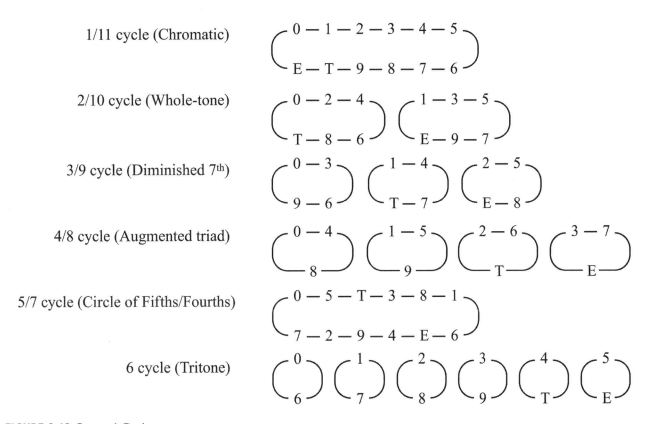

**FIGURE 2.13** Interval Cycles

**Compound interval cycles** are patterns with more than one interval and its inversion. One such cycle is the octatonic scale, which may be defined as a 1/2 or 2/1 cycle. The excerpt in Example 2.10 contains a compound 5/1 cycle. Here the notes of the collection are presented both melodically and harmonically.

**EX. 2.10**—Béla Bartók, String Quartet No. 4, V, mm. 31–34 (Compound 5/1 Cycle)

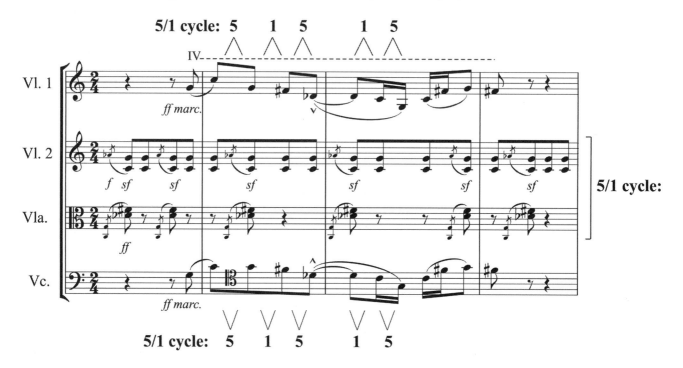

As defined by Edward Gollin, a **multi-aggregate cycle** is "a compound interval cycle that covers (or runs through the tones of) more than one aggregate."[6] A nearly complete version of a multi-aggregate 3/4/4 cycle, scattered throughout the piece, occurs in George Crumb's *The Sleeper*. Figure 2.14 contains a notated version of the complete cycle with brackets indicating the location of various fragments of the cycle. In this case, the multi-aggregate cycle comprises three aggregates. This means that there are three uniquely positioned instances of each pc in the complete cycle. (Play through the cycle to familiarize yourself with its sound. Then play a recording of the piece and listen for ascending and descending fragments of the cycle in the vocal and piano parts.)

**FIGURE 2.14** 3/4/4 Cycle

Cycles may also be fragmented to form partial cycles. Four-note partial cycles consisting of chromatic, whole-tone, and octatonic fragments are referred to as cells. These cells, most often associated with Béla Bartók, have been given the names **cell x** (chromatic fragment), **cell y** (whole-tone fragment), and **cell z** (octatonic fragment).[7] These are shown in Figure 2.15. Cell z may be conceptualized either as two interlocking tritones or a 5/1 cycle.

**FIGURE 2.15** Cells x, y, and z

Example 2.11 contains an example of a piece organized around a succession of cells; here the principal motive in the piece is cell z followed by cell x.

**EX. 2.11**—Béla Bartók, *Mikrokosmos*, Vol. 3, No. 92, "Chromatic Invention," mm. 1–5 (Excerpt with Cells x and z)

Example 2.12 contains a more subtle combination of cells. In this excerpt, cell x and its subsets appear in boxes. Instances of cell y are bracketed. Fragments of both cells are combined to create new melodic patterns in the first violin, viola, and cello parts. The B♭–B♮–C–D♭ cell, moreover, is divided into two isolated two-note groupings. Dividing the cell in this way highlights a relation known as **transpositional combination**. As illustrated in Figure 2.16, transpositional combination is a property of certain sets, including cells x, y, and z, which allows them to be divided into transpositionally equivalent subsets.[8] The chromatic cell B♭–B♮–C–D♭ contains two two-note subsets, precisely those that are circled in Example 2.12.

**EX. 2.12**—Béla Bartók, String Quartet No. 5, Andante, mm. 744–49 (Excerpt with Cells x and y)

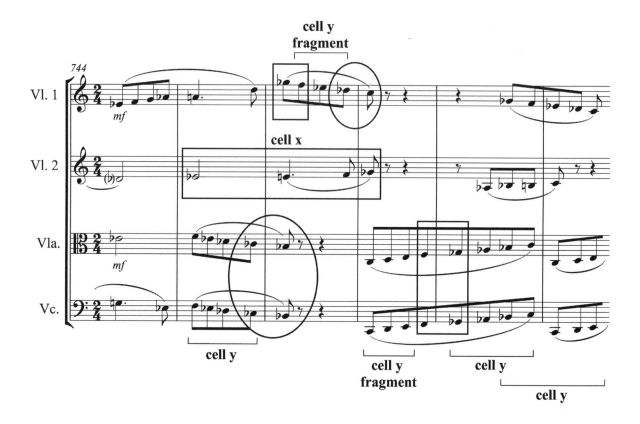

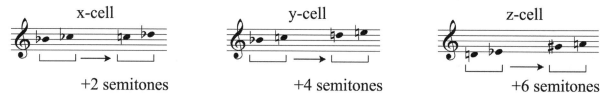

**FIGURE 2.16** Transpositional Combination

As the analyses in this chapter suggest, our comprehension of music does not rely solely on pitches and intervals in isolation. Larger groupings—motives, themes, chords, and the like—also play an important role. In the following chapters, we will investigate several different types of groupings in both pitch- and pc-space. As we shall see, the ideas covered in the present chapter, especially those centering around various types of intervals, will continue to figure prominently in our understanding of these constructions and their operations. In Chapters 4 and 5, we will discuss unordered collections—chords, scales, and the like—along with their *unordered pitch* and *pitch-class intervals*. *Ordered pitch intervals* are especially useful for identifying relations between melodic motives and themes. These will be discussed in Chapters 3 and 6. Row compositions, works based on a predetermined succession of pcs, may be analyzed using *ordered pitch-class interval*s and will be introduced in Chapter 8.

## Chapter 2 Exercises

1) Identify the pcs below using the integers 0–11.

2) Substitute integers for the following letter names.

a)  G♯_____          f)  G♮_____

b)  C♭_____          g)  D♯_____

c)  A♮_____          h)  C♯_____

d)  E♭♭_____         i)  E♮_____

e)  B♯_____          j)  F♯_____

3) Substitute letter names with octave designations (e.g., C♯5) for the following integers. Assume that C4 is 0.

a)  5 _____          f)  −8 _____

b)  15 _____         g)  20 _____

c)  −2 _____         h)  37 _____

d)  18 _____         i)  −23 _____

e)  8 _____          j)  45 _____

4) Supply integer names for each of the following intervals.

a) Perfect fifth _____

b) Minor sixth _____

c) Minor third _____

d) Minor ninth _____

e) Augmented second _____

f) Minor second _____

g) Diminished seventh _____

h) Perfect eleventh _____

i) Diminished fifth_____

j) 15ma _____

k) Augmented fifth _____

l) Major third _____

5) Label each of the following *unordered pitch intervals* using integers.

6) Interval identification.

a) Identify the melodic ordered/unordered pitch and pitch-class intervals for the melodic figures below.

b) Place a checkmark beside the interval series that are most "patternistic." These may include integer palindromes, sequences, and/or strings of the same interval.

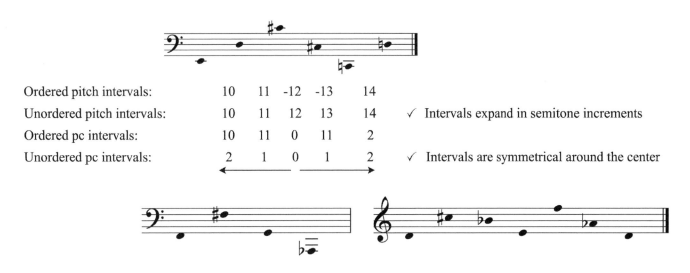

| Ordered pitch intervals: | 10 | 11 | -12 | -13 | 14 | |
|---|---|---|---|---|---|---|
| Unordered pitch intervals: | 10 | 11 | 12 | 13 | 14 | ✓ Intervals expand in semitone increments |
| Ordered pc intervals: | 10 | 11 | 0 | 11 | 2 | |
| Unordered pc intervals: | 2 | 1 | 0 | 1 | 2 | ✓ Intervals are symmetrical around the center |

Ordered pitch intervals:

Unordered pitch intervals:

Ordered pc intervals:

Unordered pc intervals:

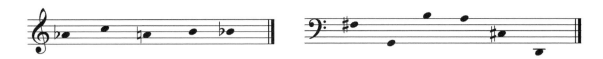

Ordered pitch intervals:

Unordered pitch intervals:

Ordered pc intervals:

Unordered pc intervals:

Ordered pitch intervals:

Unordered pitch intervals:

Ordered pc intervals:

Unordered pc intervals:

7) Convert the following ordered pitch intervals to interval classes.

a)  14 _____                          f)  9 _____

b)  −5 _____                          g)  −17 _____

c)  22 _____                          h)  6 _____

d)  −15 _____                         i)  38 _____

e)  8 _____                           j)  45 _____

8) Name the inversions for the following ordered pitch-class intervals in the axis 0 system.

a)  1 _____                           g)  11 _____

b)  3 _____                           h)  4 _____

c)  6 _____                           i)  8 _____

d)  9 _____                           j)  0 _____

e)  10 _____                          k)  7 _____

f)  5 _____                           l)  2 _____

9) Name the inversions for the following ordered pitch-class intervals in the axis 9 system.

1 _____                              11 _____

3 _____                              4 _____

6 _____                              8 _____

9 _____                              0 _____

10 _____                             7 _____

5 _____                              2 _____

10) Convert the following pitches to pcs. Assume that 0 is C4.

C♯5 _____                            45 _____

12 _____                             15 _____

−14 _____                            24 _____

G♭1 _____                            D7 _____

F6 _____                             −37 _____

11) Complete each of the following interval cycles and provide a notated version of the cycle.

5/7 cycle:   1 . . .

2/10 cycle:   3 . . .

3/9 cycle:   2 . . .

1/2 cycle:   5 . . .

1/3 cycle:   0 . . .

12) Now complete the following multi-aggregate cycles and provide a notated version.

3/4 cycle:   0 . . .

1/6 cycle:   3 . . .

# Chapter 3

# Sets and Segmentation

---

| | |
|---|---|
| Ordered pitch set | Retrograde (R) |
| Ordered pc set | Retrograde inversion (RI) |
| Unordered pitch set | Prime (P) |
| Unordered pc set | Twelve-tone operations (TTOs) |
| Pitch height | Pitch cycles |
| Adjacency interval series (AIS) | Pc cycles |
| Inversionally equivalent unordered pc sets | Rotation |
| Invariant pcs | Segmentation |
| Self-retrogradable interval series | |

## Ordered and Unordered Sets

Of primary importance to our understanding of music is the organization of pitches and/or pitch-classes into patternistic melodic and harmonic groupings. In this text, we will refer to all such groupings, whether presented as chords or melodies, as sets. Ordered sets are enclosed in angled brackets (< >) and contain either pitches or pcs arranged in a particular sequential progression. Unordered sets list either the total pitch or total pc content of a collection and are enclosed in square brackets ( [ ] ). The order of elements in unordered sets may change depending on the analytical context.

The ordered and unordered sets listed below the staff in Example 3.1 illustrate four ways of representing the harp part from the third movement of Lutoslawski's Symphony No. 1, mm. 246–47, a piece we will return to later in the chapter. The **ordered pitch set** contains six different pitches and presents each pitch in the order it occurs. The **ordered pc set** also presents the notes in the order they occur, but contains a repeated pc (pc 8). The **unordered pitch set** contains the same pitches as the ordered pitch set, but presents them bottom-to-top. The **unordered pc set** lists the pcs in ascending numerical order and has fewer elements than the other sets; because the set is unordered, it is necessary to list pc 8 only once.[1]

**EX. 3.1**—Witold Lutoslawski, Symphony No. 1, III, Harp, mm. 246–47 (Ordered and Unordered Sets)

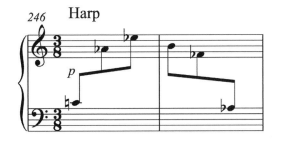

| | |
|---|---|
| Ordered Pitch set | <C4, Ab4, Eb5, B4, Fb4, Ab3> |
| Unordered Pitch set | [Ab3, C4, Fb4, Ab4, B4, Eb3] |
| Ordered Pc set | <0, 8, 3, E, 4, 8> |
| Unordered PC set | [0, 3, 4, 8, E] |

Like interval analysis, the kind of insight a particular set type provides depends on one's analytical orientation in addition to the characteristics of the passage under consideration. Both ordered and unordered pitch sets, for example, take into account the registral location of pitches in pitch-space (**pitch height**) whereas only ordered pitch sets reflect the melodic contour of a passage. Ordered pitch sets include nursery rhymes, patriotic songs, folk songs, and other familiar melodies. Not all ordered pitch sets, of course, are as "singable" as these tunes. Regardless of their makeup, however, all such sets unfold linearly and maintain their overall shape from one instance to the next.

Pc sets, whether ordered or unordered, disclose associations between octave-equivalent pitches regardless of register. The pitch realizations of pc sets, on the other hand, can vary widely since any given pc may occur in different octaves in pitch-space. As we shall see, ordered pc sets are especially relevant where the analysis of music built around various types of rows is concerned. Of these, twelve-tone rows are the most common, but rows consisting of fewer tones may also be found. (The eleven-note theme from Copland's Quartet for Piano and Strings shown in Examples 3.2 and 3.3 is one well-known example.) Row composition will be discussed in Chapter 8. Unordered pitch and pc sets are useful for analyzing collections, scales, and chords and will be covered in Chapters 4 and 5.

To make the distinctions between ordered and unordered pitch and pc sets clearer, let us look at several more examples. Example 3.2 contains two instances of the principal theme from the second movement of Aaron Copland's Quartet for Piano and Strings. Though the rhythms of the themes differ, the pitches, contour, and ordering of the two statements match exactly as do their ordered pitch set representations.

**EX. 3.2**—Aaron Copland, Quartet for Piano and Strings, II, mm. 1–2 and 9–10 (Ordered Pitch Sets)

Ordered Pitch Set <A3, Db4, Ab4, Eb4, F4, G4, A4, F#5, E5, D5, C6, Bb5>

These circumstances are reversed in Example 3.3; the melodies have nearly identical rhythms, but their pitch content differs. Both melodies, on the other hand, do articulate the same ordered succession of pcs. While the ordered pitch sets in the example do not match, then, the ordered pc sets do.

**EX. 3.3**—Aaron Copland, Quartet for Piano and Strings, II, mm. 1–2 and 5–6 (Ordered Pc sets)

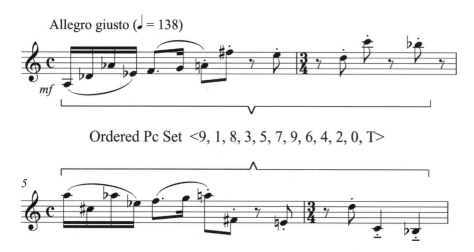

Now let's take a look at several unordered sets. The first measure of the second movement of Barbara Kolb's *Appello* shown in Example 3.4 contains a four-note untransposed pitch collection. As the brackets beneath the staff indicate, the complete collection is presented exactly four times. Though unordered, each of these iterations of the set articulate the pitches of the collection as a whole and thus belong to unordered pitch set [G4, A♭4, A♮4, D5]. (The rest of the movement unfolds in a similar manner with numerous repetitions of each measure. Be sure to listen to the entire movement, taking note of how repetition causes the pitches to coalesce into a series of composite chord-like aggregates.)

**EX. 3.4**—Barbara Kolb, *Appello*, II, "A vague chimera that engulfs the breath—Robert Pinsky," m. 1 (Unordered Pitch Sets)

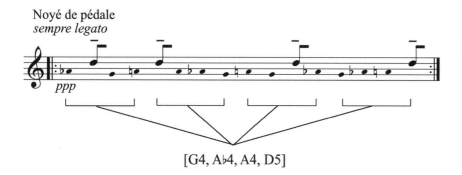

Expressing a collection as an unordered pitch set does not necessarily mean order doesn't matter. Indeed, every pitch in the excerpt from Kolb's *Appello* occurs exactly once in each ordinal position as we move from one grouping to the next. A♭4, for example, occurs in the first position, the third position, the fourth position, and finally the second position of successive four-note groupings in the example. This scheme continues throughout the movement.

The excerpt from the beginning of Debussy's prelude "Les collines d'Anacapri" (The Hills of Anacapri) in Example 3.5 is texturally more complex than those we have observed so far. Yet, each new idea seems to blend seamlessly with those around it. This may be attributed in part to the fact that, despite the wide variety of contours, pitches, and articulation in the excerpt, each two-measure unit expresses unordered pc set [1, 4, 6, 8, E], a pentatonic scale. (The only additional pc in the passage is the D♯ passing tone in m. 3.)

**EX. 3.5**—Claude Debussy, Preludes, Book 1, No. 5, "Les collines d'Anacapri," mm. 1–8 (Unordered Pc Sets)

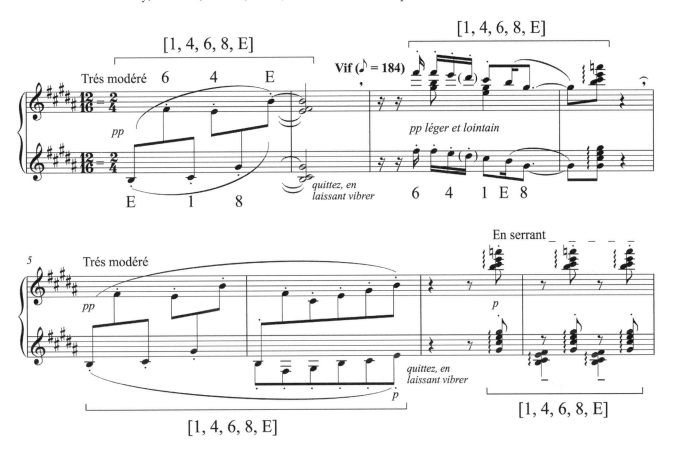

Unordered sets may also provide important information about themes with fixed contours and registers. Treating the melodic theme from the beginning of the second movement of Copland's Quartet for Piano and Strings (Example 3.2) as an unordered pc set, for example, reveals that it is only one pc shy of completing the chromatic collection. This, it turns out, is a significant aspect of the piece; the composition is based on an eleven-note row and incorporates some of the techniques associated with Schoenberg's twelve-tone method, which Copland experimented with in the 1950s.

## Inverted Sets

Like the pitches and pcs they are composed of, sets may be inverted. To invert a set, all of its elements are replaced with their complements. This has the effect of flipping the set around its axis. Take, for example, the four-note unordered pc set [1, 3, 5, 8]. To invert the set about 0, simply reverse the set and replace each pc with its inversion as illustrated in Figure 3.1. Since the index in an axis 0 system is 0, each pair of inversionally equivalent pcs will sum to 0 mod 12. (See Chapter 2, p. 47.)

Intervals are extremely important to a set's identity. Indeed, a set's interval content is often its most salient feature. The succession of intervals between consecutive pitches or pcs in a set is known as its **adjacency interval series (AIS)**. The adjacency interval series for unordered pc sets consists of unordered pitch-class intervals (ics). As Figure 3.2 illustrates, inversion reverses the order of the intervals in the adjacency interval series.

Don't allow integers to keep you from visualizing inversion in more familiar terms. Figure 3.3, for example, shows how inversion produces a mirror image of [1, 3, 5, 8] on the piano keyboard (a), alto clef staff (b), and mod 12 clock-face (c).

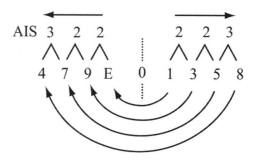

**FIGURE 3.2** Interval Inversion

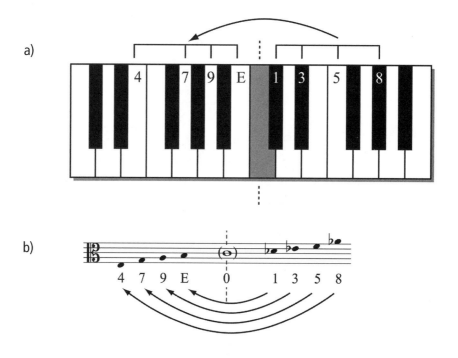

**FIGURE 3.3** Three Ways to Picture Inversion

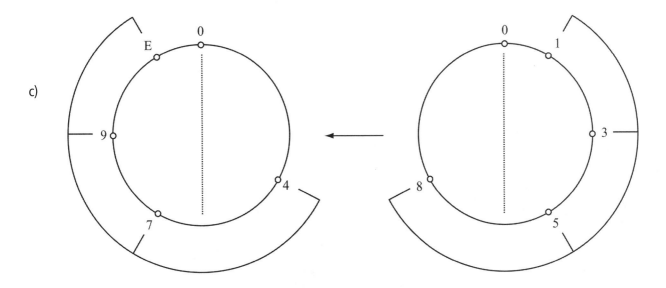

c)

**FIGURE 3.3**—continued

There are a number of sets that have multiple axes of inversion. These include interval cycles and several important referential collections, including the whole-tone and octatonic scales. As Figure 3.4 illustrates, the octatonic collection has four axes of inversion.

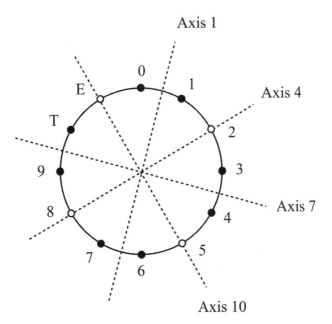

**FIGURE 3.4** Multiple Axes of Inversion for the Octatonic Scale

To see an example of how inversion can play a central role in the organization of a composition, refer to Example 3.6. In this music, the right- and left-hand parts, analyzed as unordered pc sets, are inversions of each other. Unlike the symmetrical sets in the first few measures of "Subject and Reflection" introduced in Example 2.2 (Chapter 2), however, the two parts here do not form symmetrical contours in pitch-space; the notes of the left-hand part, that is, are ordered differently than those in the right-hand part and are spread across two octaves.

EX. 3.6—Béla Bartók, *Mikrokosmos*, Vol. 6, No. 141, "Subject and Reflection," mm. 43–45 (Inversionally Equivalent Pc Sets)

Notice that the **inversionally equivalent unordered pc sets** in Example 3.6 share a number of **invariant** (i.e., common) **pcs**, namely 1 (C♯), 6 (F♯), and E (B♭). In certain cases, inversion may reproduce the complete set. One example is the unordered pc set from Debussy's "Les collines d'Anacapri" introduced in Example 3.5. This set reproduces itself when inverted about 0 because the pcs in the set are inversions of each other. In addition, the adjacency interval series is symmetrical around the center. Such interval series are **self-retrogradable**; the interval series reads the same forwards and backwards.[2] (See Figure 3.5.)

Self-retrogradable AIS

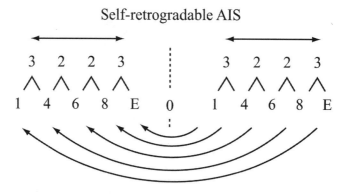

**FIGURE 3.5** Self-duplication under Inversion

The first three measures of the excerpt in Example 3.6 also exhibit inversional equivalence in *pitch-space*. As Figure 3.6 illustrates, each pitch and its inversion lie an equal distance on either side of the axis, in this case C4. Hence, the inversion of C♯5, thirteen semitones above C4, is B2, thirteen semitones below C4, and so on.

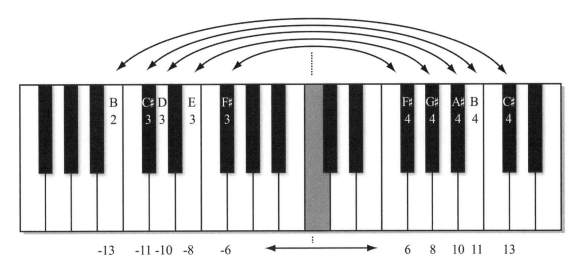

**FIGURE 3.6** Inversionally Equivalent Unordered Pitch Sets

On occasion, inversionally equivalent sets may overlap the axis as illustrated in Figures 3.7a and b. Under these circumstances the integer names of the pitch sets will contain both positive and negative numbers. These continue to be exchanged upon inversion just as complementary pcs are exchanged in inversionally equivalent pc sets.

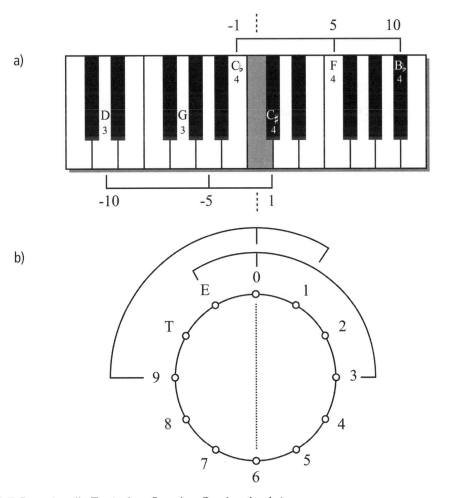

**FIGURE 3.7** Inversionally Equivalent Sets that Overlap the Axis

*Ordered* pitch and pc sets, of course, may also be inverted. In deference to their linear characteristics, ordered pc sets are usually inverted about their first note as shown in Figure 3.8. To find the index, simply add the integer name of the first pc to itself. The first pc of ordered pc set <7, 3, 2> is 7 so the index is 2 (7 + 7 = 2 mod 12). Subtract the remaining pcs from the index to complete the inversion; 2 − 3 = 11 mod 12 and 2 − 2 = 0, so the inversion of <7, 3, 2> is <0, E 7>.

**FIGURE 3.8** How to Invert an Ordered Pc Set

In this text, we will also invert ordered *pitch* sets around their first note.[3] In Figure 3.9a, B♭4, a perfect fourth above F4, is replaced by its complement, C4, a perfect fourth below F4, A♭4, a minor third above F4, is replaced by D4, a minor third below F4, and so on. F4, the axis, is its own inversion. A more intuitive way to derive the inversion is to start on the first note and reverse the contours (signs) while maintaining the pitch interval succession. This process is illustrated in Figure 3.9b. Here, +5/−2/+6 becomes −5/+2/−6 in the inversion. As the line drawings indicate, the sets are mirror reflections of each other.

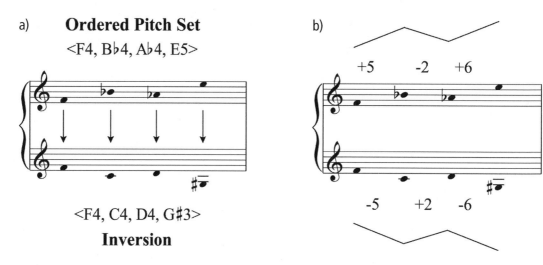

**FIGURE 3.9** Inversion in Pitch-space

## Order Operations

In addition to inversion, ordered sets may be subjected to the order operations **retrograde (R)** and **retrograde inversion (RI)**. Retrogression reverses the order of the elements in the source set—or **prime (P)**—while the retrograde inversion reverses the order of the elements in the inversion. These labels are derived from the twelve-tone method and, along with P and I, are often referred to as **twelve-tone operations** or **TTOs**.[4] The operations themselves, however, may be applied to sets of all sizes.

Figure 3.10 contains an ordered pitch set and its untransposed retrograde, inversion, and retrograde inversion. Among the most identifiable features of these sets are their shapes (indicated by the line drawings beneath the staff) and adjacency interval series: the inversion flips the shapes upside down while the retrograde and retrograde inversion present the shapes of the inversion and prime in reverse order. The operations in Figure 3.10 may also be expressed as ordered pc sets: <7, 2, 1> (P), <1, 2, 7> (R), <7, 0, 1> (I), and <1, 0, 7> (RI).

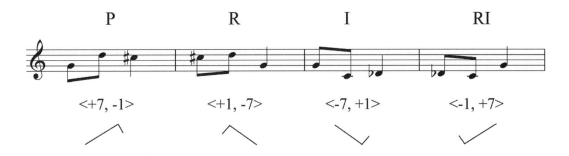

**FIGURE 3.10** TTOs

As we will learn in Chapter 6, ordered pitch sets often function as the basic melodic ideas or motives on which themes are built. (We will refer to these motives as *ordered pitch interval motives* or *shape/interval motives*.) We have already encountered several examples of this kind of motivic expansion. Both of the excerpts in Examples 2.3 and 2.4 (Chapter 2), for example, are based on short three-note melodic ideas like those in Figure 3.10. The excerpt from George Crumb's "Verte desnuda es recordar la tierra" also includes an inverted motive. (See Motive (b) in Example 2.5.)

---

### Motivic Hearing

Motives and their operations are relatively easy to identify by ear. The concepts learned in this chapter, then, can be applied directly to the ear training exercises in **Streams 2** and **3** of the *Motivic Hearing* software with little fanfare. These streams contain melodies with a series of trichords like that in Figure 3.10. For now, focus on the early exercises. The more advanced exercises include transposed and overlapping motives, processes that will be investigated more thoroughly in Chapter 6. Prime forms, which you are also asked to identify, are introduced in Chapter 4. The "Aural Skills Supplement" provides additional information on how to complete the exercises successfully, so be sure to read the instructions carefully.

## Pitch and Pc Cycles

In some cases, an ordered pitch set may be treated as a closed unit whose end connects to its beginning. Depending on their constituents, such groupings form what we will refer to either as **pitch cycles** or **pc cycles**.[5] Figure 3.11 contains a six-note pitch cycle. Notice that in addition to its cyclical properties, the set is ordered. It is therefore enclosed in angled brackets. The cyclicity of the set is indicated by the long dash that comes at the end of the set's name.

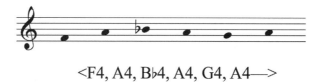

<F4, A4, B♭4, A4, G4, A4—>

**FIGURE 3.11** Pitch Cycle

Cyclicity is closely associated with **rotation**. Each rotation of a set begins with a different element and wraps around to the beginning when necessary to complete the set. Figure 3.12 shows the rotations for the pitch cycle from Figure 3.11. By convention, the first rotation of the set, the original, is designated r0. The rotation beginning on the second note of the set is r1, the rotation beginning on the third note is r2, and so on. It should be apparent that a six-element set will have six rotations each of which will begin with one of the set's six members. From this we can conclude that the number of rotations for any given set will equal the number of elements in the set.

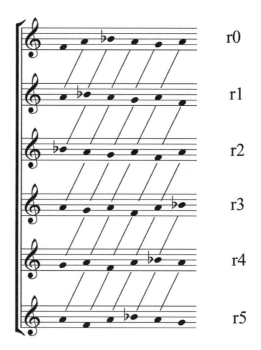

**FIGURE 3.12** Pitch Cycle with Rotations

The third beat of the excerpt in Example 3.7 contains four four-note sets, all of which are rotated to begin on their third note (r2) when the sets are repeated on the last beat of the measure.

**EX. 3.7**—Aaron Copland, Quartet for Piano and Strings, II, m. 238 (Excerpt with Rotations)

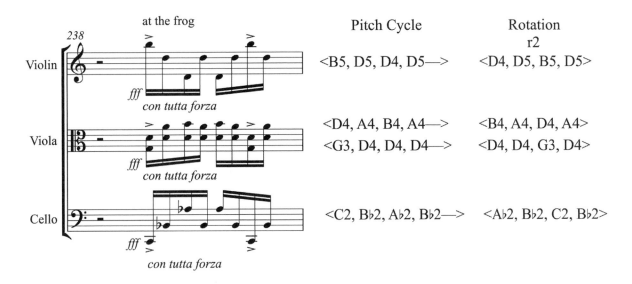

Example 3.8 contains an example of a pc cycle along with several rotations. These rotations unfold in a textbook manner, proceeding from r0 all the way to r4.[6] We consider the rotations in this example to be pc-space phenomena because some of the notes (those in boxes) are transposed either an octave above or below their position in the original.

**EX. 3.8**—Ruth Crawford, *Diaphonic Suite*, No. 1, III, mm. 1–5 (Pc Cycle with Multiple Rotations)

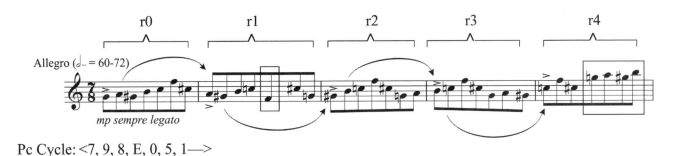

Pc Cycle: <7, 9, 8, E, 0, 5, 1—>

Scale passages can also produce rotations. The excerpt from George Rochberg's *Ukiyo-e* in Example 3.9 contains a seven-note descending scale followed by its r3 rotation beginning on B.

**EX. 3.9**—George Rochberg, *Ukiyo-e: Pictures of the Floating World*, p. 3, system 1 (Scale Treatment of a Pc Cycle)

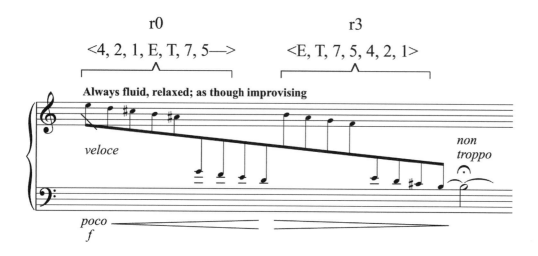

## A Brief introduction to Segmentation

The process by which music is parsed into meaningful units or sets is known as **segmentation**. Sets may be delineated through a variety of means, including, but not limited to *cadences, pauses, durations, dynamic* and *textural shifts, rhythm, articulation, register, timbre, repetition,* and *harmonic identity*.[7] The ways in which these elements are deployed in a piece is largely dependent on context and cannot be precisely defined. Even transparent markers such as double bar lines and repeat signs cannot always be trusted to delineate beginnings and endings. Regardless of the line of attack undertaken, however, it is important to remain as faithful to the aural impact of the music, as possible. The ear, then, is the final arbiter in deciding what constitutes a meaningful unit in music, although the visual effect of the score can also be extremely valuable. Let us turn now to an example.

## Analysis of Witold Lutoslawski's Symphony No. 1, III

Example 3.10 contains an excerpt from the third movement of Witold Lutoslawski's Symphony, No. 1. The passage is quite dense in terms of its pitch content and there appears to be no immediate evidence of a presiding key or tonal area. To uncover the rationale behind the passage, then, we must take other parameters into consideration. Notice, for example, that except for the first violins, cello, and contrabass, instrumental groups occupy distinct temporal regions in the score; the horns, harp, and second violins drop out in m. 242, making room for the woodwinds and celesta, which, in turn, give way to the horns, harp, second violins, and piano in m. 246.

**EX. 3.10**—Witold Lutoslawski. Symphony, No. 1, III, mm. 237–50
(Symphonic Passage with Instrumental and Temporal Groupings)

These shifts in *texture* and *timbre*, both visually and aurally apparent, provide the initial means for segmenting the music into practical analytical units. Let us consider each of these in turn. As Example 3.11 shows, the first violins—divided into three parts—open up a melodic wedge that culminates with a G♭ major seventh chord in the third measure of the passage.

**EX. 3.11**—(Violin Segment in mm. 237–39)

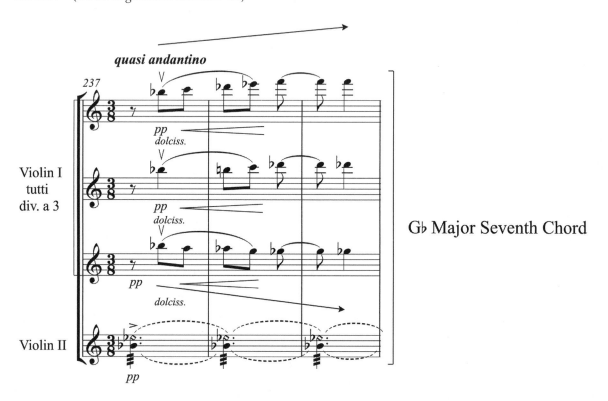

In m. 239 (Example 3.12), the horns together with the low strings and piano play a B major triad in a lower *register*.

**EX. 3.12**—(Horn/Piano/Low Strings Segment in mm. 239–40)

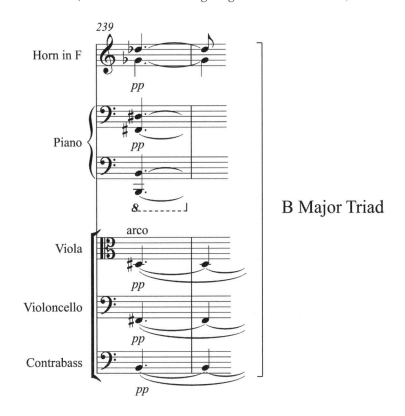

B Major Triad

At m. 246 (Example 3.13), *triadic harmony* breaks down and we are left instead with a number of bare fifths marked by their instrumental *timbres* and *tessituras*: F3/C4 in the horn parts, B2/F♯2 in the cello and contrabass parts, and E5/B5 in the first violins.

**EX. 3.13**—(Perfect Fifth Segments in mm. 246–50)

The harp part adds two more fifths: A♭4/E♭5 and F♭4(E4)/B4. (See Example 3.14.)

**EX. 3.14**—(Harp Fifths in mm. 246–47)

The appearance of numerous perfect fifths in the last five measures provides a clue as to how we might draw the excerpt's diverse strands together. The non-functional overlapping triads at the beginning of the excerpt, for example, could be reconceptualized as a series of perfect fifth *dyads* (two-note groupings), each of which occupies a discreet *register* in pitch-space as shown in Example 3.15.

**EX. 3.15**—(Dyad Analysis of mm. 236–40)

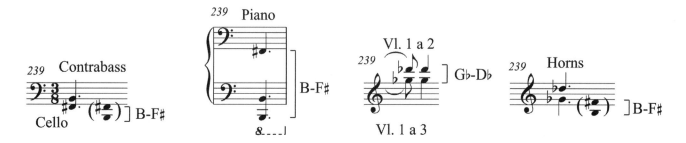

The *highest notes in the texture*—the second violin's B♭6 harmonic and the first violin's F6—invert the perfect fifth, sounding a perfect fourth instead. (See Example 3.16.)

**EX. 3.16**—(Inverted Dyad in m. 239)

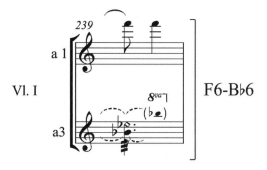

The woodwinds and celesta, meanwhile, articulate a different circle of fifths sequence (we might also call it a 5/7 cycle), D–A–E–B–F♯–C♯, as shown in Example 3.17.

**EX. 3.17**—(Woodwind and Celesta Fifths in mm. 243–45)

D - A - E - B - F♯ - C♯

The "perfect fifth" perspective on the first nine measures of the passage seems especially warranted given the fact that the harp's opening statement in mm. 239–40 (Example 3.18) also consists of a circle of fifths progression: C♭–G♭–D♭–A♭–E♭. Three of the harp's pcs, moreover, overlap with those in the horn and string parts (C♭ (B), G♭, and D♭).

**EX. 3.18**—(Harp Fifths in mm. 239–41)

Circle of fifths: C♭ - G♭ - D♭ - A♭ - E♭

As we have seen, the last five measures of the passage are overtly based on fifths. Figure 3.13 shows the pitches for the combined piano and harp parts as well as the combined string and horn parts in mm. 246–50. These are not arbitrary pairings; the piano and harp parts are associated by their simultaneous entry into the texture on the *metrical* downbeat of m. 239 and the horn and strings articulate the same *harmony*.

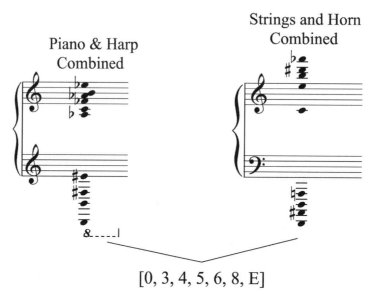

FIGURE 3.13 Unordered Pc Sets in mm. 246–50

Based on our examination of the passage, the pcs in these sets appear to be derived from the four ic 5 dyads—inclusive of both perfect fifths and fourths—most clearly delineated by *register* and *timbre* in the horn and string parts. (See Figure 3.14.) Overall the passage articulates a nearly complete circle of fifths sequence (5/7 cycle), D–A–E–B(C♭)–G♭ (F♯)–D♭–A♭–E♭–B♭–F–C. The only missing pc is G.

**TABLE 3.1** Horn and String Dyads

| | |
|---|---|
| <5, 0> | Horns |
| <3, 8> | Vl. 1 a 1 & Vl. II |
| <4, E> | Vl. 1 a 2 & 3 |
| <E, 6> | C♭. and Cello |

Texture, timbre, register, meter, harmony, and repetition all play important roles in our perception of the passage in Example 3.10. Because they engage some of music's most basic principles, such features emerge in a wide variety of musical styles. The specific details one uncovers when examining a particular musical passage, on the other hand, often have relevance only for the piece or passage under investigation. Knowing what to look and listen for, then, can be of immense help in the analytical process. Analysis would be very difficult indeed if there was no foundation on which to build. By adding layers of understanding, this chapter along with those that follow may serve as an important means for achieving this goal.

## Chapter 3 Exercises

1) Express the following as *ordered* pitch and pc sets. (You may use either integers or letter names to identify ordered pitch sets.)

a)

Ordered pitch set <A5, D5, A4, C♯5, E♯4, G♯4, C5>

Ordered pc set <9, 2, 9, 1, 5, 8, 0>

b)

_____

c)

_____

d)

_____

e)

_____

f)

_____

2) Express the following as *unordered* pitch and pc sets. Adopt your own analytical method for listing pitches and pcs. For example, you may decide to list elements in order from top-to-bottom or bottom-to-top. (You may use either integers or letter names to identify the ordered pitch sets.)

3) Pc set inversion.

   a)  List the *adjacency interval series* (AIS) for each of the unordered pc sets below.

   b)  Determine the *inversion* about 0 of each set and notate it using square brackets and commas.

   c)  Finally, list the *adjacency interval* series for the inverted sets.

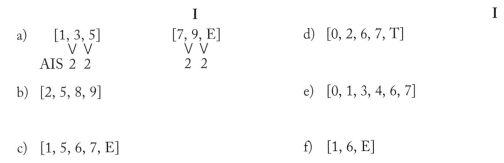

                                 I                                                I

a)   [1, 3, 5]      [7, 9, E]        d)  [0, 2, 6, 7, T]
         V V        V V
   AIS 2  2       2  2

b)  [2, 5, 8, 9]                   e)  [0, 1, 3, 4, 6, 7]

c)  [1, 5, 6, 7, E]              f)  [1, 6, E]

4)  Unordered Pitch Sets and Their Inversions.

   a)  List the *adjacency interval series* for each of the unordered pitch sets below.

   b)  Determine the *inversion* of the set about C4 and notate it using square brackets. Be sure to order the inversion from low to high. (One way to approach this task is to identify the first—i.e., lowest—note of the inversion. Then determine the remaining pitches by counting intervals in the reverse adjacency interval series.)

   c)  Finally, list the *adjacency interval series* for the inverted sets.

                                    I

a) [F♯4, B♭4, C5, C♯5]   [B2, C3, D3, F♯3]
     V   V   V        V   V   V
AIS 4    2    1       1    2    4

b)  [C4, F4, B♭4, E♭5]

c)  [D4, G4, B♭4, D♭5, G♭5]

d)  [A3, B3, C♯4]

e)  [F3, A♭3, A♮3]

5)  Ordered pitch sets.

   a)  Fill in the blanks with the ordered pitch set for each of the motives below. (Use letter names and octave designations.)

   b)  Notate the retrograde, inversion, and retrograde inversion using note heads. Remember, ordered pc sets are inverted around the first note of the set.

&lt;B♭4, F4, E♭5, A♭4&gt;

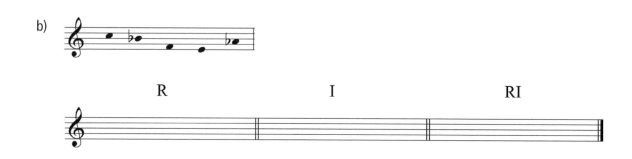

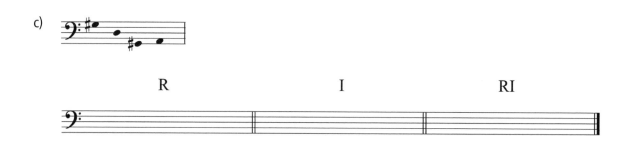

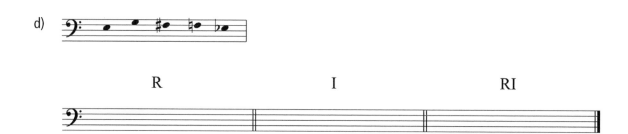

6)  Express the untransposed retrograde, inversion, and retrograde inversion of the following as ordered pc sets. (Like ordered pitch sets, ordered pc sets are inverted around the first note.)

|  | **R** | **I** | **RI** |
|---|---|---|---|
| a) <1, 3, 5, 2> | <2, 5, 3, 1> | <E, 9, 7, T> | <T, 7, 9, E> |
| b) <5, 2, 6, 3, 7, 4> | | | |
| c) <5, 4, 3, 2, 1> | | | |
| d) <6, 0, 9, 4> | | | |
| e) <1, 8, 7> | | | |
| f) <5, 9, 2, 3> | | | |

7)  Notate the indicated *rotations* using filled-in note heads. Then express the pitch-cycle for each rotation using integers enclosed in angled brackets with a long dash at the end.

r0   <5, 6, 4, 7, 3, 8—>

r1

r2

r3

r4

r5

8)  Divide the class into groups. Then segment the following excerpt from Toru Takemitsu's *Star-Isle* according to the criteria below.

  a)  Divide the passage into instrumental groups based on timbre, rhythm, register, articulation, pitch content, and/or dynamics. What instruments belong to each group and why?

b)  What role do the first and second violins play in the passage?

c)  What repeated ordered pitch interval motive occurs in the violin parts? (HINT: Look for fragments of the violin part in other instruments.)

d)  What unordered pc set occurs in the woodwinds and celesta in mm. 72–74?

e)  The set in Part d gives way to what new collection in m. 75?

f)  What does the unordered pitch set in m. 76 (woodwinds) have in common with the unordered pitch set in mm. 72–74 (Part d)?

g)  To figure out what scales occur in the harp parts, consult the tuning of the pedals. Note that there are some enharmonic tones.

h)  Name the succession of chords that occurs over the course of excerpt in the viola and cello parts. What kind of root progression do these chords outline.

i)  Can you find any other interesting features in the passage?

Toru Takemitsu, *Star-Isle*, mm. 72–76

# Chapter 4

# Unordered Sets and
# Their Operations

---

| | |
|---|---|
| Transposition | Identity operation |
| Normal order | $T_n^p$ |
| Mappings | $T_n^p I$ |
| $T_n$ | Prime form |
| $T_n I$ | Interval palindrome |

In the last chapter, we learned about ordered and unordered sets and their basic operations. In this chapter, we will undertake a more thorough investigation of *unordered* sets. There are, of course, many common musical artifacts whose temporal ordering is not among their essential features. These include chords, harmonic intervals, and referential collections. As we shall see, treating *melodic* configurations as unordered sets can also often lead to productive insights.

## Transposition

In addition to inversion and rotation, sets may be transposed, shifted to a different location in pitch- or pc-space.[1] The **transposition** of an unordered pitch set is easy enough to accomplish: simply shift the contents of the entire set the specified number of semitones in pitch-space. *Analyzing* transpositionally equivalent unordered sets is more difficult since transposition, like inversion, alters the elements of the original set. The interval content of transpositionally equivalent sets, on the other hand, remains unchanged. One way to identify sets related through transposition, then, is to compare their adjacency interval series (AIS).

The passage in Example 4.1a contains a succession of dyadic pairs, constituting a musical metaphor for the leaps and landings of a grasshopper.[2] While major seconds always follow perfect fourths in these gestures, the order of the pitches in the dyads remains unspecified. As we learned in Chapter 2, such groupings may be expressed as unordered pitch sets enclosed in square brackets. To make the sets easier to compare, list their elements in order from lowest to highest. Here, the low-to-high ordering is [C5, D5, E♭5, A♭5].

**EX. 4.1**—Benjamin Britten, *Two Insect Pieces*, "The Grasshopper," mm. 8–9 and 12–13 (Transposed Unordered Pitch Sets)

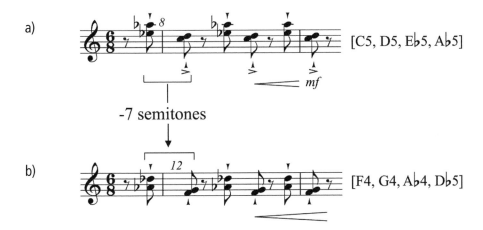

The four-note gestures in Example 4.1a are transposed a perfect fifth (seven semitones) lower in mm. 12–13 (Example 4.1b). Both sets articulate the same unordered pitch intervals bottom-to-top (2/1/5) at different pitch levels as illustrated in Figure 4.1.

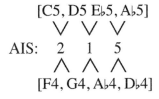

**FIGURE 4.1** AIS for the Transposed Unordered Pitch Sets in Britten's "The Grasshopper"

In some situations, the pitches of transpositionally equivalent groupings may be rearranged in pitch-space, in which case their adjacency interval series will not match, making connections harder to see. Example 4.2 shows two isolated groupings of an important six-note idea from Schoenberg's Op. 47 *Phantasy*. Here, the relations between the groupings are less transparent than those in the Britten example because we hear a different succession of melodic and harmonic intervals in pitch-space from one excerpt to the next. Under these conditions, expressing the groupings as unordered pc sets provides little clarification regarding the relations between the groupings because the notion of "lowest note" is unspecified in pc-space.

**EX. 4.2**—Arnold Schoenberg, *Phantasy for Violin and Piano Accompaniment*, Op. 47, mm. 1 and 21–22 (Transposed Unordered Pc Set)

The associations between unordered pc sets, like those in Example 4.2, can be made clearer by reducing each set to its **normal order**. The normal order is the chord position that spans the *smallest overall intervallic distance bottom-to-top*. To find the normal order of a pc set:

1)   Reduce the set to a single octave by listing its pcs in ascending numerical order like a scale.
2)   Then sort through its "chord inversions" (i.e., rotations) one by one to find the ordering that spans the smallest interval bottom-to-top.[3]

Figure 4.2 shows the rotations for the two sets identified in Schoenberg's *Phantasy* (Example 4.2).[4] The distance spanned by each rotation appears above it. The normal orders, those with the tightest packing, appear in boxes. Putting the sets in normal order makes the connections between them more transparent because both sets now have the same adjacency interval series as illustrated in Figure 4.3.

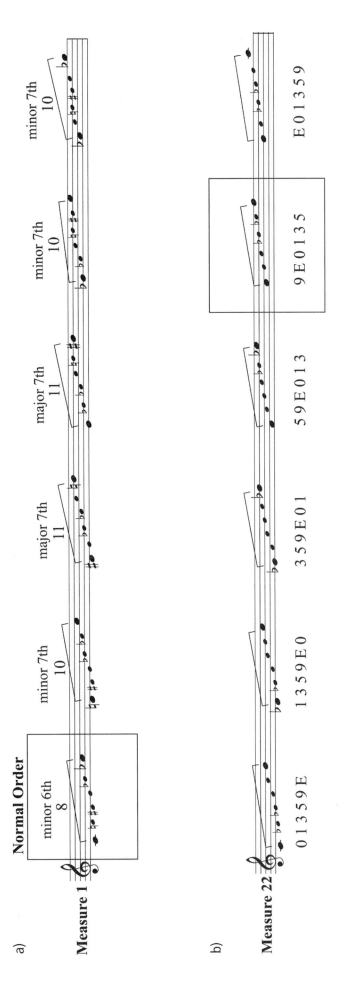

**FIGURE 4.2** Rotations and Normal Orders in Schoenberg's *Phantasy*

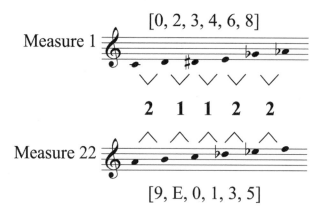

FIGURE 4.3 Comparison of Normal Orders in Schoenberg's *Phantasy*

The normal order of a chord corresponds roughly to its "root position." To determine the root position of a triad or seventh chord, we typically condense all of its pcs into a single octave and then choose the inversion (rotation) consisting of stacked thirds. Where triads are concerned, the root position is also the chord's normal order as illustrated below.

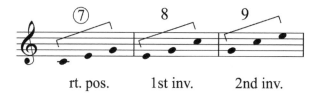

Reducing chords to their root position allows the analyst to make direct comparisons; all major triads, for example, have the same configuration, a major third on the bottom and a minor third on top. Because the chords encountered in music written since 1890 may include non-tertian intervals, it has become necessary to create a different kind of "root position," one that does not require chords to be built in thirds.

In some cases, there may be more than one rotation with the same degree of compression between its outside members. When this happens, choose the rotation that has the tightest packing of inner intervals nearer the bottom of the set. To do this, check the packing of the remaining pcs from the bottom of the set to the second-to-last pc. If the intervals on the first pass match, continue with the next set of inner intervals (i.e., from the first pc to the third-to-last, etc.). Figure 4.4 shows one example. In this case, the normal order is the rotation on the right.

Normal Order: [8, T, 0, 3, 5]

FIGURE 4.4 Rotations with the Same Degree of Compression Bottom-to-Top

If, after exhausting all possibilities, no set emerges with the best packing, choose the rotation that has the smallest integer on the bottom as shown in Figure 4.5.

Normal Order: [2, 3, 6, 7, T, E]

**FIGURE 4.5** Normal Order with the Smallest Integer on the Bottom

The method for determining normal orders shown in Figure 4.2 is somewhat tedious. *As long as the rationale behind the normal order is fully understood,* a shortcut may be used to speed up the process. Notice that the pcs at the top and bottom of each rotation of the set in Figure 4.2a, excluding the first, occur next to each other and in reverse order in the first pc set starting on 0; D ascends to C in the second rotation, D♯ ascends to D in the third rotation, and so on. This suggests that we can determine the spans of all the rotations *except the first* by calculating the ics between each pc and the pc that precedes it. Let us use [1, 6, 9, E] as an example.

1) Begin by calculating the ics between consecutive pcs in the set. Then do the same for the first and last pcs.

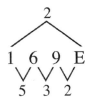

2) Now, identify the largest ic since its inversion will translate to the smallest interval between outside voices when the set is rotated.

a) If the largest ic occurs between the first and last pcs, the normal order is the same as the original unordered pc set. (See, for example, Figure 4.2a.)

b) If the largest ic occurs between any two pcs other than the first and last, begin with the top-most pc of the interval and fill in the normal order with the remaining pcs, wrapping around as necessary to complete the set.

Here, the largest ic is 5 so the normal order begins with 6 and spans seven semitones, the inversion of 5. If there is more than one rotation with the same degree of compression, use the method shown in Figure 4.4 to determine the normal order.

## $T_n/T_nI$ Mappings

Operations that transfer the elements of one set to corresponding elements in another are known as **mappings**. Sets that map onto each other under transposition or inversion followed by transposition are denoted by the expressions $T_n$ ("T sub-n") and $T_nI$ ("T sub-n of I") where n is the distance between each member of the first set and its corresponding member in the second. For $T_nI$, we invert the set first, then transpose it. The untransposed version of a set is denoted by the expression $T_0$, which is known as the **identity operation** because it maps the set onto itself. The concept of mapping gives us a way to state the relations between transpositionally equivalent sets in a straightforward and efficient manner while avoiding the inelegant passive voice construction "is transposed by."

To determine the transposition level of a set, compare its normal order to that of the source set. The normal order of the set in Example 4.2a is [0, 2, 3, 4, 6, 8] while that of the set in Example 4.2b is [9, E, 0, 1, 3, 5]. (See Figure 4.2.) To find the value of n in $T_n$, subtract any member of the first set from the corresponding member of the second. The set in Example 4.2a maps onto the set in Example 4.2b at $T_9$, 9 − 0 = 9, 11 − 2 = 9, etc. (See Figure 4.6.)

$$[9, \text{E}, 0, 1, 3, 5]$$
$$T_9 \uparrow \quad \uparrow \quad \uparrow \quad \uparrow \quad \uparrow \quad \uparrow$$
$$[0, 2, 3, 4, 6, 8]$$

**FIGURE 4.6** Transposed Pc Set

Normal orders can also be helpful for analyzing inversionally equivalent pc sets like those in Example 4.3. Here, the adjacency interval series of the normal orders do not match. They are, however, similar; the second series is merely the reverse of the first and vice versa.

**EX. 4.3**—Toru Takemitsu, *Rocking Mirror Daybreak*, I, "Autumn," mm. 1 and 13 (Inversionally Equivalent Unordered Pc Sets and their Normal Orders)

Normal Order:  6  9  T  0  1
              ∨  ∨  ∨  ∨
AIS:           3  1  2  1

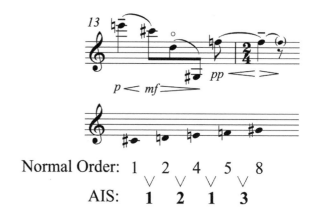

Normal Order:  1   2   4   5   8
                ∨   ∨   ∨   ∨
AIS:            1   2   1   3

The axis for sets that map onto each other under $T_nI$ is 0 and the value of n is the index (i.e., the sum of inversionally equivalent pcs). (If necessary, revisit Chapter 2 to review these ideas.) Figure 4.7a lists the pcs of the two sets from Takemitsu's "Autumn." Notice that since the sets are inversions of each other, inversionally equivalent pcs appear in reverse order in the two sets. In this case, the index is 2; 1 + 1 = 2, 0 + 2 = 2, 10 + 4 = 2 (mod 12), 9 + 5 = 2 (mod 12), and 6 + 8 = 2 (mod 12). The sets thus map onto each other at $T_2I$ as illustrated in Figure 4.7b.

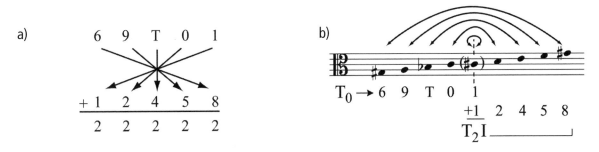

**FIGURE 4.7** Inversionally Equivalent Sets in Takemitsu's "Autumn"

The reason the index can be used to indicate the transposition level of inversionally equivalent sets is because it expresses how far the *transposed* inversion is from the untransposed inversion about 0. To get a better idea of how this process works, consider the two sets denoted by dark brackets in Figure 4.8. These two sets are axis 2 inversions of each other; 3 is the inversion of E, 5 the inversion of 9, and 6 the inversion of 8. As the gray brackets illustrate, however, [3, 5, 6] and the inversion about 0, [1, 3, 4], are two "hours" apart. To map [1, 3, 4], onto [3, 5, 6], we must therefore shift it two steps, the value of the index. The student can verify that the result is the same whether we begin with pc set [8, 9, E] or pc set [3, 5, 6].

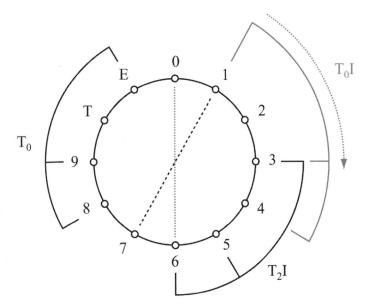

**FIGURE 4.8** Indices of Inversion and their Effect on $T_nI$ Mappings

The normal orders of inversionally equivalent sets may have adjacency interval series that are not the reverse of each other. In these cases, the inversion can be found in another rotation. To determine whether two unordered pc sets are inversionally equivalent, then, it is usually best to check through all of the rotations of at least one of the sets. If the AIS of one of the rotations is the reverse of the other set's AIS, the sets are inversionally equivalent. As a general rule, we may rotate the set whose first interval is the largest, although the result is the same regardless of the set chosen.

Figure 4.9 shows the normal orders for the non-diatonic seventh chords from Arnold Schoenberg's Op. 11, No. 1 first seen in Example 1.1 (Chapter 1). The two normal orders have the same ics but in a different order. Hence, the two sets do not map onto each other in an obvious way.

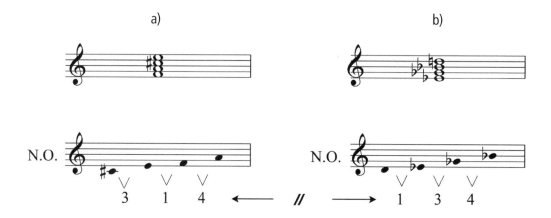

**FIGURE 4.9** Normal Orders of the Chords from Schoenberg's Op. 11, No. 1

We have already learned that the pitch intervals of the first chord are projected in the opposite direction in the second chord (see Example 1.1). To confirm that the chords are inversions of each other in pc-space, we can sort through all of the rotations of one of the sets to determine whether there is an ordering that produces the AIS of the other in reverse order. Here, we will choose set a because its first interval (3) is larger than the first interval of set b (1). Figure 4.10a shows all four rotations of set a. As the figure shows, the last rotation does indeed present the AIS of set b in reverse order (Figure 4.10b). (Notice too that the smallest ic has now migrated to the top of the set.) The sets thus map onto each other under inversion.

a)

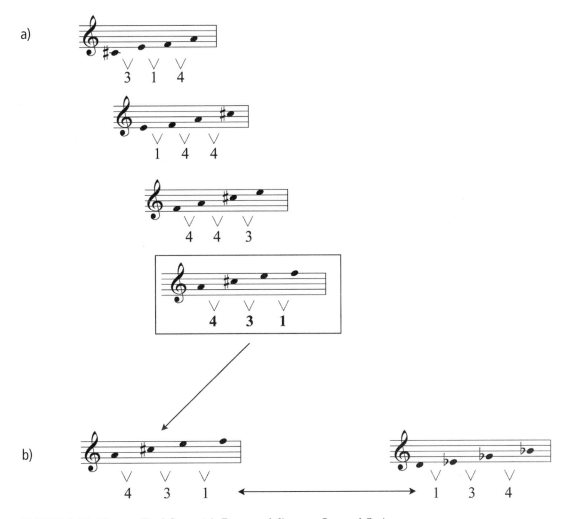

b)

**FIGURE 4.10**  How to Find Sets with Reverse Adjacency Interval Series

Figure the transposition level by finding the sum of inversionally equivalent pairs of pcs in the two rotations whose adjacency interval series are the reverse of each other. Here the index is 7, so the correct expression is $T_7I$. (See Figure 4.11.)

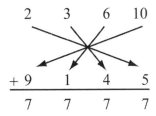

**FIGURE 4.11**  Index for the Sets in Figure 4.10

## $T_n^p/T_n^p I$ Mappings

The method for determining transpositions for unordered *pitch* sets is similar to that used for unordered *pc* sets, the only exception being that all operations take place in pitch-space. To differentiate these operations from their counterparts in pc-space, the letter "p" is added to their expressions. Hence, we use the forms $T_n^p$ ("Teepee sub-n") and $T_n^p I$ ("Teepee sub-n of I") instead of $T_n$ and $T_n I$. Unordered pitch sets may be transposed higher or lower. A negative sign is added to the expression to denote a downward transposition. The sets in mm. 12–13 of Britten's *The Grasshopper* found in Example 4.1 are seven semitones lower than those in mm. 8–9. This shift can be concisely stated using the expression $T_{-7}^p$ as illustrated in Figure 4.12. (cf. Example 4.1.)

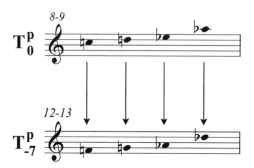

**FIGURE 4.12**  Transposed Unordered Pitch Set

Whereas the adjacency interval series of transposed unordered pitch sets match, the adjacency interval series of *inversionally* equivalent unordered pitch sets are the reverse of each other. The excerpt in Example 4.4, for example, contains several chords (accompanied by an ostinato in the low strings and woodwinds) that are both inverted *and* transposed. Here, the intervals of the first chord and its transpositions are projected in the opposite direction in the inversions.

**EX. 4.4**—Igor Stravinsky, *The Rite of Spring*, Part II, "Glorification of the Chosen Maiden," m. 28 (Inverted and Transposed Chords)

As Figure 4.13 illustrates, the index in pitch-space for the first two inversionally equivalent chords in Example 4.4 is 11. Hence, the chords map onto each other at $T^p_{11}I$. The chord on the fourth beat is two semitones lower or $T^p_9I$.

$$
\begin{array}{rrr}
-1 & 5 & 10 \\
+12 & 6 & 1 \\
\hline
\text{INDEX} \quad 11 & 11 & 11
\end{array}
$$

**FIGURE 4.13** Pitch-space Index

Figure 4.14 illustrates this process using notation and a piano keyboard diagram.

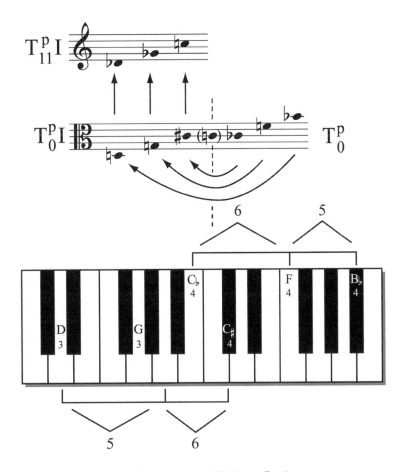

**FIGURE 4.14** How Inversion followed by Transposition Works in Pitch-space

In this case, the indexes in pitch-space and pc-space are the same. The index in pitch-space will differ from that in pc-space when the transposition is descending, larger than a major seventh, or both. Figure 4.15 shows one example.

$$\text{Index in Pitch-space} \qquad\qquad \text{Index in Pc-space}$$

$$
\begin{array}{rrr}
-17 & -8 & 5 \\
+\;\;4 & -5 & -18 \\
\hline
-13 & -13 & -13
\end{array}
\qquad\qquad
\begin{array}{rrr}
7 & 4 & 5 \\
+4 & 7 & 6 \\
\hline
11 & 11 & 11
\end{array}
$$

**FIGURE 4.15** Pitch-space vs. Pc-space Indexes

## Prime Form

To account for family resemblances between sets like those in the previous examples, we may express them in terms of a single representative set known as the **prime form**. Simply put, a prime form is a set of integers beginning with 0 that spans the smallest possible interval bottom-to-top with the added stipulation that the smallest intervals must be packed most closely toward the bottom. Prime forms give us a way to classify sets in much the same way we classify triads according to type (e.g., major, minor, diminished, and augmented).[5]

Here are the three basic steps for calculating the prime form.[6]

1) Determine the rotations of the set that span the smallest interval bottom-to-top. Most often, there will be only one of these, the set's normal order.

2) a) Reading from both the top and bottom of the rotation(s) from step 1, find where the tightest interval packing occurs to one side or the other. (To find the interval packing toward the top of a set, simply duplicate the process for determining the normal order starting on the right instead of the left.)

   b) If the smallest intervals are more closely packed toward the top of the "winning" rotation from steps 1 and 2a, reverse them so that the smallest intervals will be on the left or bottom when you build the prime form.

3) Start with 0 and calculate the elements of the prime form in increments corresponding to the intervals in Step 2.[7]

As an example, let us determine the prime form for the set that occurs in m. 13 of Takemitsu's "Autumn" (Example 4.3). In this case, the rotation with the smallest interval between the top and bottom pcs corresponds to the set's normal order (**Step 1**). What remains is to make sure the smallest intervals are packed toward the bottom of the set (**Step 2**). To do this, compare the intervals one at a time *starting at both ends of the set* until the set with tightest packing emerges as illustrated in Figure 4.16. If the smallest intervals are most tightly packed toward the top of the set, the integers representing the intervals will have to be reversed, relocating them to the left. In this case, the circled ic 4 on the bottom is smaller than ic 6 at the top. It is therefore *not necessary to reverse the intervals* because the smallest intervals overall are already packed toward the bottom.

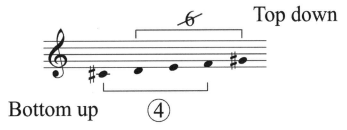

**FIGURE 4.16** Procedure for Finding the Tightest Interval Packing

The prime form contains the same intervals as the rotation from step 2, but begins with 0. To construct the prime form, then, set the first member to 0 and determine the remaining members by counting intervals in the adjacency interval series: 0 + 1 = "1", 1 + 2 = "3", and so on (**Step 3**). The complete process is illustrated in Figure 4.17. Prime forms are enclosed in parentheses without commas.

Most Compact Rotation: [1,  2,  4,  5,  8]
V  V  V  V
AIS:  1  2  1  3
∧ ∧ ∧ ∧
**Prime Form:** (0  1  3  4  7)

**FIGURE 4.17** Procedure for Determining the Prime Form of an Unordered Pc Set

To see how this procedure works when the smallest intervals are at the top of the rotation, let us now look at the set that occurs in mm. 1–2 of Takemitsu's "Autumn." Again, the most compact rotation is the same as the set's normal order, [6, 9, T, 0, 1]. In this case, however, the smallest interval, ic 4, occurs at the top of the rotation as shown in Figure 4.18. According to **Step 2**, the intervals must therefore be reversed, as illustrated in Figure 4.19, to make sure the smallest intervals occur at the bottom of the prime form. (Alternatively, you may simply start at the top of the rotation and count the number of descending steps beginning with 0 to figure the prime form.)

The prime form in Figure 4.19 matches that in Figure 4.17 despite the fact that the sets are inversions of each other. This reflects our intuition that sets and their inversions are closely related because they articulate the same constellation of intervals. A set's prime form is essentially a label, one that keeps track of the set's interval content. Because they begin with 0, prime forms put all sets on equal footing, making comparisons easier.

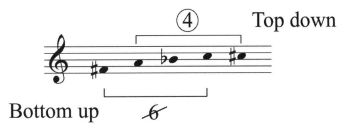

**FIGURE 4.18** Rotation with the Smallest Interval on the Top

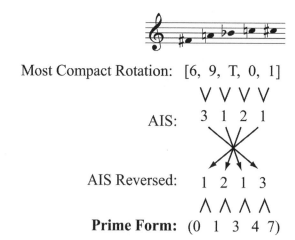

Most Compact Rotation:    [6, 9, T, 0, 1]

                ∨ ∨ ∨ ∨

AIS:            3   1   2   1

AIS Reversed:      1   2   1   3

                ∧ ∧ ∧ ∧

**Prime Form:**   (0   1   3   4   7)

**FIGURE 4.19** Procedure for Determining the Prime Form of an Inverted Set

## Some Further Observations about Prime Forms

There are a couple of idiosyncrasies involving prime forms the student should be aware of. These require no changes to the prime form algorithm itself, but might not be anticipated by the newly initiated. The first of these involves matching intervals at the top and bottom of a set. When this happens, continue checking the intervals one at a time until the smallest interval emerges. The normal order for the unordered pc set reproduced in Figure 4.20 from Schoenberg's Op. 47 *Phantasy*, m. 1 (cf. Example 4.2) may serve as an example. Here, the interval between the first and next-to-last pcs is the same as the interval between the second and last pcs (6). If we move to the next two intervals closer to the top and bottom, however, we find that the circled ic 4 between the first and fourth members near the bottom of the set is smaller than the ic 5 between the third and sixth members nearer the top. This indicates that the smallest intervals overall are packed toward the bottom of the set. The correct prime form is thus (0 1 3 6 7).

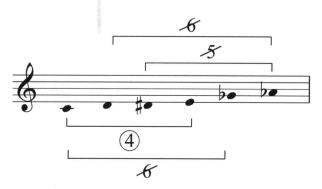

**FIGURE 4.20** Rotation with Matching Outer Intervals

If a set has more than one rotation with the same degree of compression bottom-to-top, simply compare all competing rotations. In Figure 4.21 the set on the left has the best packing of intervals top-to-bottom. We must therefore reverse the intervals to arrive at the correct prime form, (0 1 2 3 6 7 9).

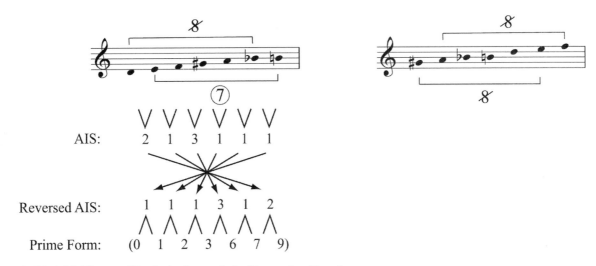

FIGURE 4.21 How to Check the Intervals in Competing Rotations

In some cases, the packing is the same bottom-to-top as it is top-to-bottom. Under these circumstances, the procedure outlined in Figures 4.15 and 4.17 does not produce a "winner." One such set is shown in Figure 4.22. Notice that the set is symmetrical about its center and thus forms an **interval palindrome**. Such sets generate the same prime form whether or not they are inverted, in this case (0 1 3 4 5 7 8).

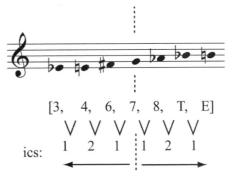

FIGURE 4.22 Normal Order with Interval Palindrome

There is an alternative way for deriving prime forms that uses two sets of rotations rather than one. The steps in this method are:

1) Determine the normal orders of the pc set *and* its inversion.
2) Test to see which normal order has the smallest intervals most tightly packed toward the left or bottom.
3) Transpose the normal order with the tightest packing of intervals toward the bottom to begin on 0 or simply begin with 0 and derive the prime form by calculating intervals based on the adjacency interval series as demonstrated in Figure 4.23.*

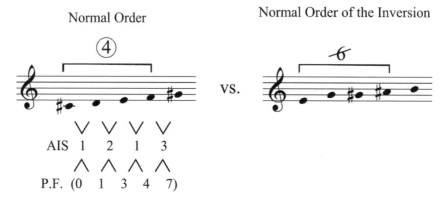

**FIGURE 4.23** Alternative Prime Form Algorithm

If the intervals between the first pc and the next-to-last pc in Step 2 match, compare the interval between the first pc and the second-to-last pc of each normal order. Continue checking intervals closer to the bottom until a "winner" emerges. If the two normal orders match, either one may be used to derive the correct prime form.

* This method for calculating prime forms is similar to that advocated by Joseph N. Straus in *Introduction to Post-tonal Theory*, 3rd ed. (Upper Saddle River: Prentice Hall, 2005), 58. In Straus's method, both of the normal orders are transposed to 0 before checking the interval packing to the left. See also John Rahn, *Basic Atonal Theory* (New York: Schirmer Books, 1980), 81.

Regardless of the method used, prime forms essentially require us to treat unordered pc sets like chords. Prime forms themselves, however, can be used to identify a variety of musical structures, including melodic configurations. Example 4.5 shows the beginning of the main theme from the first movement of César Franck's Symphony in D Minor. The passage begins with an important three-note melodic idea whose ordered pitch interval succession is −1/+4. This is followed by a similar contour in which the second interval expands by a semitone to +5, creating an (0 1 5). The bracketed motives in m. 31 incorporate different shapes and intervals, but are nonetheless related to the melodic idea in m. 29 and have the same prime form, (0 1 4).[8] The string of (0 1 4)s in mm. 31–32 finally breaks down with the reordering that occurs on the second beat of m. 32.

**EX. 4.5**—César Franck, Symphony in D Minor, I (Violin I), mm. 29–32 (Melodic Motives and their Prime Forms)

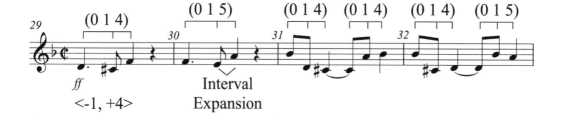

Prime forms may also serve as labels for ordered sets. Webern's 1905 String Quartet, shown in Example 4.6, begins with the same ordered pitch interval configuration found in Franck's Symphony in D Minor, −1/+4. In the first violin and cello parts, however, the grouping is treated like an ordered pitch set; it either retains its crooked shape and pitch interval content or is inverted in pitch-space. Expressing the ordered pitch sets in the passage in terms of their prime forms makes it easier to see how they relate to the highlighted unordered pc sets in the second violin and viola parts; all are members of (0 1 4).

**EX. 4.6**—Anton Webern, String Quartet, mm. 1–6 (Mixed Ordered and Unordered Sets Belonging to (0 1 4))

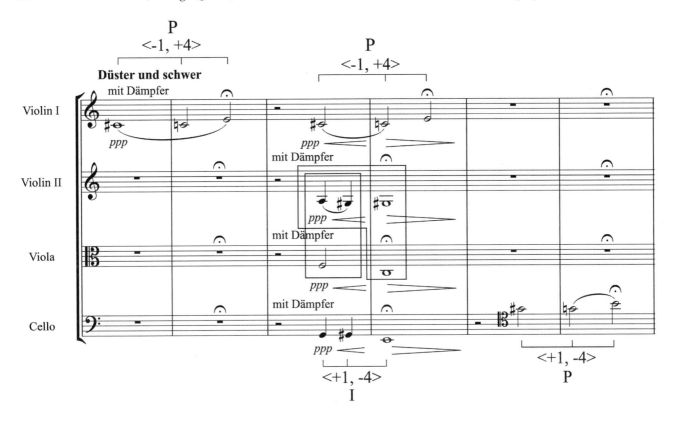

Unordered pc sets and their operations are among the most important tools used to analyze post-tonal music. Although such sets and their operations are abstractions based on the music we listen to, they involve processes that are musically viable at their core. It is in listening to music, then, that we can gain the deepest understanding of them.

## Motivic Hearing

With the discussion of prime forms behind us, the student is now prepared to begin identifying prime forms by ear in the Exercises found in the *Motivic Hearing* program discussed in the "Aural Skills Supplement."

## Chapter 4 Exercises

1) Use the adjacency interval series to determine whether the second unordered pitch set in each exercise below is a transposition of the first unordered pitch set (**P**) or the inversion followed by transposition (**I**) and write the answer in the blank. For a more advanced activity, specify the value of n in the expressions $T_n^p$ and $T_n^pI$. Remember, the value of n in $T_n^pI$ is equal to the index, the sum of the integer names of inversionally equivalent pitches.

a)

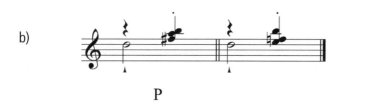

$$P \qquad\qquad I$$

_____

b)

$$P$$

_____

c)

$$P$$

_____

d)

$$P$$

_____

e)

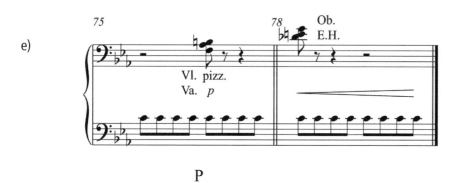

$$P$$

_____

2) Now, supply the normal order and prime form for the sets on the left in Exercise 1.

|  | Normal Order | Prime Form |  | Normal Order | Prime Form |
|---|---|---|---|---|---|
| a) | _____ | _____ | d) | _____ | _____ |
| b) | _____ | _____ | e) | _____ | _____ |
| c) | _____ | _____ |  |  |  |

3) Identify the $T_n$ mappings of the chords in the left column onto the chords in the right column. Begin by putting both chords in normal order. Then determine the distance (difference) between them.

$$T_n$$

| a) | [5, 6, 8, T] | _____ | [1, 3, T, E] |
|---|---|---|---|
| b) | [2, 5, 9] | _____ | [2, 6, E] |
| c) | [3, 5, 9, T, E] | _____ | [3, 4, 5, 9, E] |
| d | [1, 3, 5, T] | _____ | [0, 4, 6, 8] |

4) Identify the $T_nI$ mappings of the chords in the left column onto the chords in the right column. After putting the sets in normal order, sort through the rotations of the sets in the left column to find the inverted adjacency interval series. Then determine the distance (difference) between the sets.

$$T_nI$$

| a) | [5, 6, 8, T] | _____ | [6, 8, T, E] |
|---|---|---|---|
| b) | [1, 2, 4, 6, 9] | _____ | [1, 4, 6, 8, 9] |
| c) | [2, 3, 7, 9] | _____ | [3, 5, 9, T] |
| d) | [2, 3, 9] | _____ | [1, 2, 7] |

5) Fill in the boxes with the *normal order* and *prime form* for each set below.

| | Pc Set | Normal Order | Prime Form |
|---|---|---|---|
| a) | | | |
| b) | | | |
| c) | [0, 5, 6, T] | | |
| d) | G♮, C♮, F♯ | | |
| e) | | | |
| f) | [0, 1, 2, 6, 9, T] | | |
| g) | C♯, F♮, B♭, B♮ | | |

6) Fill in the boxes with the *prime form* for the following sets. Each of these sets involves one of the conditions described in the "Further Observations" section of Chapter 4 such as multiple rotations with the same degree of compression and matching intervals at the top and bottom of the set.

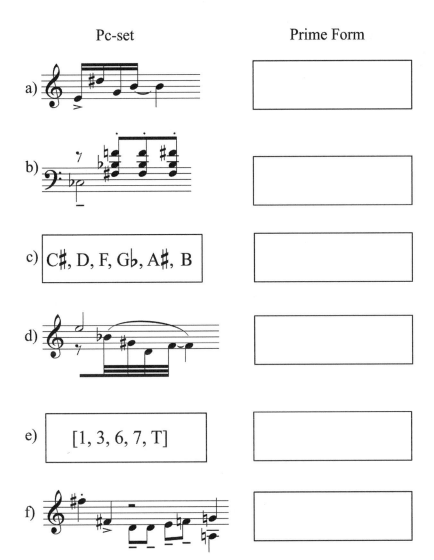

Pc-set                                    Prime Form

c) C♯, D, F, G♭, A♯, B

e) [1, 3, 6, 7, T]

7) Trichords.

   a) List the total interval-class content for each of the twelve trichords below.

   a) (012) __1 /1 /2__          e) (016) _____          i) (027) _____

   b) (013) _____          f) (024) _____          j) (036) _____

   c) (014) _____          g) (025) _____          k) (037) _____

   d) (015) _____          h) (026) _____          l) (048) _____

b) Notice that each trichord in Exercise 4.4a has a unique total interval-class content. Use this information to quickly determine the prime forms for the trichords below.

_____    _____    _____    _____    _____    _____

8) Analysis.

a) Write the prime form for the bracketed figure in the following excerpt in the space below.

b) Now, bracket ( ⌐‾‾‾‾⌐‾‾‾‾⌐ ) as many instances as you can find of this figure in the violin and right-hand piano parts. The notes of the figure may be rearranged and/or occur in any octave. Figures may also overlap (e.g., ⌐‾‾‾⌐‾‾‾⌐ ).

Lukas Foss, _Elegy for Anne Frank_, mm. 14–18

# Chapter 5

# Set-Class Analysis

---

| | |
|---|---|
| Set class | Self-mappings |
| Cardinality | Invariants |
| Interval-class vector (ICV) | Transpositionally symmetrical sets |
| Z-related sets | Inversionally symmetrical sets |
| All-interval tetrachords | Degrees of symmetry |
| Subsets | Atonal voice leading |
| Inclusion relations | Inverse |
| Supersets | K-net (Klumpenhouwer network) |
| Set saturation | |

## Set Classes

A **set class** is a family of sets that subsumes all $T_n$ and $T_nI$ forms of an unordered pc set. Set classes have two labels. One of these is the prime form, already discussed in some detail in Chapter 4. The other is a hyphenated number. The number to the left of the hyphen indicates the **cardinality** of the set (i.e., its size) while the number to the right of the hyphen indicates the set's order position on the list of set classes provided in Appendix B.[1]

Table 5.1 lists the set classes for the twelve trichords.[2] These set classes account for all possible combinations of three pitches regardless of register and order. Having a classification system such as this is extremely useful because it gives us a way to highlight musically relevant connections between sets that to the eye might at first appear to be unrelated. (The ear is probably much less easily fooled.)

**TABLE 5.1** Trichords

|       | *Prime Form* |       | *Prime Form* |
|-------|--------------|-------|--------------|
| 3–1   | (0 1 2)      | 3–7   | (0 2 5)      |
| 3–2   | (0 1 3)      | 3–8   | (0 2 6)      |
| 3–3   | (0 1 4)      | 3–9   | (0 2 7)      |
| 3–4   | (0 1 5)      | 3–10  | (0 3 6)      |
| 3–5   | (0 1 6)      | 3–11  | (0 3 7)      |
| 3–6   | (0 2 4)      | 3–12  | (0 4 8)      |

The *complement* of a pc set is the set that completes the aggregate (the collection consisting of all twelve pcs) when combined with the first. The *literal* complement of [0, 1, 4] is [2, 3, 5, 6, 7, 8, 9, T, E], the set consisting of those pcs not found in [0, 1, 4]. The set classes for these two sets, 3–3 (0 1 4) and 9–3 (0 1 2 3 4 5 6 8 9), are said to be *abstract* complements of each other. Notice that abstract complements may share elements; all the elements of (0 1 4), for example, may be found in (**0 1** 2 3 **4** 5 6 8 9). Complementary cardinalities always generate the same number of set classes. For example, there are twelve three-member and twelve nine-member sets. In order to highlight these relations, complementary sets have been lined up side by side in Appendix B.[3]

Set classes are essentially repositories for intervals. It is the interval content of a set, then, that contributes most strongly to its character. To keep track of the intervals in a set, we may refer to its **interval-class vector (ICV)**. Interval-class vectors are ordered arrays enclosed in square brackets without commas. Each position in the array represents one of the six non-0 ics; the first position corresponds to ic 1, the second to ic 2, and so on. The pc set in Figure 5.1 contains two ic 1s, no ic 2s, one ic 3, two ic 4s, one ic 5, and no ic 6s. Hence, its interval-class vector is [201210].

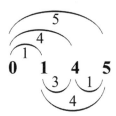

ics:  1  2  3  4  5  6
ICV [2  0  1  2  1  0]

**FIGURE 5.1** Procedure for Determining the Interval-class Vector of a Pc Set

Among other things, interval-class vectors may be used to predict the number of invariant pcs produced under transposition since transposing a set by any of the intervals present in the set will duplicate one of its members. If there are two such intervals, two members will be duplicated, and so on. The number of invariant pcs doubles for ic 6. The interval vector for [0, 1, 4, 5] is [201210]. Since there are 2 ic 1s in the set, $T_1$ produces 2 common tones as illustrated in Figure 5.2. Continuing in the same way, $T_2$ produces no common tones, $T_3$ one common tone, $T_4$ two common tones, $T_5$ one common tone, and $T_6$ no common tones.

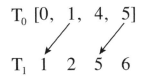

**FIGURE 5.2** Invariant Pcs under Transposition

Given the emphasis on interval content, one might assume that each prime form has a unique interval-class vector. This turns out not to be true. In some instances, two sets may share a vector. Such sets are said to be **Z-related sets**. The interval-class vector for both set class 4–Z15 and set class 4–Z29, for example, is [111111]. These two sets are known as the **all-interval tetrachords** because they are the only tetrachords that contain all six ics.

While we will not discuss them here, theorists have developed a number of ways to rate the degree of similarity between interval-class vectors. These are known as "similarity relations."[4] One can use interval-class vectors to analyze music, however, even without these relations. Alban Berg's Op. 2, No. 2, *Schlafend trägt man mich*, provides a case in point. The text of the song along with an English translation appears in Figure 5.3. As the text proclaims, the protagonist sinks into a deep sleep, dreaming of a return home after a long journey. The song itself begins and ends with references to the homeland (*Heimatland*) accompanied by a series of whole-tone chords belonging to set class 4–25, (0 2 6 8). These are highlighted in Example 5.1.

Some of the melodic tones at the beginning of the song serve an embellishing function. Notice, for example, how B♭ and A♭ step down to the chord tone, G♭, in m. 2. The progression as a whole consists of a succession of $T_{11}$ transpositions of the (0 2 6 8) tetrachord, a pattern expressly communicated by the semitone melodic descent in mm. 2–4.[5] The series is presented in reverse order beginning with the last chord in m. 4.

*Schlafend trägt man mich in mein Heimatland.*
*Ferne komm' ich her,*
*über Gipfel, über Schlünde, über ein dunkles Meer*
*in mein Heimatland.*

Sleeping, I am carried back to my homeland.
I come from far away,
over hills, over valleys, over a dark sea
to my Homeland.

**FIGURE 5.3** Text and Translation of Alban Berg's *Vier Lieder*, Op. 2, No. 2

**EX. 5.1**—Alban Berg, *Vier Lieder*, Op. 2, No. 2, mm. 1–4 (Whole-tone Chords)

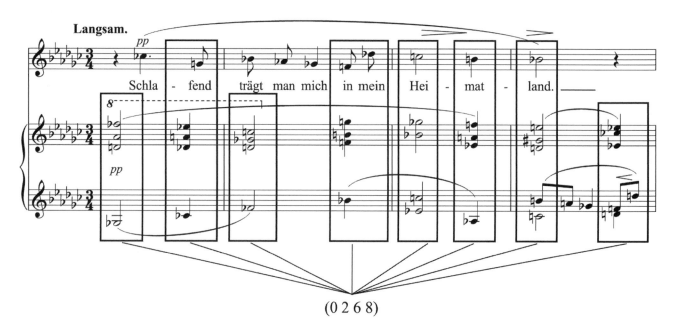

(0 2 6 8)

In mm. 9–12, the protagonist reminisces about the long journey from far away (*Ferne*) across mountains (*Gipfel*) and the dark sea (*dunkles Meer*). The music at this point echoes the notion of distance by introducing a number of non-whole-tone chords. Figure 5.4 lists several of these along with their interval-class vectors. Comparing the vectors in the figure to the remaining tetrachord vectors in Appendix B reveals that they are among the select few (nine in all) that have the fewest instances of the intervals found in set class 4–25, (0 2 6 8), and at least one each of the intervals *not* contained in set class 4–25. This idea dovetails nicely with the sense of distance portrayed by the text; in terms of their interval content, the chords in mm. 9–12 are as "distant" from the chords at the beginning and end of the song as possible.[6] The opening series of (0 2 6 8)s reappears at the end of the song, reinforcing the notion of the return home expressed in the final line of the poem.

Berg, of course, would not have been aware of interval-class vectors as such. At the same time, it is wholly within the realm of reason to assume that he would have chosen chords—whether by intuition or design—appropriate to the task of setting the text to music.

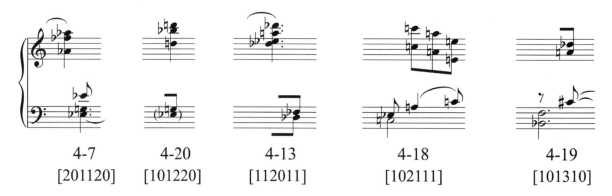

| 4-7 | 4-20 | 4-13 | 4-18 | 4-19 |
| [201120] | [101220] | [112011] | [102111] | [101310] |

**FIGURE 5.4** Selected Chords in mm. 9–11

Despite their abstract mien, set classes often correspond to familiar pitch structures. Appendix C lists a number of these structures along with their subsets and set-class representations. Many of these collections, of course, are not usually thought of as being invertible. Under the set theory perspective, for example, major and minor triads belong to the same set class, 3–11 (0 3 7), because the smallest interval, a minor third, always ends up on the bottom. On the other hand, diatonic chords *are* typically treated like unordered pc sets; their pitches, that is, are often unordered and spread across many octaves, a process that brings the total interval-class content expressed by their interval-class vectors into the limelight.

## Inclusion Relations

We have just seen how disparity can reinforce the dramatic impact of a piece (cf. note 6). In other situations musical expression may be communicated by collections that have a close affinity for one another. This affinity can often be revealed through the identification of the nested sets or **subsets** shared by different pitch groupings in a passage. Such relations between sets are called **inclusion relations** because they involve groupings that are embedded (i.e., *included*) in larger groupings known as **supersets**.

Figure 5.5 shows a tetrachord and its four trichord subsets. Here, the pcs of the subsets match their counterparts in the superset. In other cases, the relations between subsets and supersets may be more abstract. Abstract subsets and supersets involve set classes and their elements. A minor third, (0 3), for example, may be considered to be a subset of triads in general, (0 3 7), without specifying pitches. Where the relations between subsets and supersets are concerned, both the set class and its inverted representations should be considered.

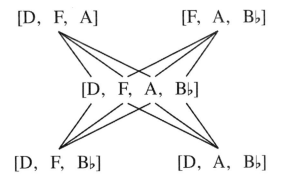

**FIGURE 5.5** Tetrachord and its Trichord Subsets

Example 5.2 provides a piano reduction of the first three measures of the third movement of Leonard Bernstein's *Chichester Psalms* along with a set-class analysis of the chords in the passage. Notice that the excerpt contains both trichords and tetrachords. In addition, the excerpt contains a number of non-matching trichords and tetrachords. Yet when we listen to this music, we hear a coherent and sensible progression. This may be owing, at least in part, to the abundance of thirds and fifths in the passage. Indeed, the progression ends on a C minor triad and there are two diatonic seventh chords in the first measure: E♭maj⁷, (0 1 5 8), and Dmin⁷, (0 3 5 8).

**EX. 5.2**—Leonard Bernstein, *Chichester Psalms*, III, mm. 1–3 (Set-Class Analysis)

Although they are not triads, many of the remaining set classes also span a perfect fifth. This is indicated by their uppermost element, 7. Three of the sets, (0 1 4 8), (0 2 3 7), and (0 2 4 7), also contain a nested triad.[7] We can easily see, for example, that (0 3 7), the prime form for major and minor triads, also occurs in (0 2 3 7). (See Figure 5.6.)

$$
\begin{array}{cccc}
& (0 & 3 & 7) \\
0 & 1 & 4 & 8
\end{array}
$$

**FIGURE 5.6** (0 2 3 7) and its Embedded (0 3 7) Subset

Subsets whose elements do not match those of the superset can be quickly determined by comparing the intervals in the respective adjacency interval series of the sets. Using this method, we find that ic 3 and ic 4 in (0 3 7) occur between 1, 4, and 8 in (0 1 4 8). (See Figure 5.7.) Hence, (0 1 4 8) also contains an embedded triad.

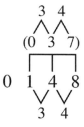

**FIGURE 5.7** (0 1 4 8) and its Embedded (0 3 7) Subset

Subsets may also be inverted as illustrated in Figure 5.8.

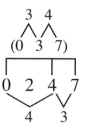

**FIGURE 5.8** (0 2 4 7) and its Embedded (0 3 7) Subset

The passage in Example 5.2 begins with the non-triadic trichord (0 1 3), which may be interpreted as a minor third with an added note for effect. This trichord, inverted, is also embedded in (0 2 3 7). (See Figure 5.9.)

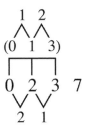

**FIGURE 5.9** (0 2 3 7) and its Embedded (0 1 3) Subset

In addition to its tertian features, the (0 2 3 7) tetrachord introduces a new trichord, (0 2 7). This trichord not only matches the sole (0 2 7) in m. 2, but also accounts for the origins of the non-triadic (0 2 5 7) in m. 2; as Figure 5.10 illustrates, (0 2 5 7) contains two versions of (0 2 7). In this case, then, the superset completely absorbs the subset, a phenomenon we will refer to as **set saturation**. Notice too that [C, D, G], which enters on the last beat of m. 2, is also a *literal* subset of the chord that precedes it, [C, D, E, G].

(0   2   7)

0   2   5   7

(0   2   7)

**FIGURE 5.10** Set Saturation of (0 2 5 7) by (0 2 7)

In this remarkable passage from Bernstein's *Chichester Psalms*, chords—even if informed by triadic harmony—do not function according to tonal protocol. The music is essentially "non-tonal," then, despite the fact that it does not fully embrace the "atonal" language of second Viennese composers such as Arnold Schoenberg.[8] On the other hand, Bernstein's music may not be as different from Schoenberg's as it appears; not only does the (0 1 4 8) sonority play an important role in Schoenberg's Op. 11, No. 1, for example, but it is consistently spelled in thirds, first as an augmented/major seventh chord and then as a minor/major seventh chord (cf. Example 1.1 in Chapter 1).

Although the (0 1 4 8) chords in Schoenberg's Op. 11, No. 1 are spelled in thirds, the piece in general does not highlight triadic harmony. Example 5.3 shows the melody that occurs at the beginning of the piece. This melody articulates two trichords, (0 1 4) and (0 1 5). These two trichords play prominent roles throughout the movement and are embedded in many of the larger pitch structures in the piece. Among these is (0 1 4 8), which, in addition to its tertian features, can be interpreted as an amalgam of both trichords. This is illustrated in Figure 5.11a. In this case, the correspondence between (0 1 5) and the elements 0, 1, and 8 in the figure may not be immediately apparent. To arrive at this interpretation, it is necessary to take into account the interval between 8 and 0 as illustrated in Figure 5.11b.

**EX. 5.3**—Arnold Schoenberg, *Three Piano Pieces*, Op. 11, No. 1, mm. 1–3 (Trichord Partitioning of the Theme)

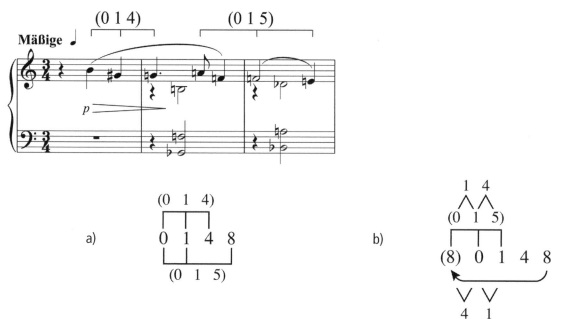

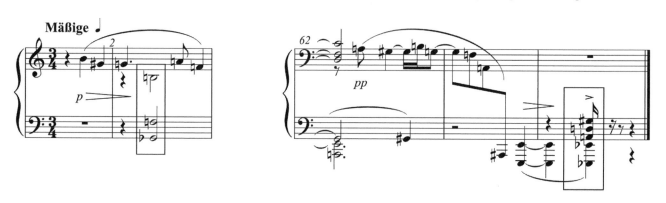

**FIGURE 5.11** Trichord Partitioning of (0 1 4 8)

In some cases, there may be many overlapping subsets in a superset. Consider the chords that "bookend" Schoenberg's Op. 11, No. 1 shown in Example 5.4, (0 1 6) and (0 1 6 7).

**EX. 5.4**—Arnold Schoenberg, *Three Piano Pieces*, Op. 11, No. 1, mm. 1–2 and 62–64 (Beginning and Ending Chords)

Two of the most obvious occurrences of (0 1 6) in (0 1 6 7) are shown in Figure 5.12a. In order to identify *all* of the (0 1 6) subsets in (0 1 6 7), however, it is necessary to treat the set as a pc cycle whose end connects to its beginning. (cf. Figure 5.11b.) This allows for the additional subsets shown in Figure 5.12b.

**FIGURE 5.12** (0 1 6) Subsets in (0 1 6 7)

## $T_n$ and $T_nI$ Self-Mappings

Among the properties of a set are the ways in which it maps onto itself under transposition or inversion followed by transposition. These are known as **self-mappings**. Sets that map onto themselves under $T_n$ or $T_nI$ are said to be **invariants** of one another because they contain the same pcs. All sets, of course, map onto themselves under the identity operation $T_0$. The collection in Example 5.5, on the other hand, also maps onto itself at non-0 levels of transposition as well as inversion.

**EX. 5.5**—George Crumb, *Madrigals*, Book III, No. 1, "La noche canta desnuda sobre los puentes de marzo," mm. 2–3 (Unordered Pc Set with Multiple $T_n$ and $T_nI$ Mappings)

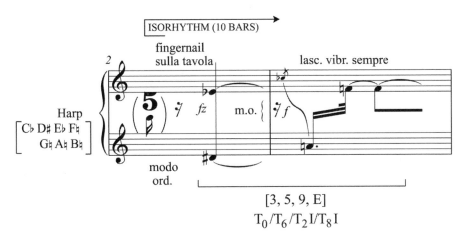

$$[3, 5, 9, E]$$
$$T_0/T_6/T_2I/T_8I$$

All $T_n$ and $T_nI$ versions of a set express the same sequence of intervals either forwards or backwards. To determine specific $T_n$ and $T_nI$ self-mappings, then, we may refer to a set's adjacency interval series. The set in Figure 5.13 has a self-retrogradable adjacency interval series and, hence, maps onto itself under both transposition ($T_0$) and inversion ($T_9I$). Sets that map onto themselves under transposition are known as **transpositionally symmetrical sets**. Those that map onto themselves under inversion are called **inversionally symmetrical sets**.

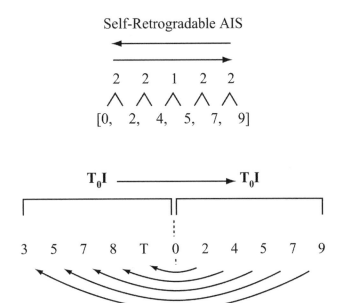

**FIGURE 5.13** $T_nI$ Self-Mapping

The number of ways a set maps onto itself under $T_n$ and $T_nI$ are known as its **degrees of symmetry**. The set in Figure 5.13 has one degree of transpositional symmetry ($T_0$) and one degree of inversional symmetry ($T_9I$). In some cases, a set may map onto one or more of its rotations. For this reason, it is best to use two complete rotations of a set and its inversion to determine $T_n$ and $T_nI$ self-mappings. The set in Figure 5.14, [0, 3, 6, 9], has four degrees each of transpositional and inversional symmetry. This set, which may be conceptualized as a diminished seventh or 3/9 cycle, subdivides the octave into four equal three-semitone segments. Hence, transposing the set by multiples of 3 in pc-space causes the set to replicate itself.

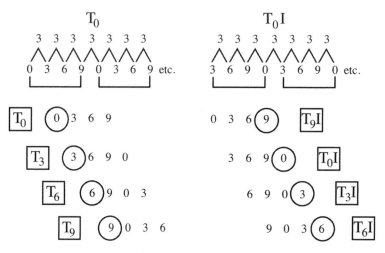

**FIGURE 5.14** Set with Multiple Self-Mappings

There are a number of sets that map onto themselves under $T_nI$, but do *not* have a self-retrogradable adjacency interval series. One such set is [0, 1, 5, 8] shown in Figure 5.15. As the figure illustrates, the inversion does not have the same adjacency interval series as $T_0$, but the rotation beginning on E does. The set thus maps onto itself under $T_1I$.

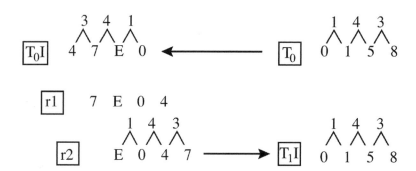

**FIGURE 5.15** Set with Non-self-retrogradable Adjacency Interval Series

There are only six set classes with multiple $T_n$ and $T_nI$ mappings.[9] These are shown in Table 5.2. All have multiple axes of inversion and a self-retrogradable adjacency interval series. Several of these set classes are also known by other names, including the diminished seventh or 3/9 cycle, (0 3 6 9), the augmented triad or 4/8 cycle, (0 4 8), cell z, (0 1 6 7), the whole-tone scale or 2/10 cycle, (0 2 4 6 8 T), the octatonic scale, (0 1 3 4 6 7 9 T), and the hexatonic or augmented scale, (0 1 4 5 8 9).

**TABLE 5.2** Sets with Multiple $T_n$ and $T_nI$ Mappings

| Degrees of Symmetry | | $T_n$ | $T_nI$ |
|---|---|---|---|
| 3–12 | (0 4 8) | 3 | 3 |
| 4–9 | (0 1 6 7) | 2 | 2 |
| 4–25 | (0 2 6 8) | 2 | 2 |
| 4–28 | (0 3 6 9) | 4 | 4 |
| 6–7 | (0 1 2 6 7 8) | 2 | 2 |
| 6–20 | (0 1 4 5 8 9) | 3 | 3 |
| 6–35 | (0 2 4 6 8 T) | 6 | 6 |
| 8–9 | (0 1 2 3 6 7 8 9) | 2 | 2 |
| 8–25 | (0 1 2 4 6 7 8 T) | 2 | 2 |
| 8–28 | (0 1 3 4 6 7 9 T) | 4 | 4 |
| 9–12 | (0 1 2 4 5 6 8 9 T) | 3 | 3 |

Self-mapping can play an integral role in the compositional design of a work. George Crumb's "La noche canta desnuda sobre los puentes de marzo," for example, begins with the four-note tetrachord shown in Example 5.6 (cf. Example 5.5). The set is transposed six semitones in mm. 42–45, producing a duplicate of the set in which its two dyads are inverted, a clear instance of self-mapping used to expand the range of a piece.

**EX. 5.6**—George Crumb, *Madrigals*, Book III, No. 1, "La noche canta desnuda sobre los puentes de marzo," mm. 2–3 and 42–43 (Expansion through Self-Mapping)

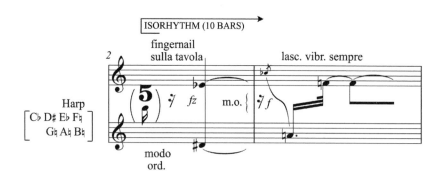

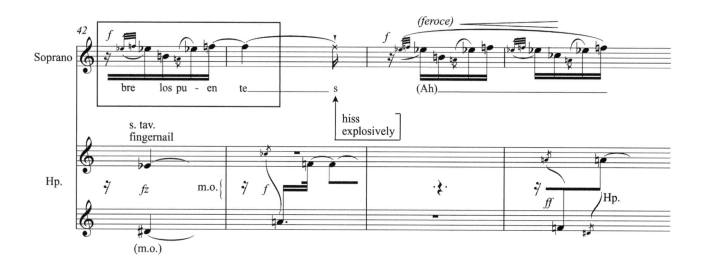

[3, 5, 9, E]          [9, E, 3, 5]

# Atonal Voice Leading

So far, we have been using $T_n$ and $T_nI$ to describe the relations between pairs of sets. $T_n$ and $T_nI$ may also be used to keep track of the **atonal voice leading** in a passage; that is, how the individual notes of sets of the same cardinality map onto each other in a succession of sets.[10] Atonal voice leading differs from traditional voice leading in that connections do not necessarily occur in the same part. Consider the series of violin trichords found in Igor Stravinsky's *Rite of Spring* shown in Example 4.4 from the previous chapter. We have already seen that the passage alternates between prime and inverted versions of the chord. To show the atonal voice leading in the passage, we not only need to identify the $T_nI$ operation that maps each chord onto the next, but also to trace the mappings of the individual voices. The atonal voice leading for the chords in this passage is shown in Example 5.7. For convenience, the letter T may be dropped from the expression $T_nI$ when labeling mappings in atonal voice leading. Notice that the repetition of $I_0$ at the end of the excerpt has the effect of reinstating the third chord on the last beat of the measure. This is because inversion is its own **inverse**; it undoes itself when repeated.[11]

**EX. 5.7**—Igor Stravinsky, *The Rite of Spring*, Part II, "Glorification of the Chosen Maiden," m. 28 (Atonal Voice Leading)

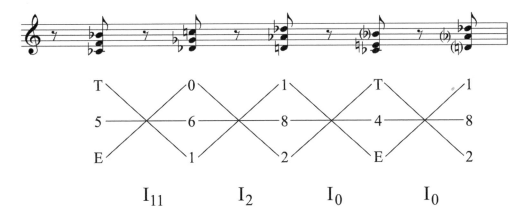

Atonal voice leading may also take the form of a series of transpositions (as in Example 5.1) or mixed $T_n$ and $I_n$ mappings as illustrated in Figure 5.16.

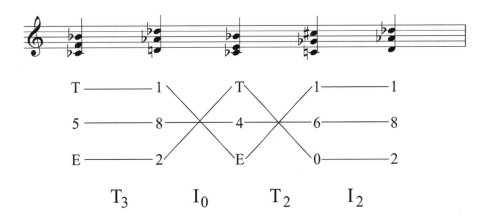

**FIGURE 5.16** (Atonal Voice Leading with Mixed Mappings)

The chords in non-triadic passages, of course, do not always map onto each other under $T_n$ or $I_n$. Example 5.8 contains an excerpt from the first movement of Paul Hindemith's *Symphonie Mathis der Maler*. The passage consists of a lyrical melody in the strings and woodwinds punctuated by two three-chord progressions in the brass. These appear on the top-most grand staff of the example in boxes. The chords in these progressions do not map onto each other under either $T_n$ or $I_n$. The voice leading from one progression to the next, on the other hand, is quite consistent; two of the voices ascend by semitone while the third voice descends by semitone. Figure 5.17, for example, shows how each voice combines with the others in mm. 54–55, forming a parallel ascent and two wedging formations consisting of contrary motion.

**EX. 5.8**—Paul Hindemith, *Symphonie Mathis der Maler*, I, mm. 53–59 (Contrapuntal Wedges)

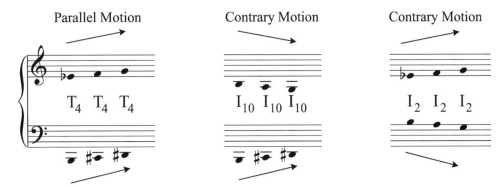

**FIGURE 5.17** Voice Leading in mm. 54–55

The relations between the voices in this kind of contrapuntal figure may be illustrated using a **K-net** or **Klumpenhouwer network**.[12] K-nets combine transposition and inversion within a single network graph. In the K-nets we produce here, we will place transpositionally related pcs at the top and bottom of the set while the third voice, that which is related by inversion to the other two voices, will be placed in the middle. This creates one $T_n$ operation and two $I_n$ operations.

The K-nets for the chords in mm. 54–55 are shown in Figure 5.18. The $T_n$ operation is the distance (difference) between the outer voices. The $I_n$ operations are the indexes (sums) of the remaining pairs of pcs and account for the two axes of inversion for the wedges.

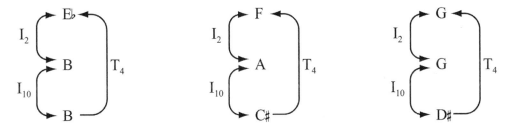

**FIGURE 5.18** K-nets in mm. 54–55

Although the chords in m. 57 follow a similar trajectory to those in mm. 54–55, they produce different graphs. This is because the transposition of the progression as a whole shifts the axes of inversion. (See Figure 5.19.)

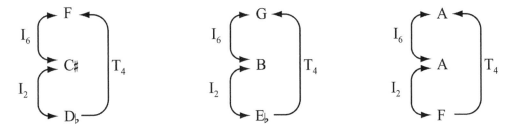

**FIGURE 5.19** K-nets in m. 57

K-nets can be modified to represent the relations between chords in passages that have wedges formed by tetrachords instead of trichords. The chords found in mm. 9–10 of Bernard Herrmann's score for the movie *Psycho* shown in Example 5.9, for instance, may be analyzed as two pairs of parallel thirds moving in contrary motion, forming alternating tetrachords.[13]

**EX. 5.9**—Bernard Herrmann, *Psycho*, "Prelude," mm. 9–10 and 35–36 (Parallel Thirds)

*Measures 9-10 & 35-36*

As Figure 5.20 illustrates, tetrachord networks require an additional transposition operation. There are also two additional axes of inversion, although these are unambiguously defined by the two at the top and bottom of the network graph and may be excluded.

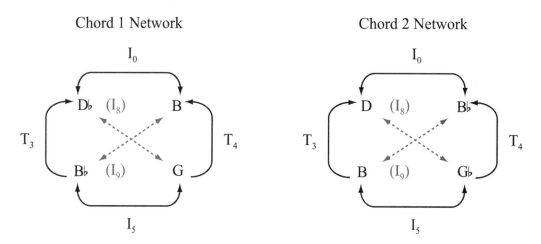

**FIGURE 5.20** Chord Networks in Bernard Herrmann's *Psycho* Soundtrack

While set classes and their prime forms are less discriminating than tools that specify contour and register, they do provide an effective means for comparing and contrasting pitch structures in post-tonal music. In addition, they may serve as convenient labels for non-triadic pitch groupings. Regardless of the uses to which they are put, however, it should be remembered that set classes are more than mere abstract mathematical expressions of a pc set. They embody the very essence of a set by articulating its interval content and, thus, capture its aural impact.

# Chapter 5 Exercises

1) Prime forms and their vectors.

   a) Fill in the blanks with the prime forms for each of the chords in the passage below.

   b) Refer to the interval vectors in Appendix B to determine which interval class occurs most often in the passage and write it in the space below.

   Circle the two all-interval tetrachords.

2) Self-mappings.

   a) Identify all of the ways [0, 2, 6, 8] maps onto itself under $T_n$ and $T_nI$.

   b) Now, identify all of the ways [0, 4, 8] maps onto itself under $T_n$ and $T_nI$.

3) Inclusion relations.

   We have already undertaken a partial analysis of Schoenberg's Op. 11, No. 1 using inclusion relations. (See Chapter 5, pp. 121–22.) In this analysis, we discovered that the main theme in mm. 1–3 could be parsed into the two trichords (014) and (015). These were subsequently mapped onto the chord in m. 14, (0148). Another important idea, shown below, arrives in mm. 4–5. This melody embeds all of the chords described above.

a)   Determine the prime form for this melody and write it in the blank space below. Then bracket
     ( ⌐⌐⌐ ) all the ways (014) maps onto it.

b)   Repeat the process using (015). (HINT: To determine all the ways (015) maps onto the set,
     you will need to treat the set as a cycle that wraps around to connect to its beginning.)

c)   Finally, show all the ways (0148) maps onto the set. Here again, you will need to treat the set
     as a cycle.

d)   The music of the right-hand part in mm. 34–36 shown below may be segmented into a series
     of trichords. What is this important trichord? (HINT: It is easier to arrive at the answer to this
     question by ear than by eye!)

e)   Where have you heard the music in mm. 34–36 before? What is unique about its presentation
     here?

4)   Complete the atonal voice-leading diagram for the chord progression below.

9

4

2

5) Label the arrows in each K-net.

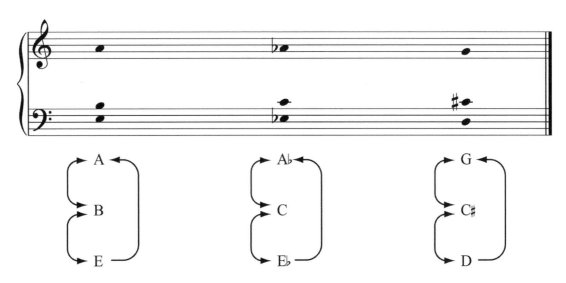

6) (Optional) Undertake each of the following operations.

# Chapter 6

# Ordered Pitch Sets and Their Operations

---

<table>
<tr><td>

($T_n^p$ and $T_n^p I$)

$T_n^p R$ and $T_n^p RI$

Ordered pitch interval motives (a.k.a. shape/interval motives)

Motive chain

Pitch imbrication

Interval imbrication

Interpolation

Interpolation with imbrication

Non-motivic tones

</td><td>

Intervallic expansions and contractions

Shape hybrid

Fragmentation

Truncation

Additive melodies

Subtractive melodies

Reordering

Signature transformation

Motto

</td></tr>
</table>

Having investigated unordered sets, we will now take a closer look at ordered pitch sets. As we shall see, the shapes (contours) and intervals of ordered pitch sets are among their most salient features and will play a crucial role in our analysis of them.

## Transposed Ordered Pitch Sets ($T_n^p$)

Among the basic operations of ordered pitch sets are inversion, retrogression, and retrograde inversion. Ordered pitch sets may also, of course, be transposed. We will continue to designate the transposition of a pitch set, whether ordered or unordered, as $T_n^p$, where n is the number of semitones the set is shifted up or down. The letter "p" is added to show that the operation takes place in pitch-space. Unsigned expressions indicate an upward transposition. A negative sign added to the expression indicates a downward transposition. The *identity operation* maps the set onto itself and is denoted by the expression $T_0^p$.

The bottom staff in Example 6.1 shows the ordered pitch-set that occurs at the beginning of Aaron Copland's *Piano Variations* (mm. 2–3). As the example indicates, the entire motive is transposed two octaves plus a semitone in mm. 119–20, twenty-five altogether, producing a new motive with the same ordered pitch interval content as that in mm. 2–3. The effect is that of a tune that has been transposed to a different "key" and register. To find the value of n mathematically, determine the distance (i.e., the difference) between the pitches of each set by subtracting the first pitch of the first set from the first note of the derived set: 17 (F5) – (–8) (E3) = 25.

**EX. 6.1**—Aaron Copland, *Piano Variations*, mm. 1–3 and 119–20 (Transposed Ordered Pitch Set)

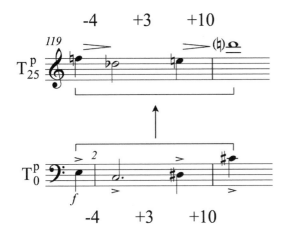

## Inversion Followed by Transposition ($T_n^p I$)

As we learned in Chapter 3, inversion has the effect of flipping the contour of an ordered pitch set upside down. (As a reminder, we are inverting ordered pitch sets around their first note. (This is essentially the same as assigning 0 to the first note.) Example 6.2 contains a particularly poignant example of this process in that both of the upper parts are inversions of the lower two parts, creating a symmetrical quartet texture bottom to top. In both cases, the inversions of the sets are transposed ten semitones, +10 if we treat the viola and cello parts as primes, –10 if we treat the first and second violin parts as primes. Subtracting the first violin's F♯4 (6) from the cello's A♭3 (–4), for example, leaves –10, the value of n in $T_{-10}^p I$.

**EX. 6.2**—Alfred Schnittke, Concerto Grosso No. 6, III, mm. 40–42 (Inverted and Transposed Pitch Sets)

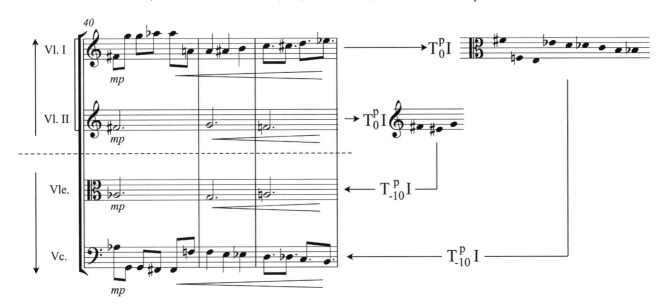

## Retrograde and Retrograde Inversion

We will use the expressions $T_n^p R$ and $T_n^p RI$ to specify the transpositions of the retrograde and retrograde inversion. When calculating the transposition level for R and RI, it is important to remember that retrogression flips the set around its endnote on the horizontal plane, thus shifting the beginning note to the end. (See Figure 6.1.) In Example 6.3, the ordered pitch set in m. 190 is first transposed up an octave. The retrograde, transposed yet another octave higher, arrives a few moments later. Since the first note of $T_0^p$ occurs last in the retrograde, we can determine the transposition of the retrograde by comparing its last note to the first note of $T_0^p$. (Another way is to compare the last note of $T_0^p$ to the first note of the retrograde. This option is especially useful when the prime and retrograde occur back-to-back.) In Example 6.3, the first and last notes are the same, making comparisons easier. Notice that since the operations take place in pitch-space, octave transpositions count despite the fact that all the sets articulate the same pcs.

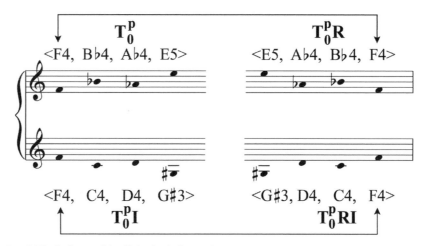

**FIGURE 6.1** Ordered Pitch Set and its Principal Operations

**EX. 6.3**—Béla Bartók, Violin Concerto No. 2, I, mm. 190–92 (Transposed Retrograde)

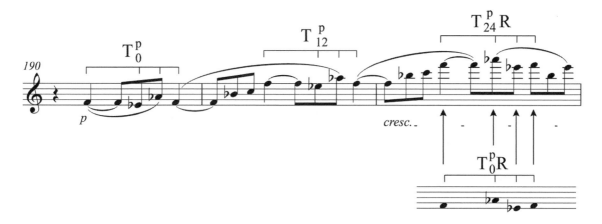

The transposition level of the retrograde inversion may be determined in the same way as the retrograde or by comparing it to the inversion. In Example 6.4, the retrograde inversion is transposed two semitones higher, allowing it to begin on the same pitch as the untransposed prime. This preserves the key as well as B's centricity in the passage.

**EX. 6.4**—Modest Mussorgsky, *Boris Godunov*, Act III, Scene 1, mm. 1–5 (Transposed Retrograde Inversion)

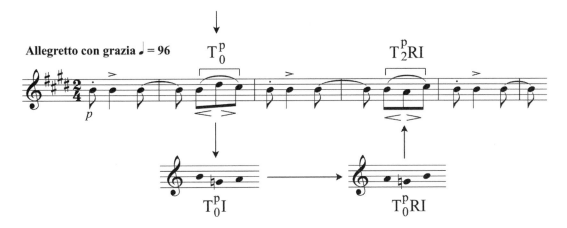

## Motives

As we learned in Chapter 3, themes, such as those in Examples 6.3 and 6.4, are often built up from germinal ideas or motives consisting of only a few notes. Among the most important of these germinal ideas are motives consisting of ordered pitch intervals. We will refer to such motives as **ordered pitch interval motives** or, to highlight their dual nature, **shape/interval motives**. The two principal features of shape/interval motives, shapes and intervals, may be combined into a single expression using ordered pitch intervals enclosed in angled brackets as illustrated in Example 6.5.[1]

**EX. 6.5**—George Crumb, *Madrigals*, Book 4, No. 1, "¿Por qué naci entre espejos?," m. 15 (Shape/Interval Motive)

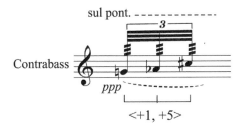

Figure 6.2 shows the P/I/R/RI operations for the motive in Example 6.5. Any of these motive forms may be subjected to transposition; the inversion and retrograde inversion are transposed, for example, in the excerpt from Crumb's "¿Por qué naci entre espejos?" shown in Example 6.6.

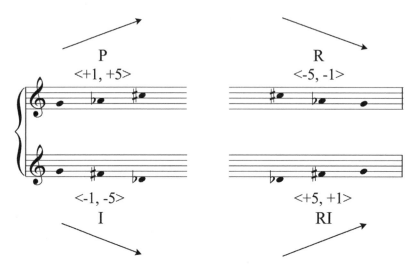

**FIGURE 6.2** P/I/R/RI Group in Crumb's Madrigals, Book 4, I

**EX. 6.6**—George Crumb, *Madrigals*, Book 4, I, "¿Por qué naci entre espejos?," mm. 15–16 (Shape/Interval Motive and its Operations)

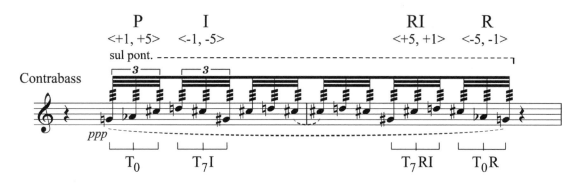

In some music, themes may be only loosely organized around motives, in which case motives may occur in isolation or in isolated groups as in Example 6.6. In other cases, themes may consist entirely of motives, forming a **motive chain**. Example 6.7 contains a particularly elegant example of a motive chain since the two transposed versions of the motive are equally balanced above and below the original.

**EX. 6.7**—Alexander Scriabin, Prelude, Op. 74, No. 3, mm. 9–12 (Motive Chain)

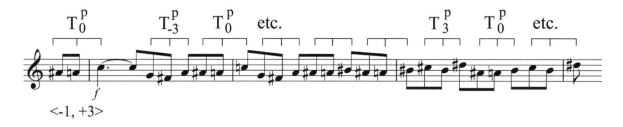

## Imbrication and Interpolation

Although motives may occur back-to-back as in Examples 6.6, and 6.7, they can also overlap. In this section, we will discuss two principal types of overlapping motives, those that share pitches (imbrication) and those in which the pitches of one motive are inserted between the pitches of another motive (interpolation).

Example 6.8a contains an excerpt from Nicolai Rimsky-Korsakov's *Scheherazade*. Although the passage could be parsed into larger groupings, the <+2, +1> grouping has been selected as the principal motive in this analysis; dividing the passage into three-note motives allows us to see how the larger gestures might themselves be derived from the repetition of a few basic shapes and intervals.[2] In this passage, P and I forms of the motive share a pitch. The overlapping motives in Example 6.8b, on the other hand, share two pitches and, by extension, an interval. We will differentiate between these two types of transformations by referring to that in Example 6.8a as **pitch imbrication** and that in Example 6.8b as **interval imbrication**.

**EX. 6.8a**—Nicolai Rimsky-Korsakov, *Scheherazade*, IV, mm. 38–42 (Pitch Imbrication)

**EX. 6.8b**—Arnold Schoenberg, *Pierrot Lunaire*, "Nacht," m. 19 (Interval Imbrication)

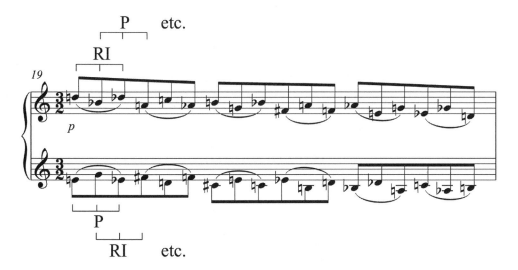

Whereas any two motives may be imbricated by pitch, interval imbrication is more selective since the interval that occurs at the end of one motive must also occur at the beginning of another. As the figure illustrates, a motive can always be imbricated by interval with its own transposed retrograde inversion while the inversion can always be imbricated by interval with the retrograde.* The arrows in the figure illustrate why this is so. The final ordered pitch interval of the prime is replicated at only one other location in the diagram, the beginning of the retrograde inversion. Similarly, the final ordered pitch interval of the inversion is replicated only at the beginning of the retrograde. These pairings remain the same even when the motives occur in reverse order.** The prime and retrograde motives in Example 6.8b, for instance, overlap with each other on both ends. Primes and inversions can only be imbricated by interval if they begin and end with the same interval or intervals. The same is true for the retrograde and retrograde inversion.

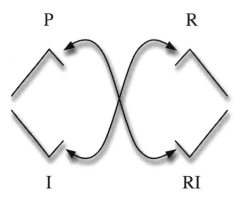

* This figure is a reproduction of Example 6e from the previously cited article on shape/interval motives by Pearsall and Schaffer, "Shape/Interval Contours and Their Ordered Transformations," 64.
** More than one overlapping interval is possible if a motive contains a repeated ordered pitch interval. The retrograde of <–2, +1, +1>, for example, is <+1, +1, –2>. The duplicate +1/+1 contour of these two motives allows motive chains with three overlapping notes to be created.

In **interpolation**, notes are inserted between those of another more drawn out motive. The interpolated motives in Example 6.9 stand out owing to their registral separation from the large-scale motive that embeds them.

**EX. 6.9**—Stravinsky, *Rite of Spring*, Part I, "Introduction," mm. 48–51 (Interpolated Motives)

As Example 6.10 illustrates, interpolation and imbrication may also be combined, a process we will refer to as **interpolation with imbrication**. The interpolated motive in this kind of overlapping structure often serves to elaborate the notes of the more global motive that embeds it. The elaborative effect of the interpolated motive is especially apparent when the first note of each interpolated motive is metrically stressed as in Example 6.10.[3]

**EX. 6.10**—Lucas Foss, *Thirteen Ways of Looking at a Blackbird*, VIII, p. 10, second system (Interpolation with Imbrication)

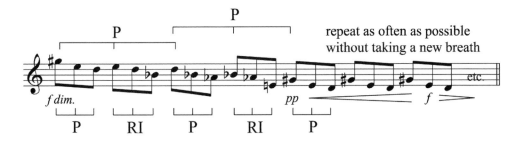

The final measure in Example 6.11a from the beginning of the sixth movement of Olivier Messiaen's *Quartet for the End of Time*, "Dance de la fureur, pour les sept trompettes" (Dance of fury, by the seven trumpets) begins with what may be considered a "false start" while the sixteenth notes in m. 12 of Example 6.11b from Mussourgsky's *Boris Godunov* may be heard as a broken-off fragment of the original. Both excerpts incorporate interpolations with imbrication and generate similar bracketing structures.

**EX. 6.11a**—Olivier Messiaen, *Quartet for the End of Time*, VI, "Danse de la fureur, pour les sept trompettes," mm. 1–4 (False Start with Interpolation)

**EX. 6.11b**—Modest Mussourgsky, *Boris Godunov*, Act III, Scene 1, mm. 11–14 (Interpolated Fragment)

We have already encountered music that contains **non-motivic tones**. (See Example 6.3.) In Example 6.12a, a number of non-motivic tones and gestures are interpolated between the notes of the principal motive in the passage. The motive itself is clearly established in the measures leading up to the excerpt, making the embellishing effect of the non-motivic tones especially salient. (See Example 6.12b.)

**EX. 6.12**—Claude Debussy, Prelude to "The Afternoon of a Faun," mm. 55–56 and 96–97 (Excerpt with Non-motivic Tones)

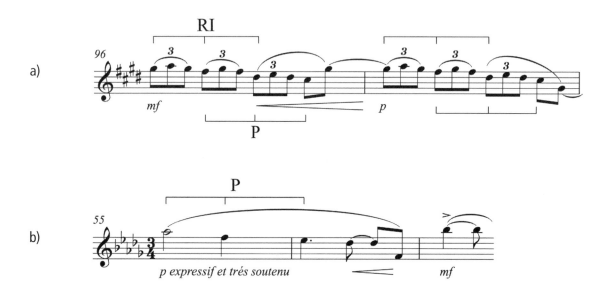

In some cases, more than one pitch of an interpolated motive may overlap with the motive that embeds it. Caution is recommended in opting for this solution, however, since such motives tend to be less accessible to the ear than those with only one imbricated pitch.

## Motivic Alterations

In addition to chaining, compositional material may be derived through changes to the basic components of motives themselves, that is, their shapes and intervals. As we shall see, altering only one of these components at a time is often the most effective way to create a sense of progression from one motive to the next.

Among the most common ways to vary a motive are **intervallic expansions** and **contractions**. Generally speaking, small changes to an interval, those consisting of a semitone or two, may have a less destructive impact on a motive, but this rule is not hard and fast. Other aspects of the texture, including rhythm and timbre, may also help to preserve a motive's identity under expansion or contraction. The excerpt from Ives's *The Incantation* in Example 6.13, for instance, may be divided into a series of motives with identical shapes and rhythms. While the first and last intervals of each motive remain constant, the size of the leap changes from one measure to the next; in mm. 13 and 14 the leap expands in size, while in m. 16 it contracts. Notice that when the middle interval changes, as it does here, the *pitches* that follow it must also change in order to preserve the remaining shapes and intervals of the motive. Shapes and

EX. 6.13—Charles Ives, *The Incantation*, mm. 11–17 (Interval Expansions and Contractions)

intervals are the most salient features of shape/interval motives, not their pitch content. Pitches serve primarily to outline these fundamental characteristics.

Shape alterations involve a change of direction, but leave the intervals of the motive untouched. Shape changes are most conspicuous when most of the shapes in a motive remain unaltered. Changing all of the shapes of a motive, moreover, simply inverts it. In Example 6.14, only one shape, the last one, is inverted.

**EX. 6.14**—César Franck, Quintet for Piano and Strings, III, mm. 73–76 and 81–84 (Theme with Shape Change)

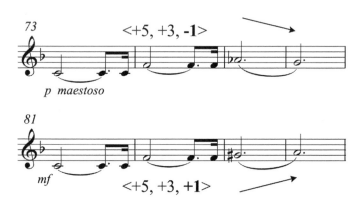

We will refer to a motive that incorporates shape alterations as a **shape hybrid** because it corresponds to the source motive through both ordered and unordered pitch intervals. Example 6.15 contains two *hybrid inversions* in which the second shape has been changed to an ascending major third, creating a jagged down/up contour instead of a smooth descent.

**EX. 6.15**—Arnold Schoenberg, *Five Pieces for Orchestra*, Op. 16, I, mm. 63–68, Horns 1 and 3 (Hybrid Inversions)

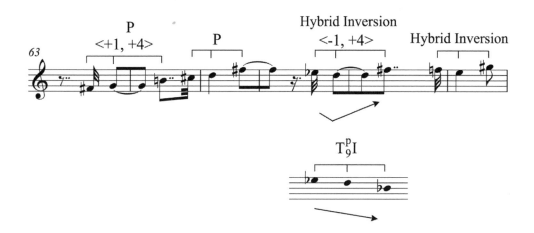

Shape alterations may also occur in the middle of a motive. In Example 6.16, the interval circumscribed by the boxed pitches is changed from the expected ascending tritone in the inversion to a descending one. Notice that the change of shape in this case has no effect on the pc content of the motive; this is because whether we ascend or descend by a tritone, we reach the same pc.

**EX. 6.16**—Roy Harris, Trio for Pianoforte, Violin, and Violoncello, I, mm. 80–82 (Shape Hybrid with Altered Internal Shape)

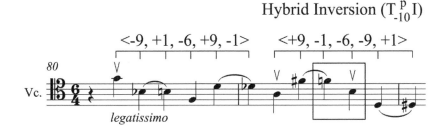

If you have not already started working on **Streams 2** and **3** of the *Motivic Hearing* software, you may do so now. With the study of transposition and imbrication behind us, the student has the information needed to take on all the exercises, including the advanced exercises, which have both transposed motives and motives imbricated by pitch. The "Aural Skills Supplement" explains how the exercises are structured and should be consulted before proceeding.

## Other Melodic Techniques

The operations discussed thus far are not the only ones composers have used to develop an idea. Other techniques, including *fragmentation, truncation, additive melodies, subtractive melodies, reordering,* and *signature transformations* are also prevalent. While the particular techniques a composer adopts are to some extent dependent on personal inclinations, those listed above appear more or less consistently across a fairly broad spectrum of musical styles, including those of the common practice period.

The first of these, **fragmentation** (breaking a motive down into smaller units), may be the most common technique of all. Fragments can be repeated untransposed, as in Example 6.17a, or transposed to generate new thematic material as in Example 6.17b.

**EX. 6.17a**—Claude Debussy, *La boîte à joujoux*, mm. 102–109 (Untransposed Fragments)

**EX. 6.17b**—Leoš Janàček, *Sinfonietta*, II, mm. 13–20 (Transposed Fragments)

Example 6.18 illustrates a type of fragmentation in which the beginning of the melody remains intact on subsequent repetitions, but the ending is cut off. This practice is common enough to warrant its own category and will be referred to as **truncation**.

**EX. 6.18**—Ernest Bloch, Sonata for Violin and Piano, I, p. 12, System 2 (Truncation)

Related to truncation is the building up of a melodic theme one note or fragment at a time. The theme is first presented in a truncated form. Upon successive repetitions, more and more pitches are added until the complete theme emerges. Such themes are called **additive melodies**. One such additive melody occurs in Steve Reich's *Nagoya Marimbas* shown in Example 6.19. In this example, the two notes in mm. 3 and 4 are carried over into m. 5 where two more notes are added to create the bracketed four-note idea. This process continues until the complete melody emerges in m. 11.

**EX. 6.19**—Steve Reich, *Nagoya Marimbas*, mm. 3–14 (Additive Melody)

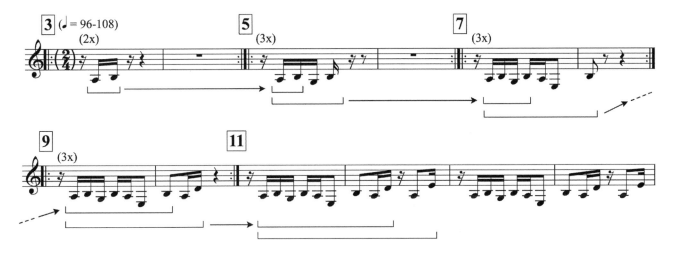

**Subtractive melodies** reverse this process; pitches are taken away upon each repetition. The passage in Example 6.20 involves both techniques. The winds, strings, and xylophone parts are subtractive while the non-pitched percussion parts are additive.

**EX. 6.20**—Peter Maxwell Davies, *Five Klee Pictures*, 1, "A Crusader," mm. 14–24 (Subtractive Melodies)

Melodies are by nature ordered. Occasionally, however, melodic fragments are treated as collections, in which case their elements may be reordered without impairing the collection's identity. We will use the term **reordering** to refer to the systematic unordering of a melodic motive used as a compositional technique. Example 6.21 contains two instances of a four-note collection that recurs throughout George Crumb's *Madrigals*, Book 3, mvt. 1. The figures present the notes in different orders, but are similar in terms of their articulation, timbre, and rhythmic organization. Reordered motives may also, of course, be analyzed as unordered pitch sets. The term reordering highlights the origins of such sets. Systematic approaches to unordering are not uncommon. We have already encountered another instance of reordering, for example, in Barbara Kolb's *Appello*. (See Chapter 3, Example 3.4.)

**EX. 6.21**—George Crumb, *Madrigals*, Book III, No. 1, "La noche canta desnuda sobre los puentes de marzo," mm. 1 and 15–16 (Reordered Motive)

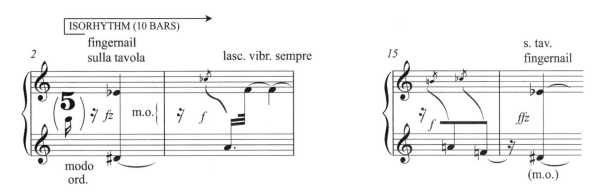

In some cases, what at first glance appears to be a reordering may in fact be a rotation. The "reordered" motive in Example 6.22, for instance, is actually a rotation (r1) of the retrograde.[4]

**EX. 6.22**—Claude Debussy, String Quartet in G Minor, I, mm. 1–2 (Reordering Based on Rotation)

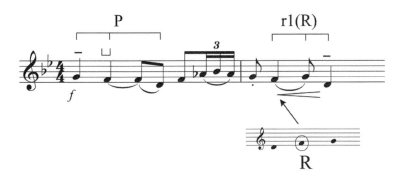

A phenomenon often observed in tonal music is the tendency to add or subtract accidentals from the key signature. This practice may also be observed in post-tonal music, where it is sometimes applied more systematically. An example of this technique may be found in Philip Glass's String Quartet No. 5. Example 6.23 shows mm. 35–50 of the first violin part. (The other parts are either unison or octave doublings of the violin.) Here, the same motive is repeated over and over, with different accidentals. These enter first in the order of flats in flat key signatures and then the subtraction of sharps from sharp key signatures. This type of motivic alteration is known as a **signature transformation**.[5]

EX. 6.23—Philip Glass, String Quartet No. 5, V, mm. 35–43 (Signature Transformations)

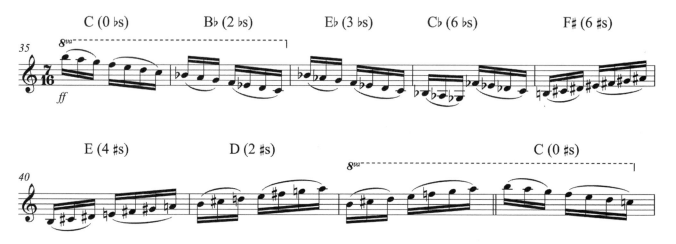

## Mottos

One particularly idiosyncratic type of ordered pitch set is the **motto**. Mottos are musical themes based on the letters of a composer's name.[6] J. S. Bach, for example, sometimes used the letters of his last name as a musical signature and others, including Schoenberg, Webern, Berg, Ravel, and Poulenc used the "Bach" motto as well. Mottos are most often based on German letter names. In German notation, B♭ is represented by the letter B while B♮ is represented by the letter H.[7] Under this system, Bach's name produces the notes B♭, A, C, and B♮. To indicate flats in German, the syllable "Es" is added to letter names. E♭ too is pronounced "Es." Hence, E♭ may be used to represent the letter "S" in a composer's name.

Example 6.24 contains the first few measures of Alban Berg's Chamber Concerto (*Kammerkonzert*), which he dedicated to his teacher and mentor, Arnold Schoenberg. The piece includes three mottos. These are based on Berg's own name (A–B♭–A, B♭–E–G) as well as those of his fellow Second Viennese School composers, Anton Webern (A, E–B♭–E) and Arnold Schoenberg (A–D, E♭, C–B♮–B♭–E–G). Notice that Berg understates his own motto by presenting it last in the muted horn part. Mottos may also be inverted and retrograded. J. S. Bach, for example, is known to have subjected his signature to the operations I, R, and RI in addition to transposition.

EX. 6.24—Alban Berg, Chamber Concerto, I, mm. 1–5 (Mottos)

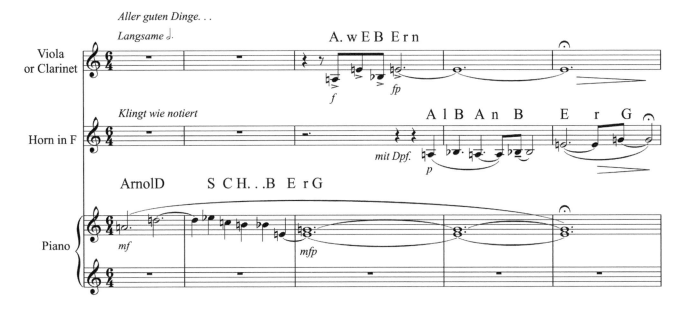

Ordered pitch motives and their transformations, of course, are not the only kinds of motives one finds in music. Other elements, such as rhythm and contour, may also serve this purpose. As we shall see in the next chapter, many of the operations we have been discussing, including inversion, retrogression, and retrograde inversion, also play a role in the organization of these important elements of music.

## Chapter 6 Exercises

1) Name the ordered pitch set and operation with transposition (e.g., $T^P_{-7}R$) for each quintuplet in the excerpt below.

Claude Debussy, Twelve Etudes, Book 1, No. 1, "pour les cinq doigts d'après Monsieur Czerny," mm. 93–94

Prime = <Gb3, Ab3, Bb3, Cb4, Db4>

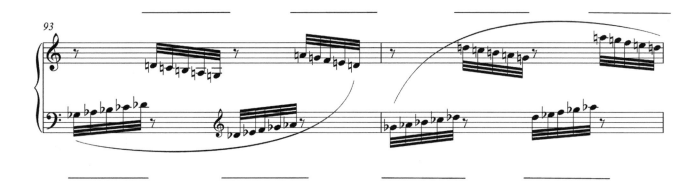

2) Motives.

    a) Determine the ordered pitch intervals for the following shape/interval motives and write them in the blank.

    b) Express the given operations using note-heads.

    c) Next provide an **interval alteration** of the prime in which *one* of the intervals contracts or expands by no more than *one* semitone.

    d) Finally, create a **shape hybrid** by altering the *final* shape of the indicated motive.

<-5, +10, -7>

$T^p_1R$        $T^p_{-3}I$        $T^p_{-3}RI$        Interval Alteration    Hybrid Prime

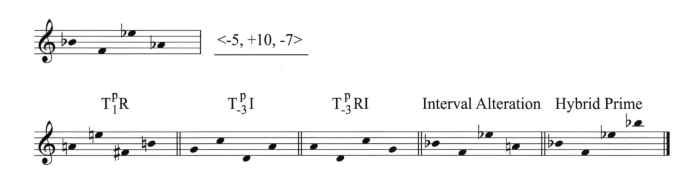

a)

$$T^p_{-4}R \qquad T^p_4I \qquad T^p_5RI \qquad \text{Interval Alteration} \qquad \text{Hybrid Prime}$$

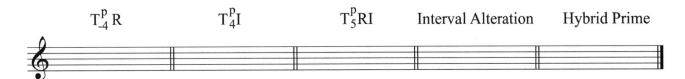

b)

$$T^p_{-6}R \qquad T^p_3R \qquad T^p_{-6}RI \qquad \text{Interval Alteration} \qquad \text{Hybrid Prime}$$

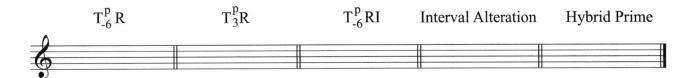

c)

$$T^p_{12}R \qquad T^p_0I \qquad T^p_{-2}RI \qquad \text{Interval Alteration} \qquad \text{Hybrid Prime}$$

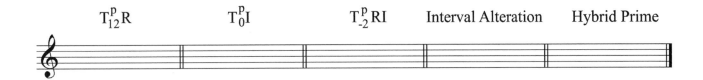

d)

$$T^p_{-1}P \qquad T^p_{-13}RI \qquad T^p_{10}I \qquad \text{Interval Alteration} \qquad \text{Hybrid Prime}$$

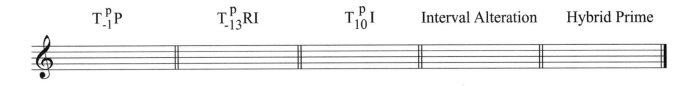

3) Imbrication.

    a)  Write the ordered pitch intervals for each motive in the blanks provided.

    b)  **Imbricate** the motives by **pitch** or **interval** in the order indicated. Then bracket
(⎡⎽⎽⎽⎤⎽⎽⎽⎤) and label (**P, I, R, RI**) both of the imbricated motives.

$\underline{+1 \quad -2 \qquad}$

Pitch Imbrication (P - I)            Interval Imbrication (P - RI)

a)

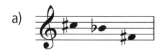

Pitch Imbrication (I - R)            Interval Imbrication (RI - P)

b)

Pitch Imbrication (P - R)            Interval Imbrication (I - R)

c)

Pitch Imbrication (P - R)            Interval Imbrication (R - I)

d)

Pitch Imbrication (RI - R)          Interval Imbrication (P - RI)

4) Interpolation with Imbrication.

   a)  Write the ordered pitch intervals for the motives in the blanks provided.

   b)  Create a motive chain using **interpolation with imbrication** as indicated. Only one note from each motive should overlap. (The interpolated motive will often need to be transposed in order to create a shared tone.)

    +5  -1

a)

I - R          I - RI

b)

R - I          RI - I

c)

RI - R                          R - P

d)

P - RI                          I - P

5) Bracket ( ⌐‾‾‾‾‾⌐ ) and label (**P, I, R, RI**) the shape/interval motives in the following excerpts. HINT: Some, but not all, are imbricated by pitch or interval.

a) Claude Debussy, String Quartet in G Minor, IV, mm. 25–26

b) Claude Debussy, String Quartet in G Minor, I, mm. 183–186

c) Charles Ives, *Walking*, mm. 16–22

the vil - lage church-bells, the road a-long the ridge,— the chest-nut burr and su-mach, the hills a-bove

d) Lucas Foss, *Thirteen Ways of Looking at a Blackbird*, VIII, p. 10, second system

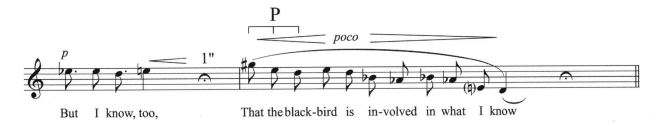

But I know, too, That the black-bird is in-volved in what I know

6) Interpolation.

    a)   Label (**P, I, R, RI**) the bracketed motives in the following excerpts.

    b)   Fill in the blank with the chaining operation used, interpolation or interpolation with imbrication.

a) Arnold Schoenberg, *Pierrot Lunair*, No. 8, "Nacht," m. 8

b) Igor Stravinsky, *Rite of Spring*, Part 1, "Introduction," mm. 10–12

c) Igor Stravinsky, *Rite of Spring*, Part 1, "Spring Roundelays," mm. 57–58

7) Bracket ( ⌐⎽⎽⎽⎽⎽⎽¬ ) and label (**P, I, R, RI**) the intervallically altered motives in the following excerpts and list their ordered pitch intervals (e.g., <−1, + 3, −5>).

a) Arnold Schoenberg, *Pierrot Lunair*, No. 11, "Rote Messe," m. 14

b) Arnold Schoenberg, *In diesen Wintertagen*, mm. 10–15

c) César Franck, Symphony in D Minor, III, mm. 19–24

d) Arnold Schoenberg, *Pierrot Lunair*, No. 7, "Der kranke Mond," mm. 23–24

e) Arnold Schoenberg, *Pierrot Lunair*, No. 18, "Der Mondfleck," mm 9–10

8) Bracket and label (e.g., **hybrid inversion**) the shape hybrids in each of the following.

a) Arnold Schoenberg, *Pierrot Lunair*, No. 7, "Der kranke Mond," mm. 22–23

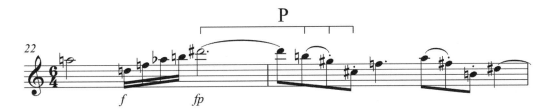

b) Darius Milhaud, *Saudades do Brazil*, Vol. 1, No. 6, "Gavea," mm. 5–8

c) Anton Webern, Five Pieces for String Quartet, Op. 5, No. 3, mm. 11–13

9) Dmitri S(c)hostakovich's musical signature consists of the first letter of his first name (D) and the first three letters of his last name spelled with a "c" (E♭, C♮, B♮). Find five versions of this signature (one of which is inverted and transposed) in his String Quartet No. 8, I, mm. 1–5. (For this assignment, you will need to acquire your own copy of the score.)

10) Béla Bartók's "From the Island of Bali" (shown below) contains examples of many of the melodic techniques discussed in Chapter 6. Identify at least one instance of each of the following:

   a)  Inversion/Retrograde
   b)  Pitch Imbrication
   c)  Interpolation with Imbrication
   d)  Fragmentation
   e)  Truncation
   f)  Rotation
   g)  Reordering
   h)  Interval Contraction

11) Except for mm. 23–30, Bartók's "From the Island of Bali" is based on what referential collection discussed in Chapter 1?

Béla Bartók, *Mikrokosmos*, Vol. 4, No. 109, "From the Island of Bali"

# Chapter 7

# Rhythm and Contour

---

| | |
|---|---|
| Contour adjacency series | Augmentation |
| Contour-pitch | Diminution |
| Contour class | Ordered duration class |
| Mixed meters | Inter-onset durations |
| Additive or asymmetrical meters | Rhythmic contour |
| Complex meters | Metric modulation |
| Alternating meters | Unordered duration class |
| Polymeter | Attack points |
| Polyrhythms | Non-retrogradable rhythms |
| Cross-rhythms | |

In Chapter 2, we learned how to segment music based primarily on pitch and textural criteria. Where melodic groupings are concerned, rhythm and contour are also among the most important means for parsing music into meaningful units. Indeed, the repetition of patterns of rhythm and contour alone can be enough to create perceptual groupings. Yet, rhythm and contour are typically communicated by means of pitches. In reality, then, all these elements reinforce each other within our holistic experience of music. We have already seen, for example, how pitch intervals and contours often combine to form ordered pitch interval motives. How rhythm merges with our understanding of pitch material will be explored more fully in the next chapter.

## Contour Analysis

As we have learned, order in music is closely linked to shape or contour. In our study of ordered pitch intervals in Chapter 2, for example, we learned that a (+) sign indicates an ascent while a (−) sign indicates a descent. These signs can be detached from their intervals and used to specify contour regardless of pitch. A series of (+)s and (−)s enclosed in angled brackets is called a **contour adjacency series**.[1] Example 7.1 contains several instances of an important melodic gesture that occurs near the beginning of the third movement of John Harbison's Piano Quintet. A comparison of these gestures reveals that while the pitch intervals and relative pitch heights differ, the succession of +s and −s remains the same from one gesture to the next; each gesture, that is, articulates a <− − + −> contour adjacency series.

**EX. 7.1**—John Harbison, Piano Quintet, III, mm. 5–9 (Contour Adjacency Series Analysis)

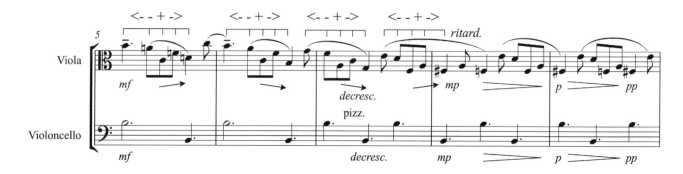

To make even finer distinctions between contours, we may appeal to their **contour-pitch** content. A contour-pitch is an integer representing the height of a pitch relative to those around it; the lowest contour-pitch in a specified region is 0, the next higher is 1, and so on. The pitch interval between contour-pitches is of no consequence. We will refer to an ordered collection of contour-pitches as a **contour class**.[2] Returning to Example 7.1, we see that the passage alternates between two different contour classes, <4 3 0 2 1> and <4 3 1 2 0>. Each of the contours in Example 7.2 from Ellen Taaffe Zwilich's String Quartet 1974, on the other hand, belongs to the same contour class, <0 1 2 4 3 5>, even though the ordered pitch intervals from one grouping to the next differ.

**EX. 7.2**—Ellen Taaffe Zwilich, String Quartet 1974, IV, mm. 35–36 (Identical Contour Classes)

We can apply the same operations used with ordered pitch sets to specify connections between non-matching contours. These include *inversion* (I), *retrogression* (R), and *retrograde inversion* (RI). Figure 7.1 shows the P/I/R/RI group for <3 1 0 2>. Notice that the lowest contour-pitch in the original or prime version (P) of the contour in the figure (0) becomes the highest contour-pitch in the inversion (3), while contour-pitches 1 and 2 switch places. The retrograde and retrograde inversion reverse the order of the contour-pitches in the prime and inversion.

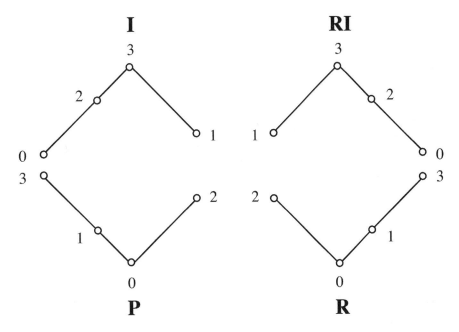

**FIGURE 7.1** <3 1 0 2> and its Principal Operations

Complementary pairs of contour-pitches sum to the number that defines the limit of the space. In Figure 7.1 the limit of the space is 3. Hence, complementary pairs of contour-pitches sum to 3: 0 + 3 and 1 + 2.

Each passage in Example 7.3 features one of the contours from Figure 7.1. The slurs and alternating two-note contour groupings found in this music favor a two-beat rather than a three-beat division, producing a hemiola. The virtuosic flourishes are marked not only by their contour and phrasing, but also by a thinning of the accompanimental texture (not shown), which allows the solo violin to emerge more prominently.

**EX. 7.3**—Béla Bartók, Violin Concerto, No. 2, III, mm. 222–25, 228–31, 234–36, and 422–26 (Contours and their TTOs)

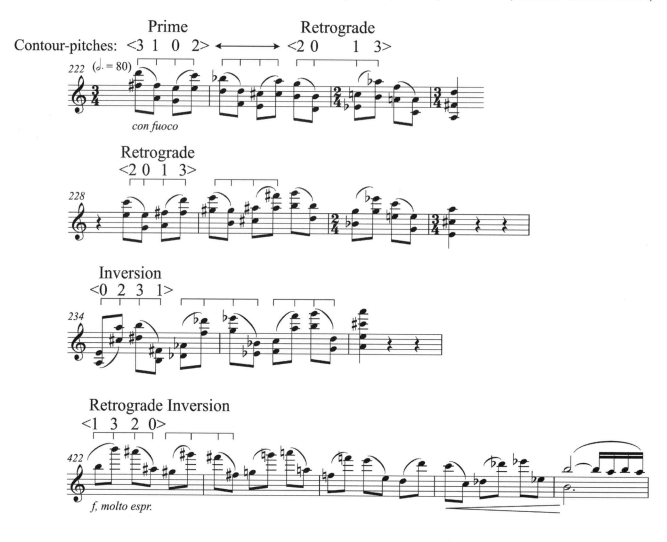

It is not uncommon for the inversion of a contour to match the retrograde and, by extension, for the retrograde inversion to match the prime. One such contour, shown in Example 7.4, occurs in Benjamin Britten's *Rhapsody*. To make the dual relations between such contours explicit, the labels may be combined as illustrated in the example.

**EX. 7.4**—Benjamin Britten, *Rhapsody*, mm. 6–7 and 120–121 (Paired Contours)

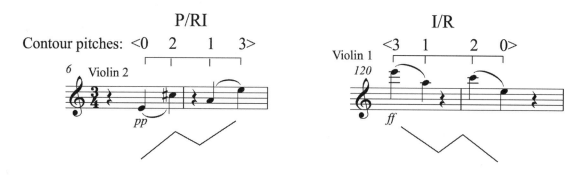

The motive from Britten's *Rhapsody* shown in Example 7.5 does not match either of the contours in Example 7.4 because it contains extra pitches. The quarter-note leap, however, immediately brings to mind the I/R contour. The subsequent descent may thus be thought of as a filled-in "leap" from G5 to D5. Understood in this way, the gesture constitutes another instance of the I/R contour. Such tempering of a theoretical concept is sometimes necessary to account for our perceptions.

EX. 7.5—Benjamin Britten, *Rhapsody*, mm. 24–26 (Filled-in Contour)

Contours may also be combined to produce longer contour strings. One example of this process is shown in Example 7.6. This excerpt, which occurs near the end of Britten's *Rhapsody*, sums up the principal idea of the piece by presenting an eight-note gesture that embeds several overlapping versions of the rhythm/contour idea presented at the beginning of the work. The contour as a whole belongs to contour class <0 2 1 4 3 5 4 7>. The three *subsets* that resemble the original contour in this set are <0 2 1 4>, <1 4 3 5>, and <3 5 4 7>. Understood in terms of their local relations, all of these subsets instance contour class <0 2 1 3>.[3]

EX. 7.6—Benjamin Britten, *Rhapsody*, mm. 249–52 (Contour Subsets)

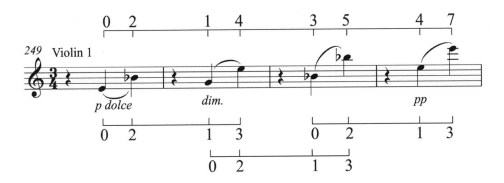

## Analysis of Rhythm and Meter

Western music written since 1890 features a wide variety of rhythmic procedures ranging from the use of relaxed non-metrical rhythms to complex divisions of the beat. Tuplet subdivisions of four, five, six, seven, and more units are common as are rapid changes of meter (i.e., **mixed meters**), **additive** or **asymmetrical meters** (e.g., $\frac{7}{8}$), **complex meters** (e.g., $\frac{4+2+3}{8}$), and **alternating meters** with double time signatures (e.g., $\frac{3}{4}$, $\frac{6}{8}$).

We will define **polymeter** as the simultaneous use of more than one meter. The two meters in the polymetrical excerpt shown in Example 7.7 are $\frac{2}{4}$ and $\frac{3}{4}$. Here, the meters are specified. In other cases, multiple meters may be conveyed through notation alone. Notice too that each part taken individually incorporates mixed meters.

**EX. 7.7**—Ernest Bloch, Sonata for Violin and Piano, I, 6 Violin Measures before Rehearsal 13 (Polymeters)

In the above example, downbeats do not line up, but the pulse or beat in both parts remains the same. **Polyrhythms** involve the simultaneous execution of different meters or rhythmic patterns. In Example 7.8, the flute, English horn, and second violin parts divide the measure into four beats. Most of the remaining parts conform to the written meter ($\frac{3}{8}$), although the top line in the clarinet, horn, and bassoon parts could be interpreted as a three quarter-note beat pattern covering two written measures ($\frac{3}{4}$).

**EX. 7.8**—Claude Debussy, *"Images" pour orchestre*, No. 2, "Iberia," I, mm. 174–78 (Polyrhythms)

Example 7.9 combines an irregular pattern of eighths in the left-hand piano part with regular subdivisions of the beat in the right-hand piano, violin, and cello parts. Here, the $\frac{4}{4}$ meter in the upper parts is disguised by the fact that beats have been grouped (i.e. beamed) in accordance with the 3 + 2 + 3 pattern in the bass. Polyrhythms that contradict the expected beat pattern are sometimes referred to as **cross-rhythms**.

**EX. 7.9**—Maurice Ravel, Trio in A Minor, I, mm. 28–32 (Cross-rhythm)

Two of the most enduring rhythmic transformations used throughout the long history of music are rhythmic **augmentation** and **diminution**. Diminution shortens the durations in a rhythm from one grouping to the next while augmentation lengthens them. Example 7.10 from David Del Tredici's "Turtle Soup I" contains an example of rhythmic diminution. Measure 31 in this example is three-quarters of the length of mm. 29–30 combined and each of its notes is exactly three-quarters of the length of the corresponding note in the first iteration of the melodic idea; each triplet eighth, that is, is worth four triplet thirty-seconds compared to the corresponding sixteenth's three triplet thirty-seconds in m. 30. These proportional relations, expressed in terms of the beat, can be represented explicitly using fractions as shown in Figure 7.2. In this figure, the number 1 is assigned to the beat and the proportions of the other durations calculated accordingly. Superscripts denote repeated durations.[4]

**EX. 7.10**—David Del Tredici, *Pop-pourri*, "Turtle Soup I," mm. 31–33 (Rhythmic Diminution)

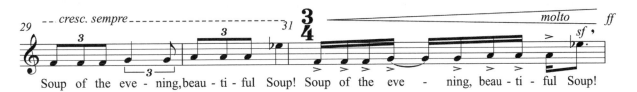

$$\text{mm. 29-30} \quad < \frac{1^3}{3}, \frac{2}{3}, \frac{1^4}{3}, 1 > \qquad \text{m. 31} \quad < \frac{1^3}{4}, \frac{1}{2}, \frac{1^4}{4}, \frac{3}{4} >$$

**FIGURE 7.2** Durational Proportions

Although their durations differ, the two sets in Example 7.10 are proportionally equivalent; their internal proportions, that is, are identical. We can express this equivalence in terms of an **ordered duration class** that shows the common multiples between the rhythms using whole numbers rather than fractions. To derive the ordered duration class for a rhythm, convert its proportions to fractions using the lowest common denominator and extract the numerators. (Use improper fractions for notes that are equal to or longer than a beat.) The proportions of the rhythms from Del Tredeci's "Turtle Soup I" expressed as fractions with the lowest common denominator appear in Figure 7.3. Both articulate the same series of numerators and superscripts in the same order and thus belong to ordered duration class $<1^3, 2, 1^4, 3>$.

**FIGURE 7.3** Ordered Duration Classes in Del Tredeci's "Turtle Soup I"

The excerpt from Milton Babbitt's *Composition for Four Instruments* shown in Example 7.11 contains an example of rhythmic augmentation. In this excerpt, the proto-rhythm is augmented by factors of 4, 3, and 2 respectively. Rhythmic values are determined on the basis of **inter-onset durations**, the distance between attacks—*including rests*—of adjacent durations in the rhythm. These inter-onset durations appear in Figure 7.4. All four of these rhythms belong to ordered duration class <1, 4, 3, 2>. The durations in the ordered duration class match the factors by which the rhythms are augmented and occur in the same order. Hence, we can see that the same scheme governs rhythmic organization on multiple levels in the piece.

**EX. 7.11**—Milton Babbitt, *Composition for Four Instruments*, mm. 1–7 (Rhythmic Augmentation)

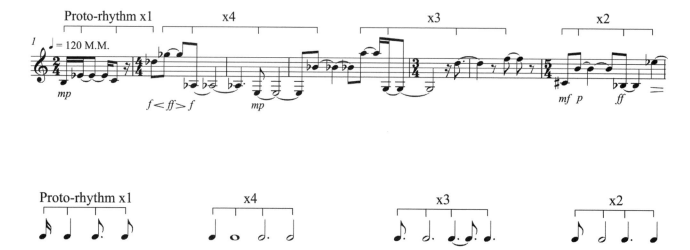

**FIGURE 7.4** Inter-onset Durations in Babbitt's *Composition for Four Instruments*

Not all rhythms related through augmentation and diminution are proportionally equivalent. The excerpt beginning in m. 255 shown in Example 7.12, for instance, may be considered a diminution of that beginning in m. 73 even though the internal proportions of the two rhythms vary somewhat; the long notes in the second excerpt are seven-elevenths as long as the corresponding notes in the first excerpt, but the shortest note, a sixteenth, stays the same. This irregularity is not enough to obscure the derivative relation between the two excerpts. While the rhythms do not belong to the same ordered duration class, moreover, they do have the same **rhythmic contour**. To determine the rhythmic contour of a passage, assign a plus sign to a duration that is longer than the one preceding it, a minus sign if it is shorter, and 0 if it stays the same.[5] As the example illustrates, both statements of the theme outline the same rhythmic contour, <− + − + 0>, accounting for our propensity to hear them as variations of the same basic idea.

**EX. 7.12**—César Franck, Quintet for Piano and Strings, III, mm. 73–80 and 255–59 (Matching Rhythmic Contours)

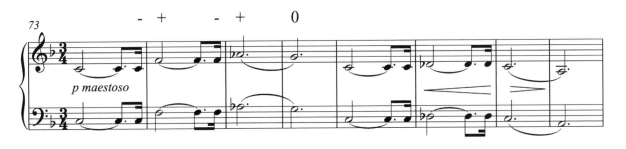

Rhythmic augmentation and diminution are essentially changes of tempo. **Metric modulation,** a phenomenon observed in Elliot Carter's music, directly engages this notion. In metric modulation, a subdivision of the beat or beat grouping in one tempo becomes the new beat in another. Example 7.13 from the beginning of the second movement of Carter's String Quartet No. 2 contains a number of metric modulations.[6] The movement begins with two overlapping tempi; ♩ = 140 in the second violin part and ♩ = 175 in the other parts. In order to keep a steady beat, the performers must keep in mind the proportional relations between the two tempi. To help in this process, the composer has provided a line below the second violin part illustrating its rhythmic organization in $\frac{4}{4}$ time. At m. 178, the first violin, viola, and cello "modulate" to the slower tempo. The second violin part plays alone in m. 178, giving the other performers an opportunity to adjust to the new beat. The tempo indication above the top staff indicates that the five sixteenth-note beat of m. 177 becomes the quarter-note beat of m. 178.

Similar modulations take place throughout the passage. In m. 183, the triplet eighth tied to a quarter in m. 182 becomes a half note. In m. 186, the dotted quarter becomes a quarter note. This last change of tempo brings back the tempo from the beginning of the piece and is probably the easiest to execute since the triplet eighths of the first violin part in m. 186 are the same length as the eighth notes in mm. 184–85. The second violin's slower tempo (♩ = 140) returns, unmarked, in m. 187.[7]

**EX. 7.13**—Elliot Carter, String Quartet No. 2, II, mm. 171–72, 177–78, and 181–87 (Metric Modulations)

Although it might seem surprising, durations, like pitches, are sometimes reordered. The two right-hand rhythms of the second piano part in Example 7.14, for instance, contain the same durations in the same quantities, but in a different order. While they have different ordered duration class labels, both rhythms belong to **unordered duration class** $[1^3, 2^2]$. Unordered duration classes correspond to the normal order of the set; durations are listed incrementally from the shortest to the longest and enclosed in square brackets.

**EX. 7.14**—Peter Maxwell Davies, *Four Lessons for Two Keyboards*, III, mm. 8–9 (Unordered Rhythms)

Jazz improvisations can sometimes produce unordered rhythms as a result of the improvisational process itself. Although most of these occurrences must necessarily be corroborated by ear (since improvisation is by nature a spontaneous event), the written-out variation of the theme from *One of Us is Over 40* by Chick Corea, John Patitucci, and Dave Weckl may serve as an example. Except for the bracketed segments shown in Example 7.15, the rhythms of the two statements of the theme are nearly the same. Despite these differences, both rhythms present the same number of eighths and sixteenths in a different order and thus belong to unordered duration class $[1^4, 2^6, 3^4]$.[8]

**EX. 7.15**—Chick Corea, John Patitucci, and Dave Weckl, *One of Us is Over 40*, mm. 24–25 and 28–29 (Unordered Rhythms)

Durations in rhythmic patterns may also be subjected to rotation, a process that effectively unorders the rhythms in subsequent units. One example from Steve Reich's *Violin Phase* appears in Example 7.16. The second violin (solo violin) accelerates periodically, producing new rhythmic relations between the two parts.

**EX. 7.16**—Steve Reich *Violin Phase*, mm. 1–5 (Rhythmic Rotations)

Although not a reordering per se, rhythms are sometimes retrograded—that is, presented in reverse order. This idea is intriguing, for it suggests that time itself might be conceptualized as a nonlinear phenomenon.[9] One example of this kind of organization is shown in Figure 7.5. This example shows the **attack points** (i.e., the beginnings of events) in the theme and first variation of Milton Babbitt's *Semi-simple Variations*. Each "measure" in the example corresponds to a beat in the original. The sixteen beats of the theme articulate all possible divisions of a quarter note into sixteenths and corresponding rests. These divisions are presented in reverse order in the variation.

Milton Babbitt, *Semi-Simple Variations*, Theme and Variation I

Theme

Variation I [Retrograde]

**FIGURE 7.5** Retrograde Rhythm

Not all rhythms produce a new sequence of durations when retrograded. Such rhythms are known as **non-retrogradable rhythms**. Figure 7.6 shows two back-to-back non-retrogradable rhythms from Olivier Messiaen's *Quartet for the End of Time*, VII, "Fouillis d'arcs-en-ciel, pour l'Ange qui annonce la fin du Temps," mm. 31–32. The rhythm in each measure forms a palindrome and remains the same whether presented forwards or backwards.

Olivier Messiaen, *Quartet for the End of Time*, VII, "Fouillis d'arcs-en-ciel, pour l'Ange qui annonce la fin du Temps," mm. 31–32

**FIGURE 7.6** Non-retrogradable Rhythms

Rhythm is essential to our understanding of music, but cannot be fully understood without considering its melodic and harmonic contexts. In the following chapter, we will see how rhythm, along with its transformations, interrelates with these other aspects of music.

## Chapter 7 Exercises

1) Contour Adjacency Series/Rhythmic Contours.

   a)  Write the contour adjacency series using (+)s and (−)s above the staff for the melodies below.

   b)  Below the staff, write the rhythmic contours (+s, −s, and 0s) for the inter-onset durations.

2) Contour Classes.

   a)  Identify the contour-classes for each of the bracketed contours below.

   b)  Fill in the blanks with the correct operation (P, I, R, or RI).

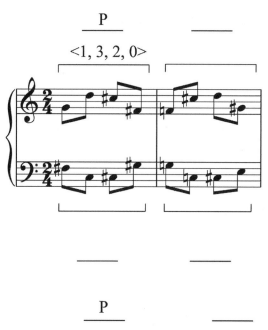

Although not a reordering per se, rhythms are sometimes retrograded—that is, presented in reverse order. This idea is intriguing, for it suggests that time itself might be conceptualized as a nonlinear phenomenon.[9] One example of this kind of organization is shown in Figure 7.5. This example shows the **attack points** (i.e., the beginnings of events) in the theme and first variation of Milton Babbitt's *Semi-simple Variations*. Each "measure" in the example corresponds to a beat in the original. The sixteen beats of the theme articulate all possible divisions of a quarter note into sixteenths and corresponding rests. These divisions are presented in reverse order in the variation.

Milton Babbitt, *Semi-Simple Variations*, Theme and Variation I

Theme

Variation I [Retrograde]

**FIGURE 7.5** Retrograde Rhythm

Not all rhythms produce a new sequence of durations when retrograded. Such rhythms are known as **non-retrogradable rhythms**. Figure 7.6 shows two back-to-back non-retrogradable rhythms from Olivier Messiaen's *Quartet for the End of Time*, VII, "Fouillis d'arcs-en-ciel, pour l'Ange qui annonce la fin du Temps," mm. 31–32. The rhythm in each measure forms a palindrome and remains the same whether presented forwards or backwards.

Olivier Messiaen, *Quartet for the End of Time*, VII, "Fouillis d'arcs-en-ciel, pour l'Ange qui annonce la fin du Temps," mm. 31–32

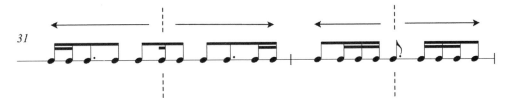

**FIGURE 7.6** Non-retrogradable Rhythms

Rhythm is essential to our understanding of music, but cannot be fully understood without considering its melodic and harmonic contexts. In the following chapter, we will see how rhythm, along with its transformations, interrelates with these other aspects of music.

## Chapter 7 Exercises

1) Contour Adjacency Series/Rhythmic Contours.

    a)   Write the contour adjacency series using (+)s and (−)s above the staff for the melodies below.

    b)   Below the staff, write the rhythmic contours (+s, −s, and 0s) for the inter-onset durations.

2) Contour Classes.

    a)   Identify the contour-classes for each of the bracketed contours below.

    b)   Fill in the blanks with the correct operation (P, I, R, or RI).

3) Find other examples of the P/RI, <0 2 1 3>, and I/R, <3 1 2 0>, contours in Benjamin Britten's *Rhapsody* discussed on pp. 166–67.

4) How do the bracketed motives in the bass part of the following excerpt from Maurice Ravel's *Sérénade Grotesque* differ from each other? How are they alike?

Maurice Ravel, *Sérénade Grotesque*, mm. 15–25

5)  Nested Contours.

    a)  Supply the contour-class for each of the melodies below from Schoenberg's *Six Little Pieces for Piano*, IV.

    b)  Like the melodic incipit in m. 1, all of the melodies below contain one or more instances of the <3 2 0 1> subset. Bracket (< >) and label these subsets in mm. 3–5, mm. 7–10, and m. 10.

Arnold Schoenberg, *Six Little Pieces for Piano*, IV

6)  Fill in the blanks with the process—rhythmic diminution or augmentation—that best describes the relation between the unlabeled passages and the proto-rhythm.

Paul Hindemith, *Symphonie Mathis der Maler*, III

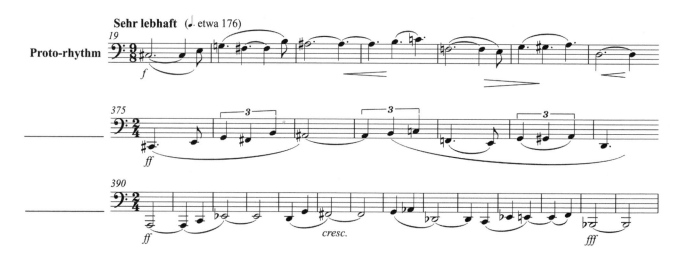

Olivier Messiaen, *Quartet for the End of Time*, No. VI, "Dance of Fury by the Seven Trumpets," mm. 45–48

Proto-rhythm

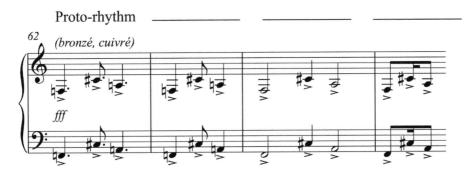

7) What ordered duration class do all of the rhythms in Exercise 6b belong to?

8) Identify the matching *unordered duration class* for the rhythms in each of the following. Use inter-onset durations for excerpt c.

a) Luciano Berio, *Sequenza* XI for Solo Guitar, p. 1, 2nd system, p. 9, 4th system, p. 10, 7th system, and p. 11, 5th system

b) Peter Maxwell Davies, *Four Lessons for Two Keyboards*, III, mm. 35–36

c) John Patitucci and Dave Weckl, *Little Things that Count*, mm. 3–4

9) Measures 2 and 3 of the Clap 2 part from Steve Reich's *Clapping Music for Two Performers* contains two rotations of the proto-rhythm in m. 1.

    a) Fill in the blanks with the rotations that occur in mm. 2 and 3 (e.g., r3).

    b) What matching unordered duration class occurs in every measure of the Clap 1 and Clap 2 parts?

    c) Perform the excerpt as a duet or acquire the piece and perform all of it.

Steve Reich, *Clapping Music for Two Performers*, mm. 1–3

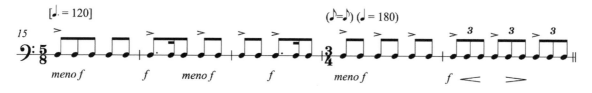

Proto-rhythm (r0) _____            _____

10) Clap or tap the following rhythms from Elliot Carter's *Eight Pieces for Four Timpani*, No. 7, Canaries. Be sure to observe the modulating tempo changes.

Elliot Carter, *Eight Pieces for Four Timpani*, No. 7, "Canaries," mm. 15–30

# Chapter 8

# Ordered Pc Sets and Rows

| | |
|---|---|
| Twelve-tone rows | Invariant trichords, tetrachords, and hexachords |
| Twelve-tone method | Derived rows |
| Right orthography | Combinatoriality |
| Twelve-tone matrix | All-combinatorial rows |
| All-interval row | Fixed register compositions |
| All-ic row | Aggregate composition |
| ic symmetry | Integral Serialism (a.k.a. total serialism) |

Ordered pc sets are similar to ordered pitch sets, one exception being that their elements (pcs) may occur in any octave in pitch-space without affecting the label. The bracketed figures in Examples 8.1a and b, for instance, are transpositionally equivalent in pc-space, but the last three pitches in the transposed version ($T_9$) have been shifted an octave lower, presumably to make the passage more singable.

Ordered pc sets are especially useful for analyzing compositions based on *rows* (temporally ordered strings of pcs). Whereas many of the ideas we have introduced in this text function primarily as analytical tools, rows and their permutations have also been used to *compose* music. The excerpt from *In Memoriam Dylan Thomas* in Example 8.2 shows Stravinsky's "row" approach to the Prelude. Notice that in his analysis, Stravinsky substitutes the term *riversion* for what we are calling retrogression.[1] All of the row forms—which could be analyzed as ordered pitch sets in the early stages of the composition—incorporate pitch substitutions (octave transpositions) as the work progresses.

**EX. 8.1**—Leonard Bernstein, *Chichester Psalms*, I, mm. 1–2 and 7–8 (Transposed Ordered Pc Sets)

a)

b)

**EX. 8.2**—Igor Stravinsky, *In Memoriam Dylan Thomas*, "Prelude," mm. 1–4 (Evidence of a Compositional Scheme based on a Five-Note Row)

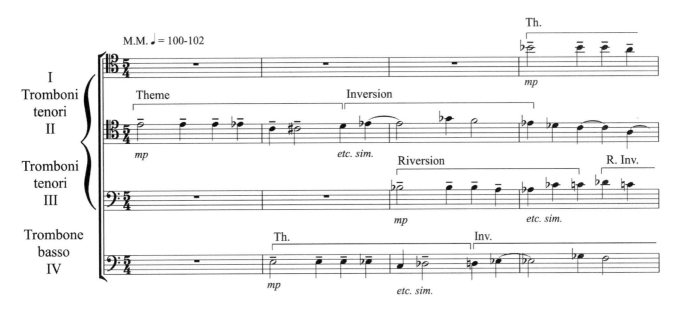

Pitch contours cannot always be relied on to identify the inversion of an ordered pc set. Ordered pitch-class intervals provide a convenient alternative. As the line drawings in Example 8.3 indicate, the contours of the two inversionally equivalent sets in mm. 1–3 of the second movement of Stravinsky's *In Memoriam Dylan Thomas* ("Song") are not inversions of each other, but the ordered pitch-class intervals of the corresponding adjacency interval series are.

**EX. 8.3**—Igor Stravinsky, *In Memoriam Dylan Thomas*, "Song," mm. 1–3 (Inverted Unordered Pc Set)

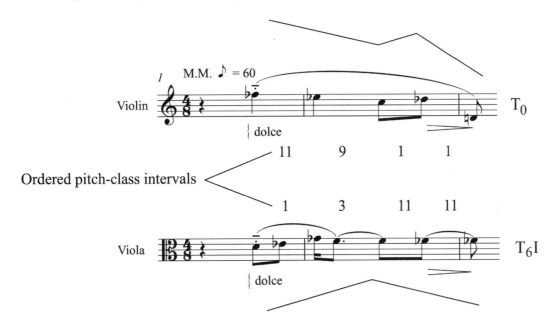

# The Twelve-Tone Method

By far the most common rows found in row compositions are those consisting of twelve tones. **Twelve-tone rows** comprise all twelve pcs presented in a specified order with no pc occurring more than once. The **twelve-tone method** incorporates several operations we have already encountered, including inversion (I), retrogression (R), and retrograde inversion (RI). As we learned in Chapter 3, these operations, along with the prime (P) and its transpositions, are typically referred to as *twelve-tone operations* or *TTOs*. The letter T is generally dropped when identifying row transpositions. Hence, we use the expression $P_2$ instead of $T_2$, $I_9$, instead of $T_9I$, and so on. Transpositions of the retrograde and retrograde inversion too are identified in this way (e.g., $R_2$, $RI_9$). Historically, $P_0$ is used to identify the original row *regardless of its initial pc*. Because it has become customary to think of pc 0 as C, we will follow a more recent practice by assigning $P_0$ to the row that begins on C.

---

The twelve-tone method was devised by Arnold Schoenberg in the early decades of the twentieth century as a means for creating formal coherence in music whose harmony and voice leading did not follow tonal conventions. Presenting all twelve tones before repeating any of them was meant to keep any particular tone from being emphasized and, hence, from being interpreted as a root or tonic. In Schoenberg's view "[e]ven a slight reminiscence of the former tonal harmony would be disturbing, because it would create false expectations of consequences and continuations."[*] If these concerns seem somewhat overwrought to the present-day reader, it may be in part because we have become accustomed to hearing harmonies of all kinds, including triads and seventh chords, outside of a functional framework. Music containing non-functional harmony, including that written by composers who continued to employ tertian chords in the modern era (e.g., Debussy), was the source of much controversy in the early part of the twentieth century.[**]

[*] See Arnold Schoenberg, *Style and Idea* (New York: Philosophical Library,1950), 108.
[**] Although the twelve-tone method reflects an attempt to equalize pitches, aesthetic demands often create conflicts with this general tenet. A pc, for example, may be emphasized agogically or by repeating it several times before moving on to the next member of the row. While there may be some disagreement over the extent to which the twelve-tone method achieves its stated goals, however, the twelve-tone method itself is not in question; all twelve-tone compositions are based on a twelve-tone row and use P, I, R, and RI as the main transformative operations.

---

Owing to their temporal ordering, twelve-tone rows may be thought of as large ordered pc sets. To identify twelve-tone rows and their operations, then, we can continue to rely on ordered pitch-class intervals. Figure 8.1 displays the $P_0$ form of the original row from Luigi Dallapiccola's *Quaderno Musicale di Annalibera* (hereafter *Quaderno Musicale*) along with the untransposed inversion, retrograde, and retrograde inversion.[2] As the figure indicates, the ordered pitch-class intervals of the prime are presented in reverse order in the retrograde inversion while the retrograde inverts the intervals of the prime.[3] Notice too that the first note of the prime occurs at the end of the retrograde and retrograde inversion just as it does in the retrograde and retrograde inversion of ordered *pitch* sets. When identifying the transposition level for the retrograde and retrograde inversion, then, it is best to think of them in relation to P and I; $R_0$ is the retrograde of $P_0$ or $R(P_0)$ while $RI_0$ is the retrograde of $I_0$ or $R(I_0)$.

The process of working through an expression from right to left is known as **right orthography**.

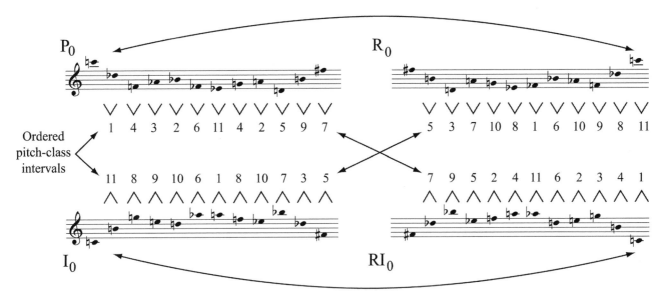

**FIGURE 8.1** Row Permutations

Example 8.4 contains the entire third movement of Dallapiccola's *Quaderno Musicale* "Contrapunctus Primus" along with an analysis of the rows in the piece. The movement begins with two overlapping versions of $P_{11}$ presented as a canon. A third voice enters in m. 9 and a fourth in m. 13. The rowforms in the example can be identified by the first few ordered pitch-class intervals we hear at the beginning of each twelve-note grouping: $P_{11}$ begins with 1/4/3/2, $R_1$ with 5/3/7/10, $RI_6$ with 7/9/5/2, and $I_{10}$ with 11/8/9/10. Some of the rows have been dispersed across several staves, indicating whether they should be played with the left or right hand. Dotted lines and cross-staff slurs show the paths of these rows in mm. 10–13 and 16–17. What Stravinsy does with brackets in the Prelude from *In Memoriam Dylan Thomas*, then, Dallapiccola does with slurs.

Row analysis alone cannot account for everything of interest in twelve-tone music. Nor must rows always be considered as a whole. Row subdivisions often play important motivic roles. The slurs in mm. 1–5 of Example 8.5, for instance, suggest two ways of partitioning the row; the right-hand part groups the row into four trichords while the left-hand part groups it into two hexachords. These groupings incorporate different rhythmic schemes. Each trichord in both the left-hand and right-hand parts, for example, has one long note and two short notes. Notice that the long notes in both cases are twice as long as the short notes. All the trichords thus belong to unordered duration class $[1^2, 2]$.[4] The notes in the right-hand part, moreover, are proportionally three-quarters of the length of the corresponding notes in the left-hand part. (The quarter-note rests ensure that the trichords in the right-hand part always follow those of the left hand, thus maintaining the canonic organization of the passage.) The hexachord segments, meanwhile, integrate the trichord rhythms into a broad arch-like scheme in which the second hexachord of each row is the rhythmic retrograde of the first. The ordered duration

**EX. 8.4**—Luigi Dallapiccola, *Quaderno Musicale di Annalibera*, No. 3, "Contrapunctus Primus" (Row Analysis)

classes of the hexachords in the right-hand part, moreover, occur in reverse order in the left-hand part as shown in Figure 8.2.

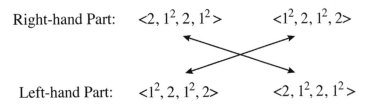

Right-hand Part:    $<2, 1^2, 2, 1^2>$        $<1^2, 2, 1^2, 2>$

Left-hand Part:    $<1^2, 2, 1^2, 2>$        $<2, 1^2, 2, 1^2>$

**FIGURE 8.2** Ordered Duration Classes in "Contrapunctus Primus," mm. 1–5

Like the rows at the beginning of the piece, the two overlapping $P_2$ rows beginning on the top staff of m. 13 may be identified by their rhythmic content. Figure 8.3 rearranges these voices onto two separate staves. This makes it easier to see that each voice incorporates a different set of proportionally related rhythms like those in mm. 1–5. Here again, the hexachord rhythms of the two voices are reversed while the corresponding rhythms in the late fourth entry are half as long as those in the third. The rhythmic scheme breaks down as the piece comes to a close, producing an automatic rhythmic *ritard*.

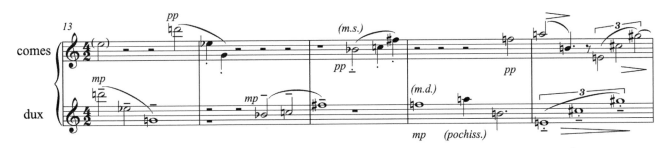

**FIGURE 8.3** Imitative Counterpoint in mm. 13–17

## Matrices

There are twelve transpositions each of P, I, R, and RI. For some applications, it is useful to compile a list of all forty-eight of these operations. These can most easily be displayed in a **twelve-tone matrix**.[5] As a demonstration, let us construct the matrix for the row from Dallapiccola's *Quaderno Musicale*. To begin, we transpose the row to 0 and write it in the top row of the matrix.

0    1    5    8    T    4    3    7    9    2    E    6

**FIGURE 8.4** Start with $P_0$

$I_0$ is then entered into the first column.

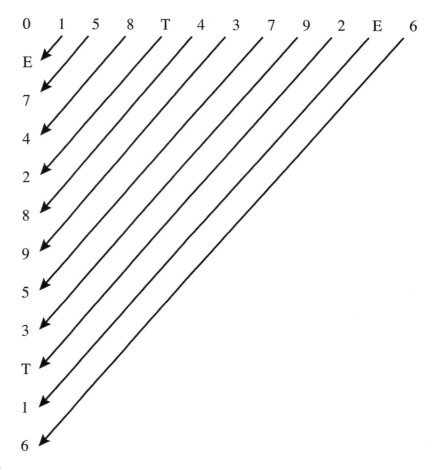

**FIGURE 8.5** Add $I_0$

Now, transpose the row to begin on each of the starting pitches in the left column as shown in Figure 8.6. If done correctly, there will be a diagonal line of 0s stretching from the top left of the matrix to the bottom right. Each row of the finished matrix will contain one of the twelve transpositions of P. To find the transpositions of R, simply read the rows from right to left, remembering to identify them by their last pc. The twelve inversions (read top to bottom) and retrograde inversions (read bottom to top) appear in columns.

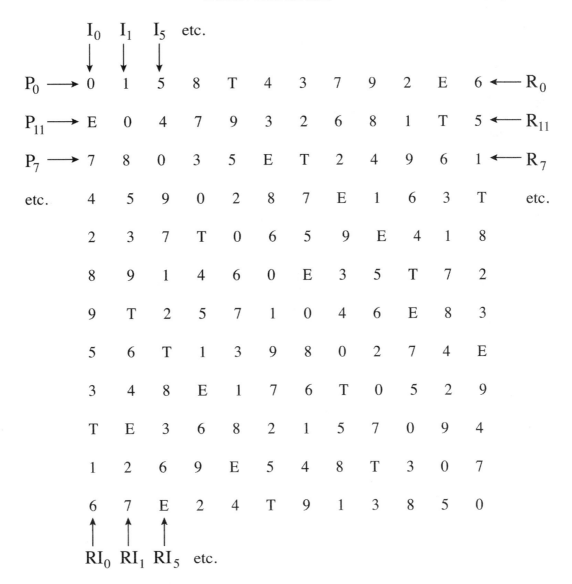

**FIGURE 8.6** Completed Matrix for Dallapiccola's *Quaderno Musicale*

Composers of twelve-tone music may or may not use matrices when composing. There is no evidence that Schoenberg and his students ever used them.[6] Nor is the identification of rows necessary for the comprehension and appreciation of twelve-tone music.[7] Matrices, however, can make it easier to uncover rows in difficult passages and doing so can be useful insofar as it gives us a way to engage more deeply with music based on rows. The members of the row at the beginning of the Menuett from Arnold Schoenberg's first twelve-tone piece, *Suite for Piano*, Op. 25, for example, are distributed onto two staves, causing the two halves of the row to overlap as shown in Example 8.5. Having a matrix at our disposal can make it easier to "hunt down" such rows. (Notice that the Arabic numerals in this example refer to row positions, not pcs.)

**EX. 8.5**—Arnold Schoenberg, *Suite For Piano*, Op. 25, Menuett, mm. 1–4 (Overlapping Row Forms)

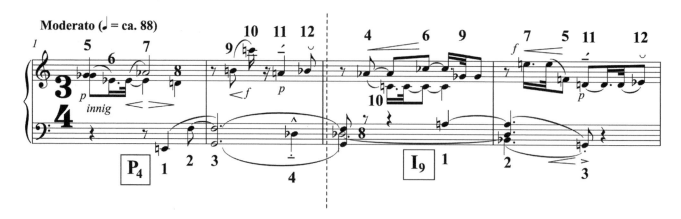

Rows may also be partitioned into chords. Under these conditions, the order of the pcs in the row may not be immediately apparent. In such cases, we may identify the row by determining the order of row segments regardless of how the pcs are ordered within each segment. The second movement of Igor Stravinsky's *Canticum Sacrum* ("Surge aquilo"—Awake, north wind), whose biblical text is drawn from the *Song of Solomon*, begins with the three tetrachords appearing in Example 8.6. These three tetrachords, expressed as unordered pc sets, are [T, E, 9, 0], [3, 4, 6, 1], and [8, 2, 7, 5]. A search of the matrix in Figure 8.7 reveals that these unordered pc sets occur *in the proper succession* only in $R_8$.

**EX. 8.6**—Igor Stravinsky, *Canticum Sacrum*, II, "Surge aquilo," m. 1 (Row Presented as a Series of Chords)

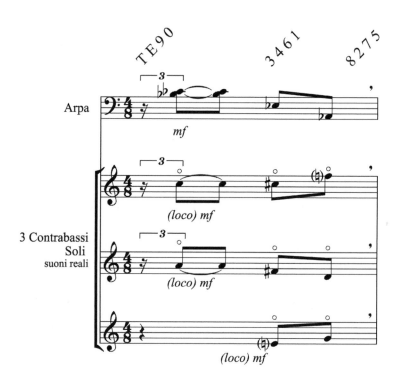

| 0 | E | 9 | 6 | T | 8 | 7 | 5 | 2 | 4 | 3 | 1 |
|---|---|---|---|---|---|---|---|---|---|---|---|
| 1 | 0 | T | 7 | E | 9 | 8 | 6 | 3 | 5 | 4 | 2 |
| 3 | 2 | 0 | 9 | 1 | E | T | 8 | 5 | 7 | 6 | 4 |
| 6 | 5 | 3 | 0 | 4 | 2 | 1 | E | 8 | T | 9 | 7 |
| 2 | 1 | E | 8 | 0 | T | 9 | 7 | 4 | 6 | 5 | 3 |
| 4 | 3 | 1 | T | 2 | 0 | E | 9 | 6 | 8 | 7 | 5 |
| 5 | 4 | 2 | E | 3 | 1 | 0 | T | 7 | 9 | 8 | 6 |
| 7 | 6 | 4 | 1 | 5 | 3 | 2 | 0 | 9 | E | T | 8 |
| T | 9 | 7 | 4 | 8 | 6 | 5 | 3 | 0 | 2 | 1 | E |
| 8 | 7 | 5 | 2 | 6 | 4 | 3 | 1 | T | 0 | E | 9 | ← **R₈** |
| 9 | 8 | 6 | 3 | 7 | 5 | 4 | 2 | E | 1 | 0 | T |
| E | T | 8 | 5 | 9 | 7 | 6 | 4 | 1 | 3 | 2 | 0 |

**FIGURE 8.7** Matrix for Stravinsky's "Surge aquilo"

## Invariance, Interval Symmetry, and All-Interval Rows

Because rows constitute the basic material of a twelve-tone composition, the choice of the row itself is a crucial consideration. It should come as no surprise, then, that many twelve-tone rows have what appear to be contrived features involving invariant pc sets, intervallic schemes, and pitch motives. These features can have a significant impact on the way a composition composed on such a row sounds.

The row in Alban Berg's *Lyric Suite*, shown in Example 8.7a, has a number of unique characteristics. For one thing, it is an **all-interval row** and thus contains all eleven non-0 ordered pitch-class intervals.[8] (See Example 8.7b.) Every all-interval row is by extension an **all-ic row**. Not every all-ic row, however, is an all-interval row. The row in Dallapiccola's *Quaderno Musicale* shown in Example 8.4, for example, is an all-ic row, but not an all-interval row.[9]

**EX. 8.7**—Alban Berg, *Lyric Suite*, I, mm. 2–4 (All-Interval Row)

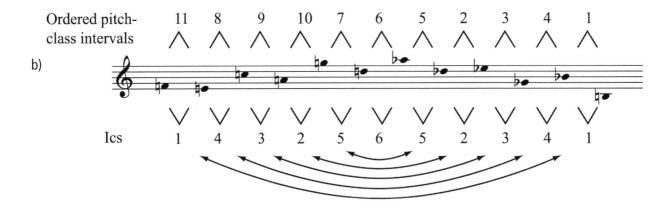

In addition to its all-interval characteristics, the row in Example 8.7 exhibits **ic symmetry**; the ics in the adjacency interval series, that is, are projected forward and backwards in the same order from the center of the collection. This is illustrated by the arrows beneath the staff in the example.

Careful structuring of a row's interval content may lead to **invariant trichords, tetrachords,** and **hexachords.**[10] (Invariant sets are those that remain the same from one subdivision of a row to the next.) Under these conditions, a series of related motives may emerge in addition to the exchange of one aggregate collection for another. Rows with invariant subsets are sometimes referred to as **derived rows.**[11] Figure 8.8 shows the invariant set classes that occur in the derived row from Berg's *Lyric Suite*. Notice that these set classes, like the ics in the row, are also arranged symmetrically around the center of the array.

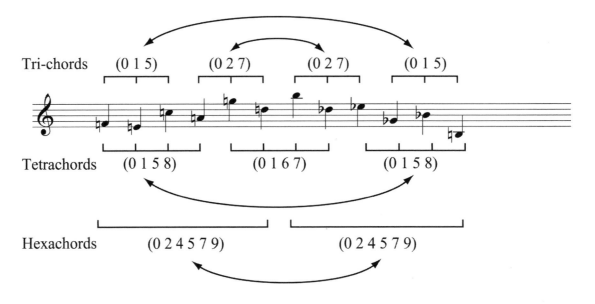

**FIGURE 8.8** Invariant Sets

## Combinatoriality

**Combinatoriality** is a property of rows that allows hexachords from different row forms to be combined to form polyphonic aggregates. Example 8.8 shows a practical application of this idea. Here, $P_{10}$ in the violin part and $I_3$ in the piano accompaniment occur simultaneously. The row in each part taken separately takes two measures to unfold. Combining the violin and piano parts, however, produces two additional aggregates, one for each measure, as indicated by the labeled brackets at the bottom of the example.

**EX. 8.8**—Arnold Schoenberg, *Phantasy for Violin with Piano Accompaniment*, Op. 47, mm. 1–2 (Combinatorial Rows)

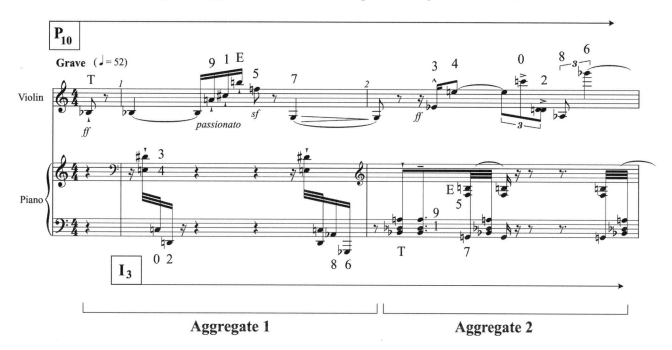

Where combinatoriality is concerned, *the order of pcs in a hexachord is not specified*. In addressing the combinatorial aspects of hexachords, then, one must essentially treat hexachords as unordered pc sets. In fact, it was in engaging with combinatorial hexachords that Milton Babbitt took the first steps toward developing the set-theoretical approach to unordered pc sets discussed in Chapter 4.[12]

Since the literal complement of an unordered set contains all those pcs that do not occur in the source set, combining a hexachord with its complement will always produce a complete aggregate. Where complementary hexachords occur in rows, then, becomes a primary concern for it is this feature that allows rows to produce aggregates in combination. In the following diagrams, arrows show the mapping of hexachords 1 (Hex 1) and 2 (Hex 2) onto various row forms. Labeled rows are combinatorial.

If the Prime row can be combined with some transposition of R to create two additional aggregates, the row is *R-combinatorial*. In R-combinatorial rows, the first hexachord of P maps onto itself, . . .

|  | Hex 1 | | | | | | Hex 2 | | | | | |
|---|---|---|---|---|---|---|---|---|---|---|---|---|
| $P_0$ | 0 | E | 7 | 4 | 2 | 9 | 3 | 8 | T | 1 | 5 | 6 |

$T_0$

. . . thus ensuring that Hex 2 (which is the first hexachord of the retrograde) contains the remaining six pcs. This allows P to be combined with R to produce two additional aggregates. *Since every hexachord maps onto itself, ALL ROWS ARE R-COMBINATORIAL.*

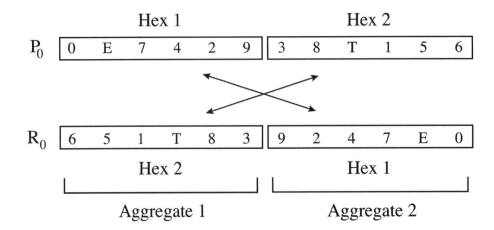

If the first hexachord of a row (Hex 1) maps onto its complement under transposition, . . .

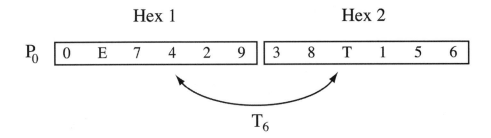

. . . the row is *P-combinatorial*; some transposition of P will have Hex 1 as its second hexachord and Hex 2 as its first, . . .

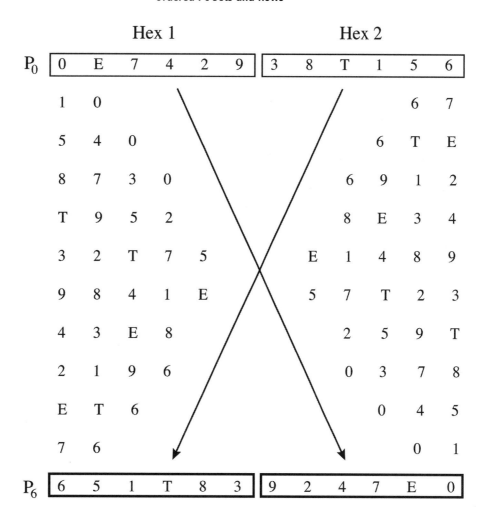

... allowing two P forms of the row to be combined to create two additional aggregates.

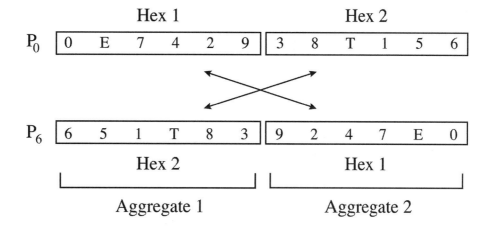

If the first hexachord of a row (Hex 1) maps onto itself under inversion, . . .

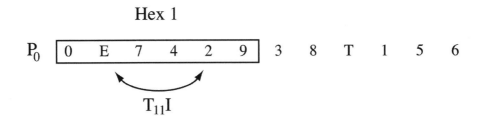

. . . the row is *RI-combinatorial*; some transposition of RI will have Hex 1 of P as its second hexachord and Hex 2 as its first, . . .

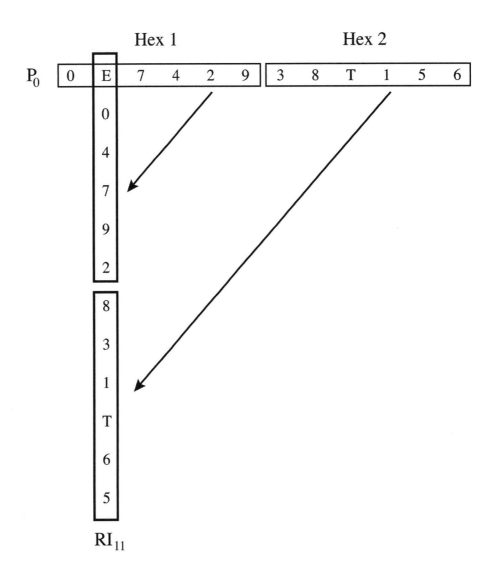

. . . allowing P and RI forms of the row to be combined to create two additional aggregates.

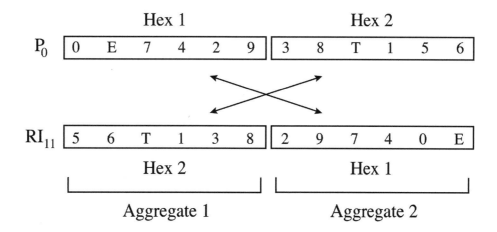

If the first hexachord of a row (Hex 1) maps onto its complement (Hex 2) under $T_nI$, . . .

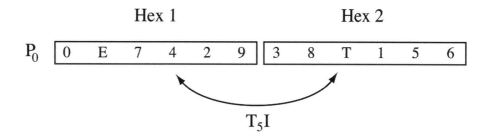

. . . the row is *I-combinatorial*; some transposition of I will have Hex 1 of P as its second hexachord and Hex 2 as its first, . . .

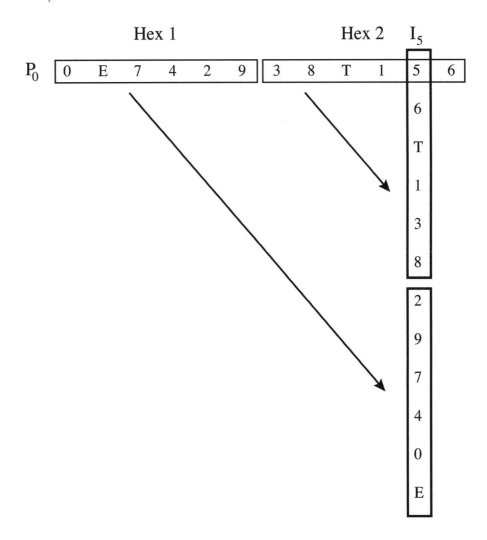

. . . allowing P and I forms of the row to be combined to create two additional aggregates.

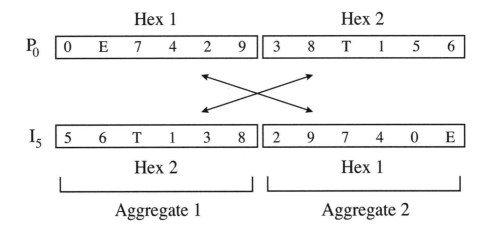

As the above diagrams illustrate, it is possible to determine a row's combinatorial properties by finding where hexachords (unordered) occur in the matrix. Rows that are combinatorial with P begin with Hex 2. The precise $T_n$ and $T_nI$ mappings correspond to the row's transposition level. The row in the above example is P-combinatorial at $P_6$, R-combinatorial at $R_0$, I-combinatorial at $I_5$, and RI-combinatorial at $RI_{11}$. Rows that exhibit all four types of combinatoriality are known as **all-combinatorial rows**. (Not every combinatorial row is all-combinatorial. The row in Stravinsky's *Surge aquilo*, for example, is I- and R-combinatorial, but not P- or RI-combinatorial.) Of the fifty hexachords in Appendix B, only six are all-combinatorial. These appear in Table 8.1 along with their combinatorial properties and relation to other familiar collections.

**TABLE 8.1** All-Combinatorial Hexachords

| | Degrees of Transposition | | | |
| --- | --- | --- | --- | --- |
| | *P* | *R* | *I* | *RI* |
| 6–1 (012345)—a chromatic fragment | 1 | 1 | 1 | 1 |
| 6–7 (012678)—gapped chromatic fragments | 2 | 2 | 2 | 2 |
| 6–8 (023457) | 1 | 1 | 1 | 1 |
| 6–20 (014589)—hexatonic/augmented scale | 3 | 3 | 3 | 3 |
| 6–32 (024579)—diatonic hexachord (major) | 1 | 1 | 1 | 1 |
| 6–35 (02468T)—the complete whole-tone collection | 6 | 6 | 6 | 6 |

Each of the hexachords in Table 8.2 have one combinatorial property in addition to R-combinatoriality. Of these, only (0 1 3 6 7 9) has more than one degree of transposition. The remaining twenty-four hexachords are R-combinatorial only.

**TABLE 8.2** Hexachords with Multiple Combinatorial Properties

| | | Combinatorial Degrees of Transposition | | | |
| --- | --- | --- | --- | --- | --- |
| | | *P* | *R* | *I* | *RI* |
| 6–2 | (012346) | – | 1 | 1 | – |
| 6–5 | (012367) | – | 1 | 1 | – |
| 6–9 | (012357) | – | 1 | 1 | – |
| 6–14 | (013458) | 1 | 1 | – | – |
| 6–15 | (012458) | – | 1 | 1 | – |
| 6–16 | (014568) | – | 1 | 1 | – |
| 6–18 | (012578) | – | 1 | 1 | – |
| 6–21 | (023468) | – | 1 | 1 | – |
| 6–22 | (012468) | – | 1 | 1 | – |
| 6–27 | (013469) | – | 1 | 1 | – |
| 6–Z29 | (013689) | – | 1 | – | 1 |
| 6–30 | (013679) | – | 2 | 2 | – |
| 6–31 | (013589) | – | 1 | 1 | – |
| 6–33 | (023579) | – | 1 | 1 | – |
| 6–34 | (013579) | – | 1 | 1 | – |
| 6–Z37 | (012348) | – | 1 | – | 1 |
| 6–Z38 | (012378) | – | 1 | – | 1 |
| 6–Z42 | (012369) | – | 1 | – | 1 |
| 6–Z45 | (023469) | – | 1 | – | 1 |
| 6–Z49 | (013479) | – | 1 | – | 1 |

## Pitch-Space Attributes of Twelve-Tone Music

Although rows are generally conceptualized in terms of pcs, it is important not to ignore their pitch content. Anton Webern, one of Schoenberg's most famous students and a member of a select group of composers belonging to the Second Viennese School, is especially notable for his attention to pitch and register as well as his propensity to exploit wide regions of registral space.

One technique that Webern employed late in his career is that of assigning pitches to a fixed register. In **fixed register compositions**, the height of each pitch is predetermined; that is, regardless of where it lies in a row, every instance of a given pitch occurs in the same octave. The excerpt from Webern's Op. 28 String Quartet shown in Example 8.9 may serve as an example. In this passage, A♮ always occurs in the fourth octave, G♯ in the sixth, C♮ in the fifth, D♭ in the fourth, and so on.

**EX. 8.9**—Anton Webern, String Quartet, Op. 28, I, mm. 1–10 (Composition with Pitches in a Fixed Register)

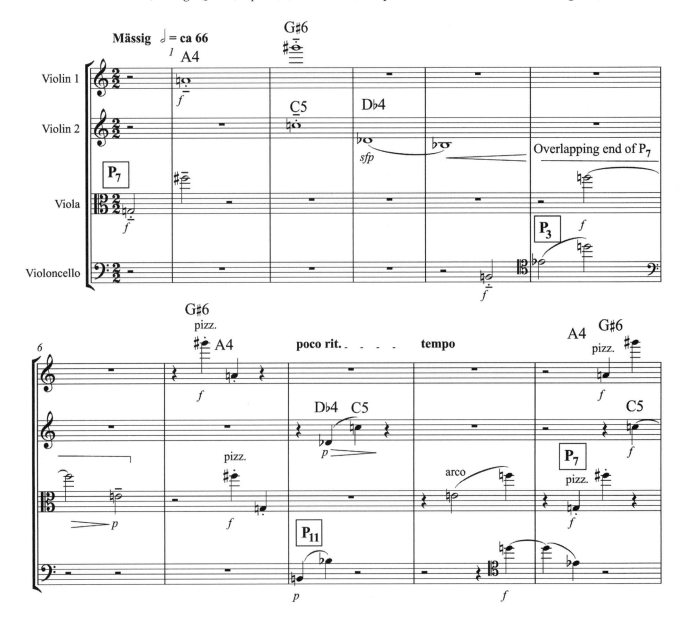

The fact that the first and last tetrachords of each row in Example 8.10 are transpositionally equivalent means that the last tetrachord of any given row also occurs at the beginning of another row. Webern takes advantage of this feature by overlapping rows with shared tetrachords as shown in Figure 8.9.

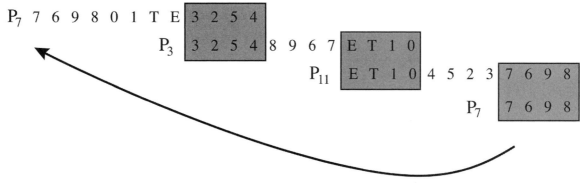

**FIGURE 8.9** Overlapping Rows in Webern's Op. 28, I

---

The row in Webern's Op. 28 String Quartet also incorporates a famous musical signature, that of J. S. "Bach" (B♭–A–C–B♮).* The row starting on B♭ is shown below. The second tetrachord is a transposed retrograde of the signature and the third tetrachord a transposition of the original.

**Figure 8.10** "Bach" Motive in Webern's Op. 28, I

| T | 9 | 0 | 11 | 3 | 4 | 1 | 2 | 6 | 5 | 8 | 7 |
|----|----|----|----|----|----|----|----|----|----|----|----|
| B♭ | A | C | B♮ | | | | | | | | |

* Musical signatures of this kind, also known as mottos, were discussed in Chapter 6.

---

The conceptual move into pitch-space leads to the possibility of parsing rows into ordered pitch interval motives. An example of this kind of organization occurs in mm. 1–5 of the first movement of Webern's *Concerto for Nine Instruments*, Op. 24. This excerpt appears in Example 8.10. Each trichord of the $P_{11}$ row in mm. 1–3 is distinguished by its instrumental timbre, rhythm, and articulation. The row thus divides into four separate motives, all of which belong to the same P/I/R/RI group. The piano articulates $RI_0$ in mm. 4–5. Here the intervals are reversed, producing a new set of related motives.[13]

**EX. 8.10**—Anton Webern, *Concerto for Nine Instruments*, Op. 24, I, mm. 1–5 (Trichord Motives)

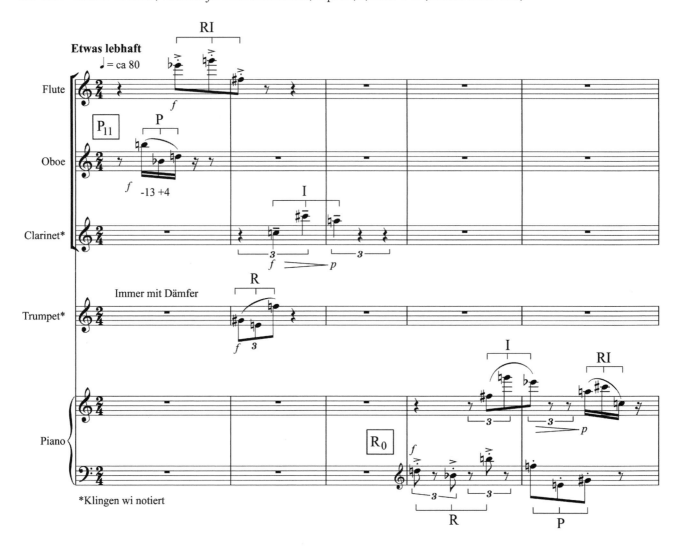

The rhythmic organization of the passage in Example 8.10 also deserves some mention. As in Dallapiccola's "Contrapunctus Primus," the durations in each motive remain proportionally the same; the flute's eighth-notes are twice as long as the oboe's sixteenths, the trumpet's triplet eighths are two-thirds of the length of the flute's eighths, and the clarinet's triplet quarter-notes are twice as long as the trumpet's triplet eighth-notes. The piano part presents the row in reverse, so the rhythms, which retain their trichord associations, are reversed as well.

## Aggregate Composition

The term **aggregate composition** (a.k.a. free atonalism or free twelve-note composition) is sometimes used to describe a piece not composed according to the twelve-tone method in which pcs are nonetheless introduced one at a time until all twelve pcs emerge.[14] This practice can be observed in the so-called "atonal" works of second Viennese school composers, those works that were composed before Schoenberg and his students adopted a more systematic approach to composition based on the twelve-tone method.

Although atonal works often resemble tonal works in terms of rhythm, counterpoint, and form, familiar pitch constructions centering around keys and triads are largely absent. In addition, melodies in atonal music may consist of a series of exceptionally wide leaps, a textural feature known as *pointillism*.[15] One such piece is Webern's Bagatelle, Op. 9, No. 2. The first three measures of this piece appear in Example 8.11. To make the succession of aggregates more conspicuous, the pcs of the first aggregate are boxed while those of the second are circled.

Also of interest in this piece is the ic 1 relation. For example, in m. 1, A is followed by G♯, F♯ by G, and so on. In some instances, pcs exhibiting the ic 1 relation are associated by tessitura: E (second violin) and F (viola) in m. 1, for example. Measure 2 introduces an interesting twist on this scheme. Here, A, which enters on the second eighth-note of the second violin part, is not immediately followed by its ic 1 correspondent. Rather, A returns later in the measure and it is only then that it is followed by B♭. There is a sense, then, that A remains active in the texture while it awaits the arrival of its ic 1 mate. Understood in this way, the piece incorporates a kind of goal-direction in which pcs or groups of pcs seek completion through association with their nearest neighbors in pc-space.

**EX. 8.11**—Anton Webern, Bagatelle, Op. 9, No. 2, mm. 1–3 (Aggregate Composition)

## Integral Serialism

Because it is based on a "series" of notes, twelve-tone music is sometimes referred to as serial music. Post-World War II composers of the Darmstadt School (e.g., Luigi Nono, Bruno Maderna, Pierre Boulez, Luciano Berio, Karlheinz Stockhausen) as well as American composers, such as Milton Babbitt, Charles Wourinen, and Donald Martino, began to apply the serial technique to parameters other than pitch, including dynamics, durations, register, and articulation. This extension of the serial technique is known as **integral serialism** (a.k.a. **total serialism**).[16]

Figure 8.11 shows the row used in Karlheinz Stockhausen's *Kreuzspiel*. Each pitch in the figure is associated with a particular dynamic and inter-onset duration measured in triplet sixteenth notes.

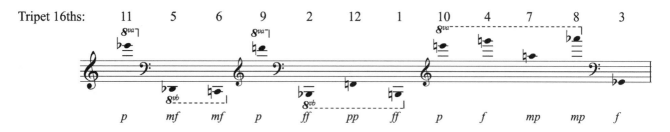

**FIGURE 8.11** Row for *Kreuzspiel*

The title of the work, *Kreuzspiel*, meaning "cross-play," hints at the work's organizational scheme.[17] Figure 8.12, for example, shows how the notes of the row "cross" over each other as the piece unfolds, ultimately leading to a complete exchange of hexachords in the twelfth statement of the theme. As the movement progresses, high pitches gravitate to lower registers and low pitches to higher registers so that by the end of the movement pitch registers have been completely exchanged.

The tumba part articulates the duration series shown in Example 8.12. As the example illustrates, there are two tumbas, one high and one low. Each inter-onset duration begins with a finger-tap on the high tumba. The duration is consequently filled in by a slightly softer series of finger-taps on the low tumba.

**EX. 8.12**—Karlheinz Stockhausen, *Kreuzspiel*, I, mm. 1–7 (Tumba Inter-onset Durations)

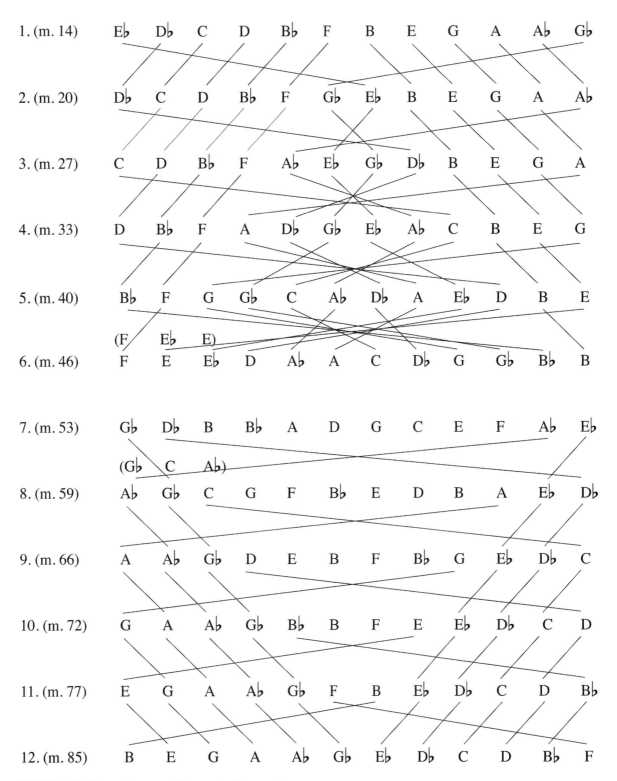

**FIGURE 8.12** Piano Crossover Pattern in *Kreuzspiel*

The tumba series in mm. 1–7 becomes the basis for a rhythmic crossover scheme in the tom-toms. As the rhythms in parentheses in Figure 8.13 indicate, some durations are filled in with multiple attacks. This is not an uncommon practice. Milton Babbitt, for example, uses a similar approach in his *Composition for Four Instruments*.[18]

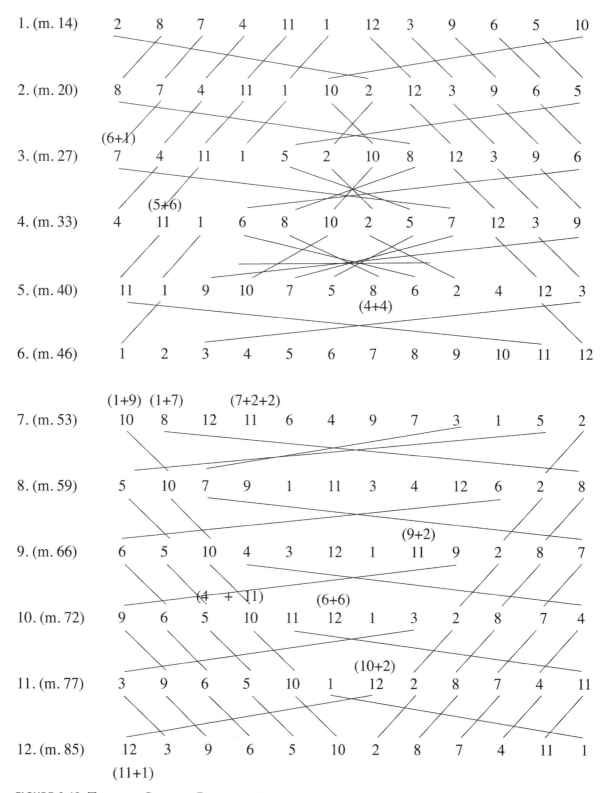

**FIGURE 8.13** Tom-tom Crossover Pattern in *Kreuzspiel*

The tumba part itself follows the somewhat simpler scheme shown in Figure 8.14. (Because the first row of the tumba part enters seven measures before the others, the tumbas have an extra row.)

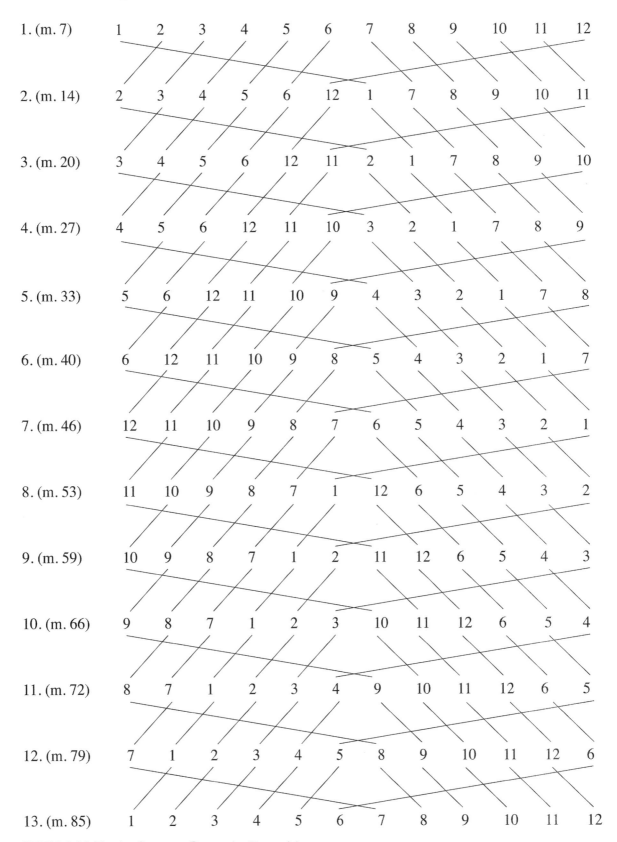

**FIGURE 8.14** Tumba Crossover Pattern in *Kreuzspiel*

As the movement continues, more percussion instruments are gradually added along with the oboe and bass clarinet. Near the end of the movement, the texture thins out again until only the piano and tumbas remain. The ensuing movement (movement 2) begins by articulating a new rhythmic row at a slower eighth-note tempo. This row becomes the basis for a new pitch row with its own durational associations as shown in Example 8.13.

**EX. 8.13**—Karlheinz Stockhausen, *Kreuzspiel*, II, mm. 99–103, Oboe and Bass Clarinet (Pitch Row)

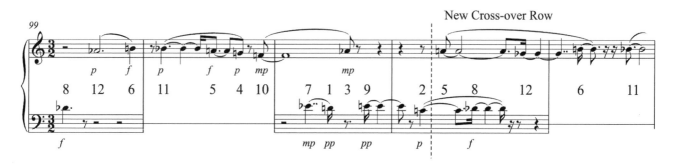

Movement 3 (m. 141) marks a return of the original inter-onset durations (expressed as sixteenths) along with their pitch affiliates from the first movement. In this movement, two rows overlap, producing a crossover effect on vertical as well as horizontal planes. The movement ends with a retrograde of the original pc row, completing a large-scale crossover scheme that spans the work's three movements. A final iteration of the gradually incrementing tom-tom rhythm, which is essentially a rhythmic ritard, along with diminishing dynamics provides a sense of dying away as the piece comes to an end. (See Example 8.14.)

**EX. 8.14**—Karlheinz Stockhausen, *Kreuzspiel*, III, mm. 198–202 (Final Measures)

Serial methods were adopted by many twentieth-century composers as a means for pushing music toward new horizons. Such ultra-rational approaches to music were meant to ensure that old habits would not reassert themselves. Composers writing in the modernist tradition today tend to rely more on intuitive means to reach the same goal. Today's composers, however, are deeply familiar with music created according to serial methods and are thus able to create similar sounding works without having to rely on serial methodology per se. Others have gone on to create their own intellectual schemes for deriving compositional material. Many composers, on the other hand, have rejected serial methods altogether, opting for more flexible approaches to composition. In all these ways, serial music continues to exert its influence.

## Chapter 8 Exercises

1) Ordered Pc Sets.

   a) Supply the untransposed inversion, retrograde, and retrograde inversion for the following ordered pc set.

$T_0P$ <1, 3, E, 5, 8>                    $T_0R$

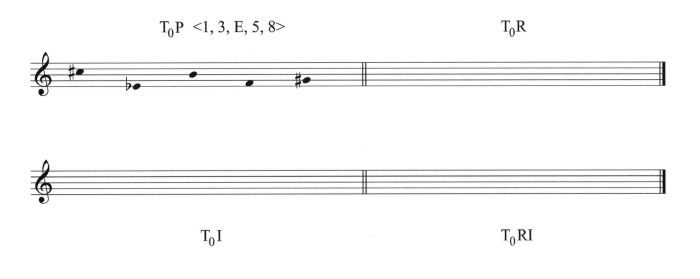

$T_0I$                    $T_0RI$

   b) Now, undertake the following operations.

$T_6P$   <1, 3, E, 5, 8>                    $T_6R$

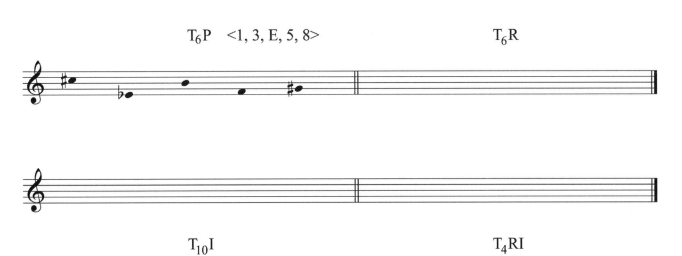

$T_{10}I$                    $T_4RI$

2)  Row Identification.

a)  Supply the ordered pc intervals for the prime row from Schoenberg's Op. 31 below.

b)  Use these intervals and their inversions to determine the other row forms and write them in the blanks. Be sure to include the correct transposition level. (HINT: Remember, the transposition level for retrograde rows is derived from their final note, not the first.)

Arnold Schoenberg, *Variations for Orchestra*, Op. 31, mm. 34–57

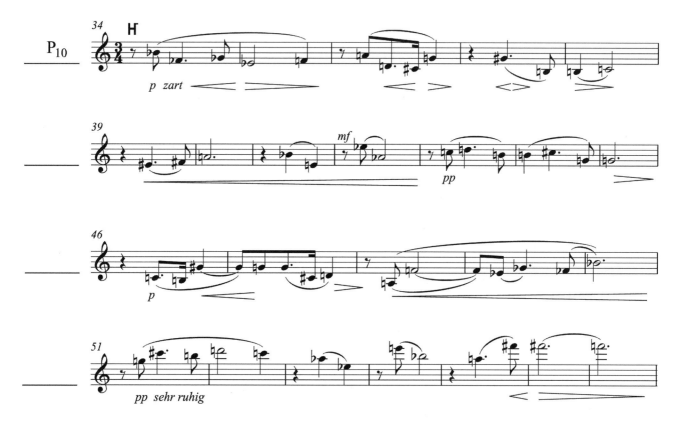

3) Complete the twelve-tone matrix for the row from Arnold Schoenberg's *Suite for Piano*, Op. 25: <0, 1, 3, 9, 2, E, 4, T, 7, 8, 5, 6>

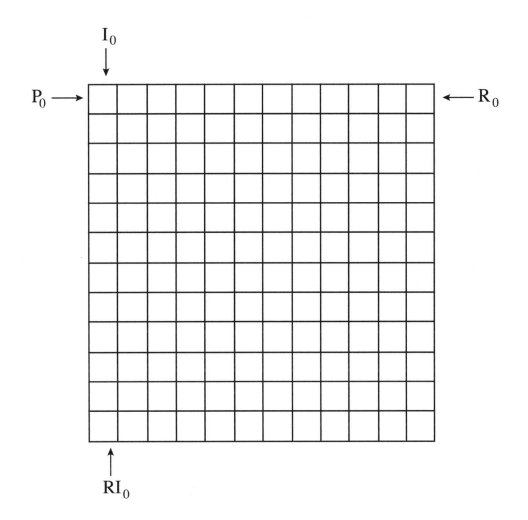

4) Now, use the matrix from Exercise 8.3 to fill in the boxes in the excerpt from the Trio below with the correct row form (**P, I, R, RI**) and transposition (e.g., $P_4$).

Arnold Schoenberg, *Suite for Piano*, Op. 25, Trio, mm. 34–38

5) Is the row for Schoenberg's Suite for Piano:

     a) P-combinatorial? _____

     b) R-combinatorial? _____

     c) I-combinatorial? _____

     d) RI-combinatorial? _____

6) Motive Analysis I.

   a) Each hexachord in the excerpt from Schoenberg's Op. 25 Trio shown in Exercise 8.4 forms a shape/interval motive. The first of these appears below. Write the ordered pitch intervals of this motive in the blanks.

— — — — —

   b) Now, write the ordered pitch intervals for the hexachords in mm. 35 and 37 and identify their operations (P, I, R, RI) based on the motive in Exercise 6a. (Transpositions are not required.)

Operation ———

— — — — —   — — — — —

7) Motive Analysis II.

   a) The sixteenth note figures in Schoenberg's Op. 25 Trio also form shape/interval motives. Begin by supplying the ordered pitch intervals for the sixteenth note figure below from m. 35.

— — — —

   b) Finally, identify the intervals and operations (P, I, R, RI) for the sixteenth-note figures in mm. 36 and 38 based on the motive in Exercise 7a.

Operation ———   ———

— — — — —   — — — — —

8) Rhythm.

    a)  How does the rhythm in the first hexachord of each row in Schoenberg's Trio relate to the second hexachord? (HINT: Add the value of the eighth-note rests to the sixteenth notes that precede them.)

    b)  What ordered duration class do all of the hexachord rhythms belong to?

    c)  What kind of contrapuntal technique is used in the passage?

9) Intervals, invariance, and symmetry.

    a)  Below, you will find a number of well-known rows. List the **prime forms** for the **trichords** and **tetrachords** under the appropriate heading in the table on the facing page. Do any of the rows appear to be derived from trichords or tetrachords?

    b)  Now indicate (yes or no) whether the rows are all-interval or all-ic rows and whether they exhibit ic or interval symmetry.

    c)  Finally, determine the combinatorial properties of the rows. Are any of the row all-combinatorial?

Famous Rows

Schoenberg, Trio, Op. 45, mm. 52-61

Webern, String Quartet, Op. 28, II

Schoenberg, String Quartet No. 4, Op. 37, I

Webern, Symphonie, Op. 21, I

Luigi Nono, Canto Sospeso, No. 4

Schoenberg, Die Jakobsleiter

|  | Trichords | Tetrachords | All-ic | All-interval | ic Symmetry | Interval symmetry |
|---|---|---|---|---|---|---|
| Schoenberg Op. 45 | | | | | | |
| Webern Op. 28 | | | | | | |
| Schoenberg Op. 37 | | | | | | |
| Webern Op. 21 | | | | | | |
| Nono Canto Sospeso | | | | | | |
| Schoenberg Die Jakobsleiter | | | | | | |

# Chapter 9

# Texture and Sound Color

| | |
|---|---|
| Pitch stasis | Klangfarbenmelodie |
| Rhythmic stasis | Spectralism |
| Ostinato | Harmonic spectrum |
| Planing | Harmonic series |
| Stratification | Overtones |
| Rhythmic stratification | Partials |
| Collage | Ring modulation |
| Quotations | Echo |
| Paraphrases | Feedback |
| Polytonality | Sound-mass |
| Pandiatonicism | Micropolyphony |
| Pointillism | Linearity |
| Timbre | Nonlinearity |
| Tone color | Performative silence |
| Acousmatic music | Microsound composition |
| Musique concrète | Glitch music |
| Digital and analog recordings | Aleatory music |
| Frequency modulation synthesis | Conceptual music |
| Additive synthesis | Danger music |
| Samples | |

# Some Textural Features of Twentieth-Century Music

Texture in music refers to the number of voices or parts in a composition and the overall sound they produce when combined. Familiar textures include those consisting of a single part (monophony), those with several voices moving independently of one another or in imitation (polyphony), and those in which multiple voices combine to form chords or chordal accompaniment for a melody (homophony). We have already encountered examples of these textures in the previous chapters. Stravinsky's *In Memoriam Dylan Thomas* and Dallapiccola's "Contrapunctus Primus" (Chapter 8, Examples 8.2 and 8.4) with their imitative counterpoint are polyphonic compositions. Ruth Crawford's *Diaphonic Suite* (Chapter 3, Example 3.8) has a monophonic texture. Among the numerous examples of homophonic textures are Alban Berg's *Schlafend trägt man mich* (Chapter 5, Example 5.1) and Leonard Bernstein's *Chichester Psalms* (Chapter 5, Example 5.2 and Chapter 8, Example 8.1).

In the absence of tonal landmarks, textural features can begin to take on a more prominent role in the delineation of formal boundaries, themes, phrases, and other structural units. **Pitch stasis** (characterized by little or no change in pitch content), for example, can be an important means for creating a sense of "repose" at the end of phrases lacking dominant/tonic closure.[1] Example 9.1 contains the final measures of "Voiles" from Debussy's Preludes, Book 1, No. 2. As the end of the piece approaches, we hear a series of repeated whole-tone scales punctuated by a C4/E4 dyad. These repetitive features impart a sense of finality despite the fact that there is no authentic cadence.

**EX. 9.1**—Claude Debussy, Preludes, Book 1, No. 2, "Voiles," mm. 62–64 (Closing Passage with Pitch Stasis)

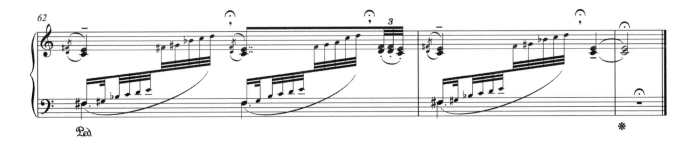

Pitch stasis, of course, can also be used to build unresolved tension in a passage. Overall, the passage in Example 9.2 is dominated by a whole-tone$_1$ collection. In this case, however, the out-of-phase overlapping motives, gradual addition of instruments, and rising dynamic levels create a sense of heightened intensity that builds to a climax in m. 20.

**EX. 9.2**—Claude Debussy, *"Images" pour orchestre*, No. 2, "Iberia," III, mm. 18–20 (Climactic Passage with Pitch Stasis)

Another means for imparting energy and drive to a composition is **rhythmic stasis** (multiple repetitions of a rhythmic pattern or phrase). In the passage from Michael Torke's *Yellow Pages* shown in Example 9.3, the inter-onset durations of the cello part are intermittently reinforced by the rhythms in the other instruments. Here, it is the rhythmic complexity of the individual parts and the way they congeal into a repetitive series of driving sixteenths that brings rhythm to the forefront. Notice too the signature transformation from one to two sharps.

**EX. 9.3**—Michael Torke, *Yellow Pages*, mm. 7–9 (Rhythmic Stasis)

One important device in which pitch and rhythmic stasis are combined is the **ostinato**. Ostinatos are repeated patterns of pitch, rhythm, and contour. As in Example 9.4, ostinatos typically serve as an accompaniment for other melodic or harmonic events.

**EX. 9.4**—Jean Sibelius, *Luonnotar*, mm. 56–67 (String Ostinato)

A widely used textural device found in twentieth-century music, most notably French music, is **planing**. Planing refers to a series of chords that move in parallel or near-parallel motion. The passage from Ravel's *Miroirs* in Example 9.5 incorporates a sequence of planing major and minor triads. In passages such as this, parallel fifths and octaves are the norm and may be thought of as harmonic doublings rather than independent voices in the texture.

**EX. 9.5**—Maurice Ravel, *Miroirs*, I, "Noctuelles," mm. 42–45 (Tertian Chords with Planing)

On occasion, non-triadic sonorities may also be subjected to planing. Example 9.6 shows a passage with quintal chords moving in parallel motion.

**EX. 9.6**—George Crumb, *Star Child*, Violins 1 and 2, p. 29, System 1 (Quintal Chords with Planing)

While planing minimizes the independence of elements in the texture, **stratification** intensifies it. In stratified textures, parts are distributed into discreet, clearly defined, layers.[2] We have already encountered an example of a stratified or layered texture in Witold Lutoslawski's Symphony No. 1, III, mm. 237–50 in Chapter 3 (Example 3.10). As you may recall, our analysis of this passage consisted primarily of a systematic segmentation of the excerpt into layers based on articulation, instrumental timbre, rhythm, tessitura, meter, and pitch content. Examples of **rhythmic stratification** communicated through the use of polymeter may be found in Examples 7.7 and 7.13 in Chapter 7.

Stratification can also occur in less dense textures, in which case layers may be represented by individual parts. In Example 9.7, the two violins are isolated, not by timbre, but by their register, rhythm, and—most strikingly—by the fact that they are based on two different scales.

**EX. 9.7**—Béla Bartók, *44 Duos for Two Violins*, No. 3, "Song of Harvest," mm. 1–5 (Stratified Melodic Texture)

A type of stratification peculiar to Charles Ives is the "parade effect," produced by dividing the orchestra into groups and having each group play a different theme.[3] The juxtaposition of different themes in a piece is known as a musical **collage**.[4] Ives's collages typically incorporate **quotations** from familiar works. In Example 9.8, the tunes are quoted from a number of sources, including Ives's own earlier work, "Country Band March." Some quotations only approximate the tune they reference. Such near-quotations are called **paraphrases** of the original. Figure 9.1 shows two instances of the paraphrase technique in "Putnam's Camp."[5]

**EX. 9.8**—Charles Ives, *Three Places in New England*, II, "Putnam's Camp," mm. 27–30 (Layered Quotations)

"Stephen Foster, "Massa's in the Cold Ground"

Charles Ives, "Putnam's Camp"

Horn

John Philip Sousa, *Semper Fidelis*

Charles Ives, "Putnam's Camp"

Trom. 3
& Tuba

**FIGURE 9.1** Paraphrase Technique in "Putnam's Camp"

The quoted tunes in a collage may or may not be in different keys. The simultaneous use of more than one key—whether or not the collage technique is present—is known as **polytonality**. The excerpt in Example 9.9 articulates two keys—B major and G major—separated by register. Some of the chords in this example could be described as polytriads. Unlike the polytriads encountered in Chapter 1, however, the right- and left-hand parts remain in different keys for the entire excerpt. The polytriads in Britten's "At Day-close in November" (Chapter 1, Example 1.5), on the other hand, are less key-centric than those in Example 9.9 even though the song as a whole is in the key of D minor.

**EX. 9.9**—Darius Milhaud, *Saudades do Brazil*, Vol. 1, No. 4, "Copacabana," mm. 53–62 (Polytonal Texture)

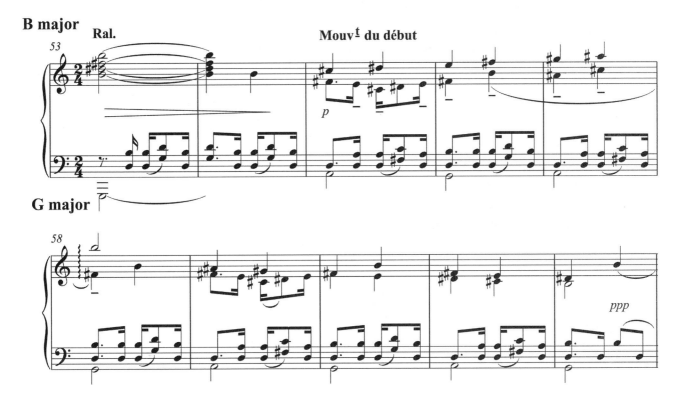

Another important trend in music written since 1890 is **pandiatonicism**, the free use of the diatonic collection without the use of functional harmony. The excerpt from Aaron Copland's *Appalachian Spring* in Example 9.10 is based on the C-major collection, but incorporates secundal and quartal harmony.

**EX. 9.10**—Aaron Copland, *Appalachian Spring*, mm. 19–22 (Excerpt with Pandiatonicism)

While many recent compositions follow conventional procedures by incorporating melodies that are primarily conjunct, others are pointillistic. In **pointillism**, the line disintegrates into a sequence of pitches separated by large skips as in Example 9.11. This allows each tone to emerge with a unique, pristine character, somewhat like the individual facets of a gem or jewel.[6]

EX. 9.11—Anton Webern, Five Pieces for String Quartet, Op. 28, I, mm. 1–9 (Pointillistic Texture)

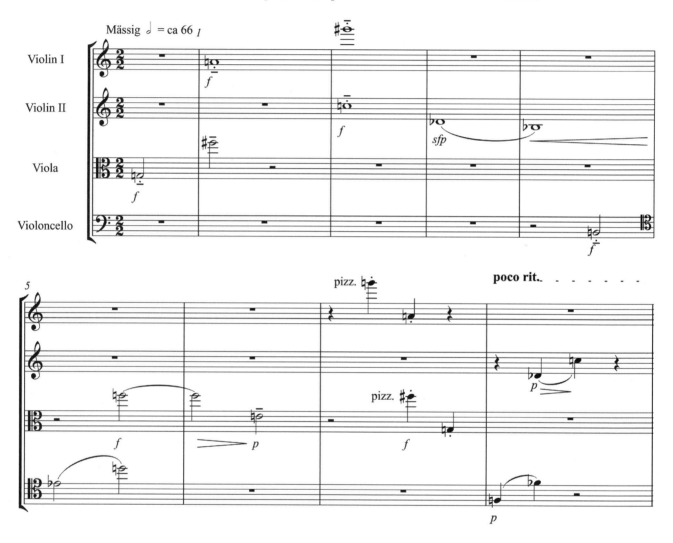

Like many of the terms used to describe recent music, the term pointillism is borrowed from art, where it connotes the technique of painting by dabbing the canvas with many tiny dots. Seen from a distance, the dots blend together to form soft images. Perhaps the most famous example of a pointillistic painting is "Sunday Afternoon on the Island of the Grand Jatte" by Georges Seurat.

The techniques discussed in the foregoing discussion provide a means for describing various aspects of musical texture. These techniques do not necessarily occur in isolation. In fact, it is typical for a passage to incorporate more than one technique. The excerpt in Example 9.12, for instance, has a *stratified* texture with an *ostinato* in the horn and clarinet parts, one that incorporates a particularly vigorous example of *rhythmic stasis.*

**EX. 9.12**—Paul Hindemith, *Mathis der Maler*, III, mm. 453–60 (Excerpt with Multiple Textural Features)

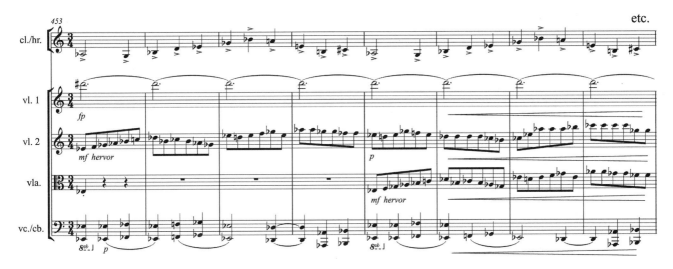

Many of the techniques and devices we have encountered in this section are not confined to twentieth-century music. It is in their contextual details, then, that they differ from earlier music. Texture, moreover, is crucial to our understanding of twentieth-century music and is therefore an integral part of the analytical process.

## Coloristic Music

An aspect of music that does not often come to the forefront in discussions of tonal music is **timbre**, which in some instances can take on a significance equaling that of pitch, rhythm, and meter in music written since 1890. Timbre—also referred to as **tone color**—has to do with orchestration and the characteristic tone quality of individual instruments. Whereas much of the music written in the last few hundred years has typically been thought of as having an "absolute" structure and can therefore be conveyed through a variety of means (Mozart, for example, transcribed many of his string pieces for winds), the full effect of some music can only be communicated through its original medium. Examples include music written for *stopped* horn (playing the horn while closing off the bell with the right hand) as well as pieces that incorporate string effects such as *sul ponticello* (bowing at or near the bridge), *col legno* (striking the string with the wooden part of the bow), *sul tasto* (bowing over the fingerboard to produce a soft, raspy sound), and *bariolage* (playing a series of tones on different strings to produce a variety of sound colors).

George Crumb is an example of a composer who focuses overtly on tone color. Crumb routinely employs instrumental effects that can only be performed by a specific instrument. In the excerpt from *Vox Ballenae* in Example 9.13a, for instance, the cellist touches the string lightly to produce an A♮6 harmonic. By sliding the finger down the string, the cellist creates a succession of harmonic glissandos that imitate the sound of a seagull. In the second excerpt, Example 9.13b, the pianist strums the strings inside the piano, producing a different sound color than the one usually associated with the piano. Other common effects that cannot be easily transferred from one medium to another include multiphonics (singing or humming while playing a wind instrument), preparing the piano by inserting objects such as paper clips and pencil erasers between the strings, and unusual uses of the voice and tongue—*Sprechstimme*, tongue clicks, and the like.

**EX. 9.13**—George Crumb, *Vox Baellenae* (Instrumental Effects)

a)

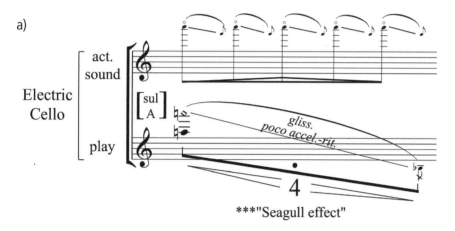

***"Seagull effect"

***This effect is produced automatically. Begin
with 4th finger (lightly touching string) an
octave above lower note. Keep same
spacing of hand throughout glissando (the
interval thereby diminishing).

b)

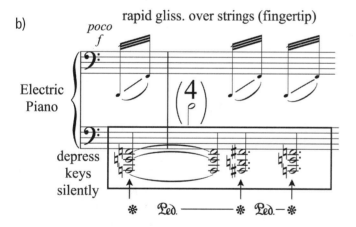

Krzysztof Penderecki, famous for composing large works based on instrumental sound effects during a brief period in the early 1960s, explored the various types of sounds that can be created using combinations of metal, wood, leather, hair, and felt.[7] The passage shown in Example 9.14 exploits several of these categories. A list of the materials and instruments, designated by abbreviations in the score, appears beneath the excerpt. Bracketed annotations indicate which materials are used. The *güiro* is played by rubbing it with the hand, the hand roughly fitting the category of leather and the *güiro* the category of wood. The filled-in upside-down triangular shape in the horn, trombone, and tuba parts indicates that the lowest note possible should be played.

**EX. 9.14**—Krzysztof Penderecki, *Fluorescences*, mm. 1–4 (Materials and Timbres)

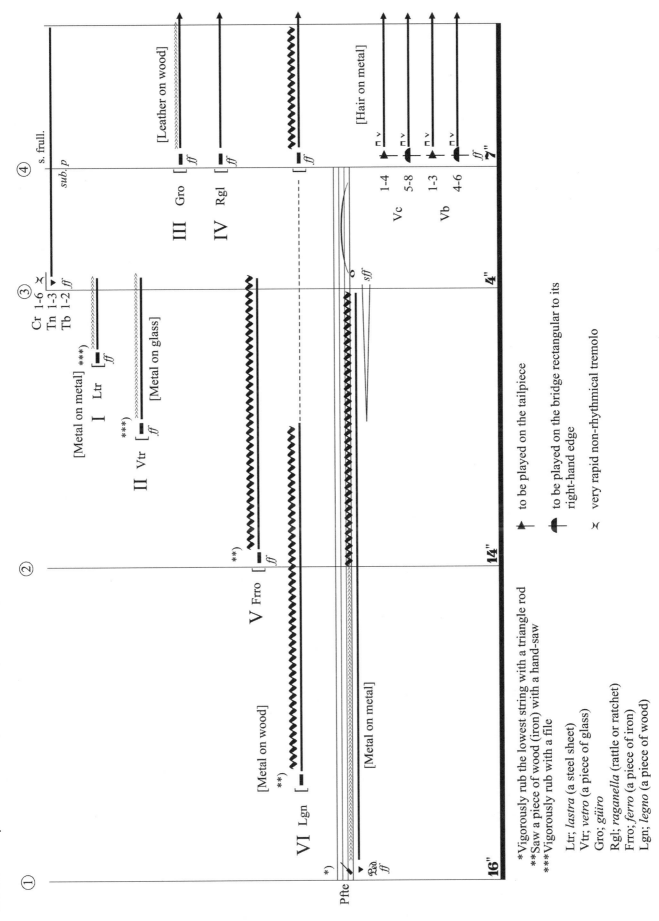

*Vigorously rub the lowest string with a triangle rod
**Saw a piece of wood (iron) with a hand-saw
***Vigorously rub with a file

Ltr; *lastra* (a steel sheet)
Vtr; *vetro* (a piece of glass)
Gro; *giiro*
Rgl; *raganella* (rattle or ratchet)
Frro; *ferro* (a piece of iron)
Lgn; *legno* (a piece of wood)

▲ to be played on the tailpiece

◖ to be played on the bridge rectangular to its
right-hand edge

ᕱ very rapid non-rhythmical tremolo

Composers such as Crumb and Penderecki generally rely on unorthodox ways of playing traditional instruments to produce interesting timbres. Other composers have incorporated tools and devices not intended for use as musical instruments to create coloristic effects. One example of a piece that uses unconventional instruments is Edgard Varèse's *Amériques*, which, in addition to a large orchestra, includes a siren, a boat whistle, a wind machine, and sleigh bells.

The electronic medium, of course, is especially suited for creating works based on timbre. Music for electronics alone is sometimes referred to as **acousmatic music**. Because composers of acousmatic music generally compose by directly manipulating electronic sounds, there is often no score.

Early electronic compositions centered on the manipulation of tape recordings and employed microphones, filters, tape loops (the playing of a relatively short recorded natural sound over and over), altering the speed and direction of the tape, and splicing (cutting the tape and then reattaching the segments at different locations).[8]

One of the earliest composers to explore electronic tape composition was the French composer Pierre Schaeffer. Schaeffer dubbed his new medium **musique concrète** (concrete music) and founded a research institute in Paris devoted to exploring tape composition.[9] Other early composers who experimented with electronic music include the previously mentioned Edgard Varèse as well as a number of American composers, including Earle Brown, Morton Feldman, Morton Subotnik, Vladimir Ussachevsky, and, more recently, David Davidovsky, Steve Reich, and Philip Glass.

Most recordings made today are digital rather than analog. **Digital recordings** register sound as a series of non-contiguous frequency bits rather than the continuous spectrum of **analog recordings**. CDs, DVDs, cell phones, and computer hard drives are all digital devices. Examples of analog media include reel-to-reel tapes, cassettes, and vinyl records.

The appearance of the *Buchla* and *Moog synthesizers* (named for their creators Don Buchla and Robert Moog) in the 1960s revolutionized electronic composition by allowing musicians to generate sounds electronically rather than having to rely on recorded acoustical signals. Developments in synthesizer technology led to a number of techniques for creating new sounds, including **frequency modulation synthesis** (FM synthesis) and **additive synthesis**. In FM synthesis, which was developed by John Chowning at Stanford University in the late 1960s, a sound is distorted through the application of another, often lower, frequency.[10] Additive synthesis is based on the work of French mathematician Joseph Fourier and relies on the process of systematically layering frequencies to produce new timbres.

These and other techniques are today most often implemented using sound editing computer programs. Computers have also been used as a tool for generating compositional material. One of the earliest and most famous examples of a computer-generated composition is HPSCHD by John Cage and Legaren Hiller for live harpsichord and one or more of a total of fifty-one computer-generated electronic tapes.

It should be noted that despite its potential for creating unique and heretofore unheard sounds and sound effects, the synthesizer has often been used to imitate traditional acoustical instruments as well as natural sounds. The most accurate analogues of natural sounds, of course, are recorded sounds and many synthesizers now include recorded **samples** in their sound arsenal. While some musicians in the 1960s and 1970s became concerned that electronic instruments would someday replace traditional acoustical instruments, this has turned out to be a false concern; music that requires expressive license continues to be produced most efficiently by human performers.

Arnold Schoenberg was one of the first to conceive of sound color as a musical parameter capable of standing on its own. Schoenberg outlined a program for creating music consisting of a succession of sound colors, giving it the name *Klangfarbenmelodie* or sound-color melody.[11] Schoenberg's discussion provides only a cursory examination of this idea and the term has generated considerable controversy.

Taken literally, *Klangfarbenmelodie* suggests a melody whose tones are played by different instruments, producing a succession of timbres. The excerpt from Webern's orchestral arrangement of J. S. Bach's *Musical Offering*, "Ricercar a 6," in Example 9.15 is often cited as an example of this technique. Notice how the original melody, confined to one voice in Bach's rendition (Example 9.16), is distributed among a variety of instruments in Webern's arrangement.

**EX. 9.15**—Anton Webern, *Fuga (Ricercata) a 6 voci*, mm. 1–9 (*Klangfarbenmelodie*)

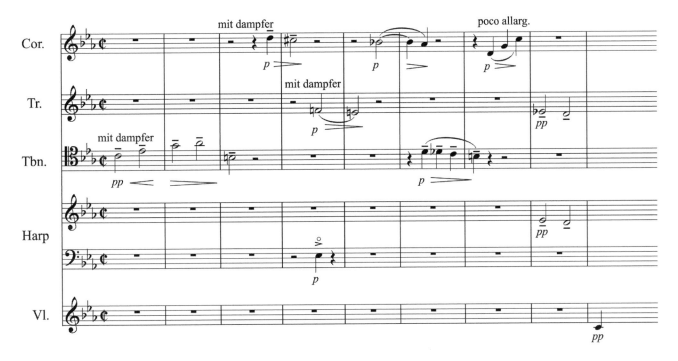

**EX. 9.16**—J. S. Bach, *Musical Offering*, "Ricercar a 6," mm. 1–9 (Original Theme)

Alfred Cramer has argued that the concept of *Klangfarbenmelodie*, as conceived by Schoenberg, may have had more to do with the sound quality produced by tones alone or in combination than with that of tones presented in succession. Understood in this way, chords and their overtones may also "be identified with (and as) timbres."[12] Composers associated with the stylistic movement known as **spectralism** have capitalized on this aspect of *Klangfarbenmelodie* by drawing on the **harmonic spectrum** to generate pitch material. Gérard Grisey's cycle of works *Les espaces acoustiques*, for example, is derived entirely from the harmonic spectrum of a low trombone E1. Example 9.17 contains a few notes from the first work in this cycle. The instructions in this re-engraved version of the piece have been translated into English. The .\ symbol designates a short fermata lasting about one second.

**EX. 9.17**—Gérard Grisey, *Les espaces acoustiques* "Prologue," (Spectral Composition based on the Harmonic Series of E1)

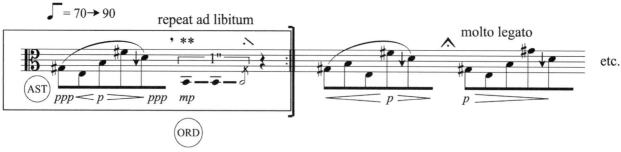

Tune string IV a half-step lower

** Like a heartbeat. The shorter note more stressed
than the longer. The speed of each section = 60 to 70,
whatever the tempo it is inserted into, and always in
ordinary position.

(AST: alto sul tasto)

> The **harmonic series** consists of a fundamental frequency and the tones generated above it
> (**overtones**). The fundamental and its overtones together constitute **partials**. Generally speaking,
> the overtones grow weaker as the series unfolds. The first seven partials shown below form the
> rough equivalent of a dominant seventh chord. As the downward pointing arrow in the figure
> below indicates, the seventh partial is flat. Notice that Grisey also uses an arrow to indicate that
> this pitch should be lowered in the excerpt shown in Example 9.18.
>
> Harmonic Series
>
>

The third piece in this same cycle, "Partiels," simulates additive synthesis. All of the notes in the piece
are members of the E1 harmonic series. Figure 9.2 shows the partials of this series and the instruments
that play them. Each instrument reinforces one of the partials, but also adds its own harmonic spectrum
to the texture, thus creating a complex new sound timbre.

**FIGURE 9.2** Simulated Additive Synthesis Based on the Harmonic Series of E1

Spectralist composers also sometimes emulate electro-acoustical techniques, including **ring modulation** (a technique for producing new sounds through the combination of waveforms), **echo**, and **feedback**. Grisey, for example, uses the symbol ⟨symbol⟩ to indicate a raspy, impure tone and ⟨symbol⟩ to indicate an instable, or wobbly tone, similar to one that might be produced through the application of a low-frequency oscillator (cf. footnote 10).

## Sound and Silence

It is a small step from here to the earlier **sound-mass** music written by such composers as György Ligeti, Edgard Varèse, Iannis Xenakis, and Krzysztof Penderecki in which tones lose their individuality altogether and instead congeal into a unitary sound conglomerate. Ligeti's sound-masses are often built up by means of many individual instruments performing a canon within a narrow pitch range, a technique known as **micropolyphony**. An example of this type of structuring appears in Example 9.18. Sound-masses are identified primarily by their sound color, a characteristic that Ligeti himself alludes to: "The blurring of successiveness combines with a hyperchromatic fluctuation of pitch to produce a strange shimmering in the *tone colour*."[13]

**EX. 9.18**—György Ligeti, *Requiem*, II, "Kyrie," mm. 60–64 (Micropolyphonic Canon)

Music that elevates sound color to a principal role often seems to make little progress, to move in "no particular direction."[14] It is this lack of goal-direction that has led some theorists to adopt the terms *nonlinearity* and *anti-teleology* to describe such music.[15] Linear music sets up expectations that are realized or denied as the music unfolds; examples include the expectation that a melody will descend as the cadence approaches or that pre-dominant harmony will lead to dominant harmony and dominant harmony to the tonic. Whereas **linearity** involves goal-direction, **nonlinearity** involves stasis. In nonlinear contexts, melodies and chords typically do not unfold in a goal-directed manner.[16] This allows the listener to concentrate on the sounds themselves rather than on formal processes. Although difficult to pin down, nonlinearity in music may be characterized by 1) a high degree of repetitiveness, 2) very thick textures in which tones lose their individuality (e.g., sound masses), and 3) blurred patterns of strong and weak beats.

Taking the idea of non-linearity further, we might envision sound masses and other types of sustained, static textures as a form of *silent* expression. We will refer to this phenomenon as **performative silence**.[17] Music that incorporates performative silence is *not* silent in the absolute sense since the music continues to sound. Rather, performative silence refers to the absence of a structural or narrative (we might say, expressive) trajectory in a work.

It is the inclusion of narrativity in this definition that most clearly differentiates the concept of performative silence from nonlinearity. Non-linearity refers mainly to the structural aspects of a work, its spatial and non-progressive features. In this particular respect, nonlinearity and silence have the same connotation; it is the music itself that is non-progressive or non-discursive (i.e., silent). The idea of silence, however, can also be conveyed by music that unfolds in a linear manner. Music, that is, can express silence, without necessarily remaining silent itself.

---

Absolute silence is difficult if not impossible to achieve. As John Cage puts it, "try as we may to make silence, we cannot." Cage elaborates on this notion with the following anecdote:

> For certain engineering purposes, it is desirable to have as silent a situation as possible. Such a room is called an anechoic chamber, its six walls made of special material, a room without echoes. I entered one at Harvard University several years ago and heard two sounds, one high and one low. When I described them to the engineer in charge, he informed me that the high one was my nervous system in operation, the low one my blood circulation. Until I die there will be sounds. And they will continue until my death. One need not fear about the future of music.*

\* John Cage, *Silence*, 8.

---

Below, you will find several examples illustrating silent *expression* (representative or semantic silence) and/or silent *music* (music that is syntactically quiet or still). In Morton Feldman's *For Samuel Beckett*, (Example 9.19), silence is primarily a structural phenomenon, although the allusion to silence in the title is inescapable; you may remember that Samuel Beckett too expressed silence in the form of an absence of activity in his narrative works, *Waiting for Godot* being one example. Speaking of his approach to composition, Feldman notes that "silence is my substitute for counterpoint," thus focusing attention on his compositional process rather than on musical meaning per se. The two excerpts in Example 9.19 are separated by forty measures, yet, except for the boxed pitches, the pc content and ambiguous metrical structure remain unchanged. (In addition, some pcs are played by different instruments in the second excerpt. Mutes remain in place.) This music embodies the notion of silence by remaining largely inactive over long periods of time. What the music is meant to express, on the other hand, is not specified.

**EX. 9.19**—Morton Feldman, *For Samuel Beckett*, mm. 1–4 and 91–93 (Structural Silence)

In other cases, music may express or *represent* silence. John Tavener, for example, describes the "silence" in his music as a kind of "frozen ecstasy" meant to *represent* one's "longing for God" (emphasis mine).[18] Tavener reveals that one of the ways he expresses silence in his music is by means of a "drone" as in Example 9.20. Although the drone in the excerpt may *represent* silence, however, the melody's progress toward the F tonal center is never in doubt. The mounting crescendo and *con molto expressione* marking reinforce the sense of goal-direction. In this passage, then, it is the expressive/dramatic content of the passage more than its structuring that engages the concept of silence.[19]

**EX. 9.20**—John Tavener, *The Protecting Veil*, m. 12 (Semantic Silence)

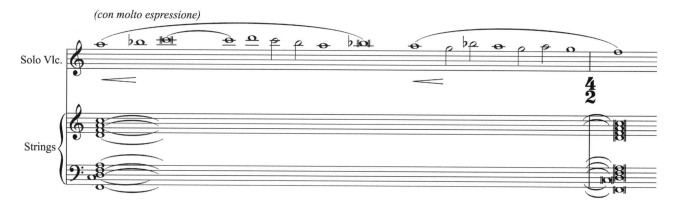

The excerpt from Olivier Messiaen's "Regard du silence" in Example 9.21 combines features from both Examples 9.19 and 9.20. This music not only *represents* silence, as its title indicates, but it also engages silence on the syntactical level.[20] The passage articulates a repetitive series of chords in the right- and left-hand parts. The left-hand series is repeated twice in each measure. The right-hand series is longer and consists of seventeen chords. The second repetition of the right-hand series begins on the second eighth note of m. 89. Notice that in this case, however, the left-hand part is "out-of-phase" with its first appearance in m. 87. Although there are some triadic sonorities in the excerpt, these are always accompanied by added notes, thwarting the formation of functional patterns. All of these features together create a sense of suspended motion on the structural level, while also expressing silence on the semantic level.

**EX. 9.21**—Olivier Messiaen, *Vingt regards sur l'enfant-Jésus*, No. 17, "Regard du silence," mm. 87–92 (Excerpt with Semantic and Syntactic Silence)

Of the composers associated with the phenomenon of silence, John Cage is probably the most renowned. Cage was intrigued by the random noises that occurred in the "silent" void surrounding music. As Cage himself put it:

> [I]n this new music nothing takes place but sounds: those that are notated and those that are not. Those that are not notated appear in the written music as silences, opening the doors of the music to the sounds that happen to be in the environment.[21]

Perhaps the most famous example of a piece that elevates environmental sounds to a featured role is Cage's 4'33". The piece consists of three movements, each of which is *tacet*. Cage provides the following performance note:

> The title of this work is the total length in minutes and seconds of its performance. At Woodstock, NY, August 29, 1952, the title was 4'33" and the three parts were 33", 2'40", and 1' 20". It was performed by David Tudor, pianist, who indicated the beginnings of parts by closing, the endings by opening, the keyboard lid. However, the work may be performed by any instrumentalist or combination of instrumentalists and last any length of time.[22]

Silence also plays a role in the music of the *microsound* movement. Microsound music consists of what Joanne Demers has described as electronically generated "sounds of extremely short duration, typically lasting only a fraction of a second."[23] Barely audible, these "grains" of sound are usually separated by long gaps or silences. **Microsound composition** is related to a species of "post-digital" electronic music that emerged in the 1990s known as *glitch*.[24] **Glitch music** is built around sounds created by errors (or glitches) in recording media (scratches, clicks, and other undesirable noises), although the sounds used in glitch recordings may also be generated purposefully.

The emphasis on incidental sounds, color, and silence challenges the very foundations of the concept of music itself for it suggests that music may take the form of something other than an "absolute" pitch structure. Many composers in the mid-twentieth century experimented with this idea by relinquishing control over the performance or by abandoning the sound medium altogether. John Cage, for example, sometimes derived pitch combinations through chance procedures to create what has come to be known as **aleatory music**. Among the sources Cage consulted to make compositional choices involving such things as pitch, dynamics, and rhythm was the *I Ching* (Book of Changes), an ancient Chinese text containing a number of rubrics for specifying the relations among the components of a system.

Related to chance music is the practice of leaving certain aspects of a performance up to the performer. In Toru Takemitsu's *Tree Line* (Example 9.22), for instance, the composer calls for the flautist to improvise using the given pitches. As the score indicates, the remaining winds play repeated tones *senza tempo* (literally, "without time, unmeasured"). The time signature here is for the accompanying string parts (not shown).

By choosing chance procedures, the composer makes a conscious decision to suppress his or her own voice, leaving it up to the environment or the performer to determine what sounds there will be. Taking the notion of silence even further, some composers have chosen to abandon the medium of sound altogether by creating **conceptual music** whose performances involve something other than the production of sound. The fifth meditation of Pauline Oliveros's *Sonic Meditations* (1974), for example, instructs the performer/listener to "Take a walk at night" and to "Walk so silently that the bottoms of your feet become ears."[25] One particularly haunting sub-genre of conceptual music is **danger music**, an idiom that arose

**EX. 9.22**—Toru Takemitsu, *Tree Line*, Woodwind Parts at Cue 6 (Excerpt with Loose Improvised Texture)

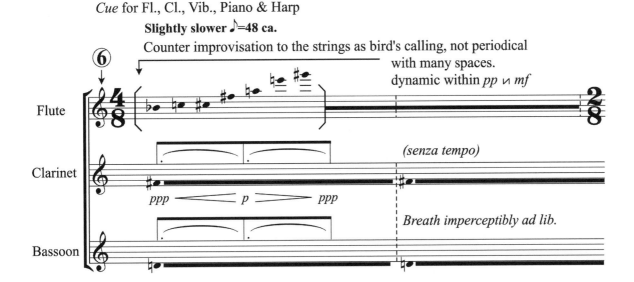

in the 1960s. Quite bluntly, if performed, danger music will cause harm to the performer. One example is Nam June Paik's "Creep into the Vagina of a Living Whale." Although one might be tempted to dismiss conceptual music as a form of *anti-music*, since it completely eschews the acoustical domain, it does share one important aesthetic property with sounded music, the ability to evoke strong, if sometimes unpleasant, emotions.

In conceptual works, music falls completely silent, signaling what may be thought of as the demise of music itself. Yet, to a large extent, all music is really a product of our imaginations. Musical artifacts, melodies, chords, progressions, gestures, patterns, all arise from the ideas we impose on the sounds we hear.[26] Understood in this way, music is brought into existence by means of interpretation and the mechanics of human perception. This idea applies as much to conceptual music as to music that is acoustically active.

Understood within an historical context, the lapse of music into "literal" silence essentially leaves composers with the task of reconstituting music anew. Such a task might seem overwhelming were it not for the fact that in the current climate of postmodern pluralism, there are a plethora of avenues today's composer might explore without risking his or her livelihood. In addition, composers have a wide range of techniques and sound sources at their disposal, including the materials and instruments of the past as well as those made available through modern technology. At the same time, as we have learned in this text, there are deep historical traditions that permeate music of many styles, eras, and cultures. The old and the new mingle in the contemporary consciousness as never before. This is the foundation on which the future of music will be built.

## Chapter 9 Exercises

1) Describe the textural features of Debussy's "La Cathédrale engloutie," using the following questions as a springboard.

   a) What term best describes the technique used in mm. 28–41 and the right-hand part of mm. 72–83?

   b) How is a sense of finality and closure achieved at the end of the piece?

   c) How would you describe the succession of chords in the right-hand part of mm. 14–15? Notice that mm. 16–18 follow a similar pattern.

   d) What term best describes the repeating pattern in the left-hand part of mm. 72–83?

   e) What referential collection occurs in mm. 1–6?

   f) How do mm. 1–6 resemble ancient church music?

   g) Thinking again of cathedrals and church music, what might the resounding low Cs in mm. 32–41 refer to?

   h) What is the referential collection in mm. 32–41?

   i) The bass begins a descent in m. 3. How far does this "sinking" bass line ultimately descend?

   j) How many instances of quintal harmony can you find?

   k) What other structural and textural features occur in the piece?

Claude Debussy, Preludes, Book 1, No. 10, "La Cathédrale engloutie"

2) Stratification.

    a) Describe each layer of the stratified texture in Toru Takemitsu's *Star-Isle* for Orchestra, mm. 72–76. (This excerpt may be found in Exercise 3.8.)

    b) Béla Bartók's "From the Island of Bali" (Exercise 6.10) contains a much subtler example of stratification. Describe the pitch and rhythmic features that produce two independent layers in mm. 1–11.

    c) Identify the layers and their content (e.g., scale material, pc sets, motives) in mm. 35–42 of Béla Bartók's Music for String Instruments, Percussion, and Celesta, III. What parts embody the notion of nonlinearity or performative silence in the passage? What parts are more linear in nature?

3) Of the terms polytonal, pandiatonic, and pointillistic, which one best describes each of the textures below?

a) Maurice Ravel, Trio for Violin, Cello, and Piano, II, "Pantoum," mm. 125–28

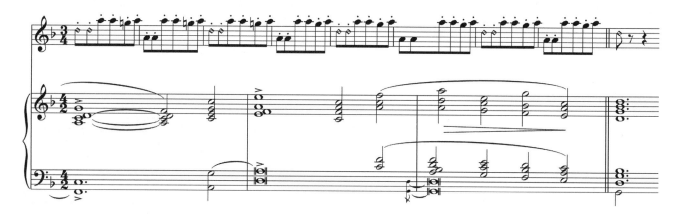

b) Darius Milhaud, *Saudades do Brazil*, Vol. 2, No. 10, "Paineras," mm. 1–10

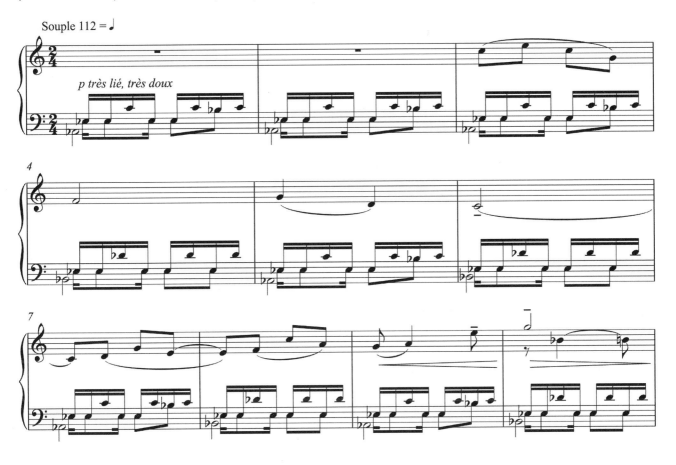

c) Anton Webern, *Drei kleine Stücke*, Op. 11, No. 1, mm. 1–6

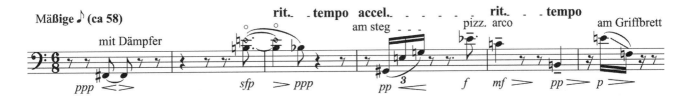

4) Identify which of the following tunes are either quoted or paraphrased in the bracketed portions of Charles Ives's *The Things Our Fathers Loved*.

a) Daniel Emmet, *Dixie*

b) Paul Dresser, *On the Banks of the Wabash, Far Away*

c) Samuel F. Bennett and Joseph P. Webster, *In the Sweet By and By*

d) George F. Root, *Battle Cry of Freedom*

e) Robert Robinson and John Wyeth, *Come, Thou Font of Every Blessing*

b) Darius Milhaud, *Saudades do Brazil*, Vol. 2, No. 10, "Paineras," mm. 1–10

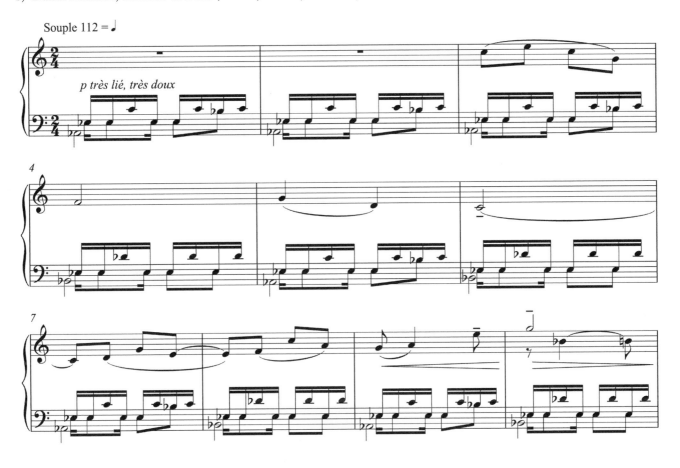

c) Anton Webern, *Drei kleine Stücke*, Op. 11, No. 1, mm. 1–6

4) Identify which of the following tunes are either quoted or paraphrased in the bracketed portions of Charles Ives's *The Things Our Fathers Loved*.

a) Daniel Emmet, *Dixie*

b) Paul Dresser, *On the Banks of the Wabash, Far Away*

Chorus

Oh, the moon-light's fair to-night a-long the Wa-bash, From the

field there comes the breath of new-mown hay,

c) Samuel F. Bennett and Joseph P. Webster, *In the Sweet By and By*

d) George F. Root, *Battle Cry of Freedom*

e) Robert Robinson and John Wyeth, *Come, Thou Font of Every Blessing*

Adagio

f) Charles Ives, *The Things Our Fathers Loved*

5) Notate the harmonic series for G1 up to the eighth partial. Place an arrow beside tones that are out of tune (i.e., sharp or flat).

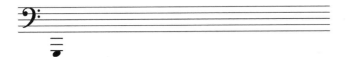

6) Create a micro-polyphonic canon for divisi violins based on the first violin part below. Introduce the C/C♯ eighth-note figure on successive beats until all instruments have entered. Complete as much of each part as possible, always keeping the canonic relationship intact.

7) Describe the nonlinear (or silent) features of the passage from Debussy's *Images pour orchestre*, No. 2, "Iberia," III, mm. 18–20 shown in Example 9.2 of the textbook. Does this excerpt embody structural silence, semantic silence or both?

8) Create a conceptual composition consisting of 200 words or less.

9) Attend a concert of electronic or electro-acoustic music and write a 1–2 page review.

# Aural Skills Supplement

## To the instructor

When listening to music that does not follow tonal protocol, students must learn to rely on other criteria to organize their hearing. This supplement appropriates intervals and contour for this purpose. Such an approach provides access to important details in a broad cross-section of recent music while limiting the skills the student must learn to a manageable few rather than including a broad spectrum of analytical approaches.

The exercises themselves are laid out in a progressive manner so that the skills acquired in earlier units may be used to complete more difficult exercises later on. STREAM 1 provides practice in identifying unordered pitch and pc intervals in trichords, tetrachords, and melodies. STREAM 2 combines intervals and contours. Each exercise contains a melody consisting of four back-to-back motives. The student must identify the correct operation for each motive based on the shapes and intervals found in the original (i.e., P, I, R, or RI). The exercises in STREAM 3 are similar to those in STREAM 2, but incorporate more rhythmic variation. The most advanced exercises in STREAMS 2 and 3 include transposition and overlapping motives. Most exercises also include an option for identifying prime forms.

The streams follow the same trajectory as the textbook. STREAM 1 centers around the identification of unordered pitch intervals, which are covered in Chapter 1. The prime form option can be added in STREAM 1 upon the completion of Chapter 4. The exercises in STREAMS 2 and 3 build on the discussion of shape/interval motives in Chapters 3 and 6. Although all the exercises may be completed without specific knowledge of twelve-tone rows, the exercises in STREAMS 2 and 3 contain several derived rows and, thus, pertain to the material in Chapter 8. Strategies for completing the exercises successfully are covered in the following discussion. Although the student's progress through the aural skills exercises does not necessarily have to remain in strict lockstep with the text, it would probably be best to avoid introducing aural skills exercises before the techniques they involve have been addressed in the textbook.

To use the exam function, contact the author at motivichearing@gmail.com. Once you have been approved, you may go to the Exam page where you will be able to select exercises to create exams and create and manage groups. Students will only be able to take an exam after they have entered the automatically generated group code and been approved by the instructor on the Manage Groups page. The scores for completed exams will appear automatically on the instructor's exam page.

## The Online *Motivic Hearing* Program

To gain access to the online ear-training program, log on to the Motivic Hearing site at www.motivichearing.com on your web browser. You will need to register before you can use the program. The required secret phrase is "goeartraining." The program is fairly straightforward. The exercises are organized into streams and sets. You can choose a complete set or one of the routines labeled A, B, C, etc. within each set. To hear an exercise, click on the "play" button ▶. You can also use the play button to start and stop at will. The moving cursor can be dragged to any location in the exercise. Pressing the "loop" button ◉ to the right of the play button causes the exercise to repeat automatically. The "snail" 🐌 button on the right can be used to toggle between fast and slow versions of the exercises. Pick the options you want by clicking on the buttons at the bottom left corner of the window. When you press the "Intervals," "Operations," and "Prime Form" buttons, you will be presented with a pop-up menu. Select your answer, then click "SUBMIT." The program will provide feedback by showing you the correct and incorrect selections. Correct your mistakes and hit the "SUBMIT" button again. To see the notated exercise, click on the "SHOW ANSWER" button. Notice that you can still make corrections after choosing this option. The "CONTINUE" button takes you to the next exercise in the set.

## Introduction to the Aural Skills Exercises

### Twentieth-century music and the ear

Twentieth-century music does not always incorporate the chords and scales we associate with tonal music, nor is it immersed in a single dominant stylistic paradigm. But neither is it incomprehensible. What we need, then, are new listening strategies to experience twentieth-century music to its fullest.

Fortunately, it is not necessary to approach each piece of new music with a different set of aural skills. This is because, despite its variety, much of the music written during the last 100 years or so has a number of shared features. Consider the excerpts in Example S.1. Excerpt a) is by Alexander Scriabin, a late nineteenth-century romantic composer, and excerpt b) by Second Viennese School composer Arnold Schoenberg.

EX. S.1a—Alexander Scriabin, Prelude, Op. 74, No. 3, mm. 9–12

EX. S.1b—Arnold Schoenberg, *Pierrot Lunaire*, "Nacht," mm. 12–13

While the two excerpts differ in terms of their stylistic details, there are also some commonalities. Notice, for example, that only three pitch intervals occur in each excerpt, a phenomenon we may refer to as **interval saturation**. Notice too that two of the intervals in each excerpt cluster together, forming a series of three-note melodic gestures. While the pitches of these gestures do not match, their intervals do. In addition, the gestures have related contours, a descent followed by an ascent in the Scriabin and an ascent followed by a descent in the Schoenberg.

While motives may take on a number of different forms, ranging from abstract ideas to highly prescribed pitch-rhythm designs, defining motives in terms of shape (contour) and ordered pitch interval content alone—as in Example S.1—can produce quite rich results when applied analytically and aurally. As in the accompanying textbook, we will refer to such gestures as **ordered pitch interval motives** (a.k.a. **shape/interval motives**). In other cases, motives may be constructed around unordered pc intervals (a.k.a. interval-classes or ics). The exercises in the software that accompanies this supplement provide practice in identifying both kinds of motives.

## The Stream Approach

The online *Motivic Hearing* program is divided into sets with multiple exercises. These are arranged according to parameter and difficulty. STREAM 1 contains exercises for learning to recognize unordered pitch intervals in trichords, tetrachords, and melodies. There is also an option for identifying prime forms. (Prime Forms are covered in Chapter 4 of the textbook. You will find a tutorial for identifying prime forms by ear on p. 260 of this supplement. STREAM 2 exercises comprise four back-to-back trichords. The first trichord is the prime (P). The objective is to identify the operations, prime (P), retrograde (R), inversion (I), or retrograde inversion (RI), of the remaining trichords. STREAM 3 presents trichords and their operations in more complex melodic contexts.

This method of aural analysis was developed by John Wm. Schaffer in collaboration with the author in the mid 1990s. We found that by concentrating on

> relatively short shape/interval motives (often consisting of only three or four pitches) along with their ordered transformations, we [were] able to account for important details in the music of a number of important composers, including Messiaen, Ives, Debussy, Shostakovich, Copland, Rorem, Crawford, Schoenberg, Scriabin, Bartók, Webern, Stravinsky, Hindemith, and Crumb.[1]

Obviously, such an approach cannot account for all the stylistic details of the broad range of music written since 1890. Indeed, one of the most important aspects of twentieth-century music is its variety and intense innovative spirit. Our individual subjective responses to this music, on the other hand, may engage similar interpretive mechanics regardless of style or genre. Schaffer's contention was that "[b]y shifting our analytical vantage point we [could] begin to see that a conceptualized world of discrete schools might actually be viewed quite productively as a set of variations on a few common themes."[2] The aural skills method outlined in this supplement stems directly from this premise by incorporating short motivic ideas identified by their shapes and intervals. What it is *not* meant to do is "teach us to identify truths about a composer's intent."[3] The method, that is, is intended only as a tool, one that combines analysis and ear training into a single endeavor, **analytical listening**.

# Stream 1

## Intervals and prime forms

Stream 1 provides practice in recognizing intervals in trichords, tetrachords, and melodies. The exercises are saturated by two or three pitch intervals, all smaller than an octave. Early exercises comprise either trichords or tetrachords, while later exercises consist of melodic phrases. This approach allows the student to improve interval recognition skills before proceeding to more complex kinds of structures involving motives and their transpositions.

In this supplement, we will adopt the general premise that dissimilar intervals are easier to distinguish than similar intervals.[4] Major and minor seconds, for example, may be more difficult for some listeners to differentiate than minor seconds and perfect fifths. In recognition of this tendency, the first group of exercises in each set (e.g., 1.1a, 2.1a, etc.) will typically contain dissimilar intervals. Similar intervals are relegated to the more advanced exercises (e.g., 1.1b, 2.1b, etc.). Where trichords are involved, the exercises are further broken down according to shape; except where indicated, jagged contours consisting of an up–down or down–up contour occur in the first group of exercises (e.g., 1.1a, 2.1a, etc.) while smooth ascending or descending contours occur in the second group (1.1b, 2.1b, etc.). Let us now turn to a detailed description of each set of exercises and consider some strategies for completing them successfully.

### Sets 1.1a–1.1d

The exercises in Sets 1.1a–1.1d consist of individual trichords . . .

**EX. S.2**—Set 1.1a Sample Exercise

Intervals:     m2     P4

Prime Form:   (0 1 5)

. . . and are organized according to the following shape and interval criteria.

**TABLE S.1** Criteria for Sets 1.1a–1.1d

| Set  | Interval Size | Shape  |
| ---- | ------------- | ------ |
| 1.1a | Dissimilar    | Jagged |
| 1.1b | Dissimilar    | Smooth |
| 1.1c | Similar       | Jagged |
| 1.1d | Similar       | Smooth |

Smooth shapes comprise either two ascents or two descents as shown in Example S.3.

**EX. S.3**—Set 1.1b Sample Exercise

Intervals:    m2      P4

Prime Form:   (0 1 6)

The instructions are to . . .

> 1) Identify the two unordered pitch intervals in the order they occur and
> 2) Identify the prime form of the set.

## Sets 1.2a–1.2b

The exercises in Sets 1.2a–1.2b are similar to those in Sets 1.1a–1.2b, but contain tetrachords. (See Example S.4.)

**EX. S.4**—Set 1.2a Sample Exercise

Intervals:    P5        m2      TT

The exercises are based on either dissimilar or similar intervals as indicated in the chart below. In general, the shapes in Set 1.2b are smoother than those in Set 1.2a.

**TABLE S.2** Criteria for Sets 1.2a–1.2b

| Set | Interval Size |
| --- | --- |
| 1.2a | Dissimilar |
| 1.2b | Similar |

The instructions are to . . .

> Identify the three unordered pitch intervals in the order they occur.

## Listening Strategies for Sets 1.1a–1.2b

To complete Stream 1 exercises 1.1a–1.2b successfully, adopt a strategy. For example, try "singing" the motive back to yourself silently. Once you have memorized it, you should be able to isolate each interval to determine its size. Although the motives do not always conform to a major or minor key, you may still be able to situate some of the motives and their intervals within a tonal context. A motive with a descending tritone followed by an ascending minor second, for example, corresponds to "fa–ti–do" in a major scale.

### Sets 1.3a–1.4b

The exercises in Sets 1.3a–1.4b contain melodies saturated by two or three intervals (See Example S.5.)

**EX. S.5**—Set 1.3a Sample Exercise

Intervals:   M2   P5   etc.

As in the other Stream 1 sets, the exercises are constructed for the most part around similar or dissimilar intervals. Set 1.4b breaks this pattern by including a mix of intervals.

**TABLE S.3** Criteria for Sets 1.3a–1.4b

| Set | No. Intervals | Interval Size |
| --- | --- | --- |
| 1.3a | 2 | Dissimilar |
| 1.3b | 2 | Similar |
| 1.4a | 3 | Dissimilar |
| 1.4b | 3 | Mixed |

The instructions are to . . .

Identify the two or three unordered pitch intervals in any order.

## Listening Strategies for Sets 1.3a–1.4b

Remember, the melodies in Sets 1.3a–1.4b are saturated by only two or three pitch intervals. Listen especially to the beginning and ending of each melody to isolate intervals for analysis. You can also start and stop the melody at will.

# Tutorial for Identifying Prime Forms

Perhaps the easiest way to identify the prime form of a trichord is to mentally rearrange its pcs into an arpeggiated chord. Once this is accomplished, simply construct the prime form in increments by counting intervals bottom-to-top or top-to-bottom starting with the smallest. You may also create a notated version of the motive to help you determine the prime form.

Some of the prime forms for trichords correspond to familiar musical chords and scale patterns. These include major and minor triads, (0 3 7), diminished triads, (0 3 6), augmented triads, (0 4 8), and the first three steps of a chromatic scale (0 1 2), major or whole-tone scale (0 2 4), and minor or Phrygian scale (0 1 3). To the extent the student recognizes these structures and their corresponding prime forms, prime forms may be assigned without counting intervals.

It is also possible to identify prime forms based on the total interval-class content of motives. The two melodic intervals in a trichord are easy enough to hear because they occur in succession. Determining the interval between the first and last pitches, however, may require a more analytical approach. In smooth ascending or descending motives, the interval between the first and last pitches can be determined by adding the two melodic pitch intervals together as illustrated in Figure S.1a. To determine the interval between the first and last pitches of jagged motives, try subtracting the smaller pitch interval from the larger one (Figure S.1b). In both cases, you will need to convert pitch intervals to ics. Use the total interval-class content to determine the prime form based on the data in Table S.4.

a) (Smooth Motive)

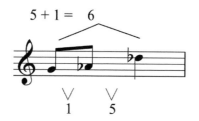

Total ic content:   1/5/6

b) (Jagged Motive)

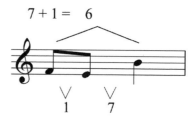

Total ic content:   1/5/6

**FIGURE S.1**  How to Determine the Total Interval-Class Content of a Shape/Interval Motive

**TABLE S.4** Trichords and their Total Interval-Class Content

|      | Prime Form | ic Content |      | Prime Form | ic Content |
|------|-----------|-----------|------|-----------|-----------|
| 3-1  | (012)     | 1/2/2     | 3-7  | (0 2 5)   | 2/3/5     |
| 3-2  | (013)     | 1/2/3     | 3-8  | (0 2 6)   | 2/4/6     |
| 3-3  | (014)     | 1/3/4     | 3-9  | (0 2 7)   | 2/5/5     |
| 3-4  | (0 1 5)   | 1/4/5     | 3-10 | (0 3 6)   | 3/3/6     |
| 3-5  | (0 1 6)   | 1/5/6     | 3-11 | (0 3 7)   | 3/4/5     |
| 3-6  | (0 2 4)   | 2/2/4     | 3-12 | (0 4 8)   | 4/4/4     |

## Stream 2

### Shape/interval motives and their P, I, R, and RI operations

Stream 2 exercises are designed to help students gain facility recognizing shape/interval motives and their operations. To the extent that shape alone cannot be used to make accurate judgments, other factors—including register and interval content—may also prove useful. All Stream 2 exercises consist of melodies with twelve notes distributed over four measures. Each measure contains a single trichord. The first trichord is the prime and maps onto the other trichords by means of the ordered operations prime (P), inversion (I), retrograde (R), or retrograde inversion (RI).

The instructions for all of the exercises in Stream 2 are the same:

> 1) Identify the two unordered pitch intervals of the prime motive in the order they occur.
> 2) Identify the operation (P, I, R, RI) of the remaining trichords.
> 3) Identify the prime form of the trichords in the exercise. (NOTE: All of the trichords in each exercise will have the same prime form.)

### Sets 2.1a–2.2b

Example S.6 contains a typical Set 2.1a exercise consisting of four back-to-back trichords with dissimilar intervals.

**EX. S.6**—Set 2.1a Sample Exercise

Notice that each trichord articulates an eighth–eighth–quarter rhythm, making it easy to distinguish between them. Sets 2.1b and 2.2b contain exercises with smooth shapes (ascents or descents) like the one in Example S.7.

**EX. S.7**—Set 2.1b Sample Exercise

The chart in Table S.5 shows how the sets are organized by shape and interval. (None of the motives is transposed.)

**TABLE S.5** Criteria for Sets 2.1a–2.2b

| Set | Interval Size | $T_n^p$ | Shape |
|-----|---------------|---------|-------|
| 2.1a | Dissimilar | No | Jagged |
| 2.1b | Dissimilar | No | Smooth |
| 2.2a | Similar | No | Jagged |
| 2.2b | Similar | No | Smooth |

## Listening strategies for sets 2.1a–2.2b

Shape alone can be a strong indicator of the operations in Stream 2 exercises. Where jagged contours occur, for example, the prime and retrograde forms of the motive have the same contour adjacency series while the inversion and retrograde inversion invert the series as in Figure S.2.[5]

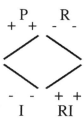

**FIGURE S.2** Adjacency Contour Series of Jagged Motives

In ascending and descending motives, the shape of the prime and retrograde inversion match while the inversion and retrograde have an inverted shape. Hence, if the prime ascends, as in Figure S.3, so does the retrograde inversion. Both the inversion and the retrograde descend.

**FIGURE S.3** Adjacency Contour Series of Smooth Motives

In addition to shape, the student may also attend to register to help identify operations. This is because the inversion and retrograde inversion often open up a new register by introducing pitches not heard in the prime and retrograde. In Example S.6, for instance, the addition of C♭3 in both the inversion and retrograde inversion expands the range of the theme.

Not all motives introduce new pitches under inversion. All of the motives in Example S.8, for instance, contain the same pitches in a different order. Even in this case, however, pitch plays a role since the prime and inversion both begin with F4 while the retrograde and retrograde inversion end on F4. Keeping track of the beginning and ending pitches may therefore be of some help.

**EX. S.8**—Motives with the Same Pitch Content

## Sets 2.3a–2.4b

Like Sets 2.1a–2.2b, Sets 2.3a–2.4b contain exercises with four back-to-back trichords. In these exercises, however, one or more of the motives is transposed. (See Example S.9.)

**EX. S.9**—Set 2.3a Sample Exercise

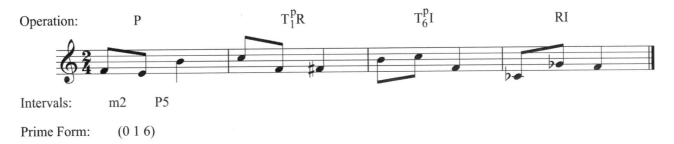

Except for transposition, the sets incorporate the same shape and interval criteria as Sets 2.1a–2.2b.

**TABLE S.6** Criteria for Sets 2.3a–2.4b

| Set | Interval Size | $T_n^p$ | Shape |
| --- | --- | --- | --- |
| 2.3a | Dissimilar | Yes | Jagged |
| 2.3b | Dissimilar | Yes | Smooth |
| 2.4a | Similar | Yes | Jagged |
| 2.4b | Similar | Yes | Smooth |

## Listening strategies for sets 2.3a–2.4b

Register and pitch cannot be relied upon to identify motivic operations under transposition since the complete motive may be shifted to another register, thus introducing a new set of pitches altogether. Under these circumstances, shapes and intervals take on more importance. In many cases, the *relative* sizes of intervals alone may be enough to establish connections between motives. It happens, for example, that if the prime motive begins with a relatively small interval followed by a larger interval, as in Example S.9, the inversion will also begin with a small interval followed by a larger interval. The retrograde and retrograde inversion reverse these so that the larger interval comes first and the smaller interval second.

The large/small interval distinction becomes less pronounced in Sets 2.2b and 2.3b where intervals are relatively similar in size and and/or type (e.g., major and minor seconds, major and minor thirds, perfect fourths and fifths). This makes it necessary to calculate intervals more precisely to determine operations. Fortunately, the shape distinctions discussed in conjunction with the exercises in Sets 2.1a–2.2b remain valid when sets are transposed; the contour adjacency series of the prime motive, for example, matches that of the retrograde in jagged motives and that of the retrograde inversion in smooth motives. (See Figures S.2 and S.3.)

## Sets 2.5a–2.6b

Sets 2.5a–2.6b incorporate **pitch imbrication**; each motive overlaps with those on either side of it as shown in Figure S.4.

**FIGURE S.4** Schematic for Imbricated Motives

Like the other sets in STREAM 2, these sets continue to be organized around similar/dissimilar intervals and jagged/smooth shapes. The fact that the motives overlap also means, of course, that motives must often be transposed since imbrication by pitch requires the first note of the second motive in each imbricated pair to match the last pitch of the first.

**TABLE S.7** Criteria for Sets 2.5a–2.6b

| Set | Interval Size | Shape |
|-----|--------------|-------|
| 2.5a | Dissimilar | Jagged |
| 2.5b | Dissimilar | Smooth |
| 2.6a | Similar | Jagged |
| 2.6b | Similar | Smooth |

## Listening strategies for sets 2.5a–2.6b

Shape and interval criteria for exercises 2.5a–2.6b are the same as those for the other exercises in STREAM 2. The main difference is that the operations occur in more rapid succession. Keeping track of downbeats is essential since all motives either begin or end on a downbeat as illustrated in Example S.10.

**EX. S.10**—Sample Exercise with Imbricated Motives

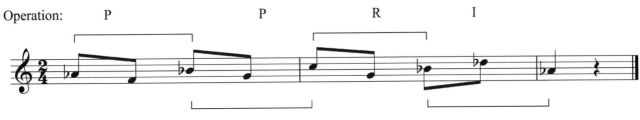

Operation:    P              P        R        I

Intervals:    m3        P4

Prime Form:    ( 0 2 5)

Smooth contours may be somewhat easier to distinguish than jagged contours since a shift in direction also constitutes a change of operation. The fact that the overall contour of the prime matches that of the retrograde, moreover, allows the listener to form a quick hypothesis about the operations in an exercise. If the prime outlines a descent, for example, so will the retrograde inversion. The inversion and retrograde, meanwhile, will outline an ascent. A pair of descents at the beginning of an exercise, then, might very well turn out to be the prime imbricated with its transposed retrograde inversion as in Example S.11.

**EX. S.11**—Sample Exercise with Overlapping P and RI

This may not always be the case, however. The prime, for example, might also be paired with a transposed version of itself, producing two ascents or descents as in Example S.12.

**EX. S.12**—Sample Exercise with Overlapping Primes

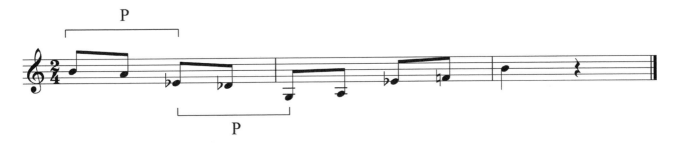

## Stream 3

### Operations and prime forms in melodies

Stream 3 exercises are similar to those in STREAM 2, with the exception that they incorporate more complex rhythmic contexts such as those in STREAM 1. As such, these exercises more closely resemble the music we play and listen to. Melodies, of course, are not always saturated by motives and their operations. In recognition of these circumstances, there are also a few exercises (Sets 3.7a–3.10b) with isolated motives.

The instructions for Sets 3.1a–3.6b are the same as those for STREAM 2:

> 1) Identify the two unordered pitch intervals of the prime motive in the order they occur.
> 2) Identify the operation (P, I, R, RI) of the remaining trichords.
> 3) Identify the prime form of the trichords in the exercise. (NOTE: All of the trichords in Sets 3.1a–3.6b will have the same prime form.)

### Sets 3.1a–3.2b

Like Sets 2.1a–2.2b, Sets 3.1a–3.2b contain four back-to-back trichords. In this case, however, the exercises incorporate more rhythmic variety than those in Sets 2.1a–2.2b and, thus, resemble the exercises in Stream 1. (See Example S.13.)

**EX. S.13**—Set 3.1a Sample Exercise

Operation:        P              R            I            RI

Intervals:        M2    TT

Prime Form:       (0 2 6)

The exercises maintain the dissimilar/similar, jagged/smooth distinctions used in STREAMS 1 and 2. None of the motives is transposed.

**TABLE S.8** Criteria for Sets 3.1a–3.2b

| Set | Interval Size | $T_n^p$ | Shape |
|-----|---------------|---------|-------|
| 3.1a | Dissimilar | No | Jagged |
| 3.1b | Dissimilar | No | Smooth |
| 3.2a | Similar | No | Jagged |
| 3.2b | Similar | No | Smooth |

## Listening strategies for sets 3.1a–3.2b

While the motives in Sets 3.1a–3.2b do not adhere to a strict rhythmic paradigm like those in STREAM 2 (e.g., eighth–eighth–quarter), for the most part, the first note of each motive or motive pairing is metrically accented. In addition, many of the exercises incorporate a repeated rhythmic idea. Thus, while the rhythms are more varied than those in STREAM 2, the student may continue to rely on rhythmic similarities and metrical accent to group pitches into motives.

### Sets 3.3a–3.4b

The exercises in Sets 3.3a–3.4b are similar to those in Sets 3.3a–3.4b, but include transposed motives as illustrated in Example S.14.

**EX. S.14**—Set 3.3a Sample Exercise

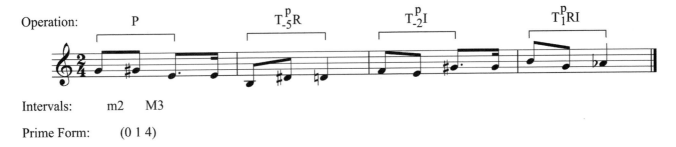

Intervals:      m2    M3

Prime Form:      (0 1 4)

The shape and interval criteria match those for Sets 2.3a–2.4b.

**TABLE S.9** Criteria for Sets 3.3a–3.4b

| Set | Interval Size | $T_n^p$ | Shape |
|-----|---------------|---------|-------|
| 3.3a | Dissimilar | Yes | Jagged |
| 3.3b | Dissimilar | Yes | Smooth |
| 3.4a | Similar | Yes | Jagged |
| 3.4b | Similar | Yes | Smooth |

## Listening strategies for sets 3.3a–3.4b

To find hints for completing these exercises successfully, revisit the Listening Strategies for Sets 2.3a–2.4b in the discussion of STREAM 2.

### Sets 3.5a–3.6b

The melodies in Sets 3.5a–3.6b incorporate pitch imbrication: some of the motives overlap. Unlike Sets 2.5a–2.6b, however, Sets 3.5a–3.6b contain two separate pairs of overlapping motives as illustrated in Figure S.5.

**FIGURE S.5** Imbrication Schematic for STREAM 3 Exercises

In addition to the criteria in the chart below, some of the motives are transposed.

**TABLE S.10** Criteria for Sets 3.5a–3.6b

| Set | Interval Size | Shape |
|-----|--------------|-------|
| 3.5a | Dissimilar | Jagged |
| 3.5b | Dissimilar | Smooth |
| 3.6a | Similar | Jagged |
| 3.6b | Similar | Smooth |

## Listening strategies for sets 3.5a–3.6b

The melodies in Sets 3.5a–3.6b can easily be divided into two five-note groupings because the first pair ends with a relatively long inter-onset duration as in Example S15 . . .

**EX. S.15**—Sample Exercise with Long Inter-Onset Duration

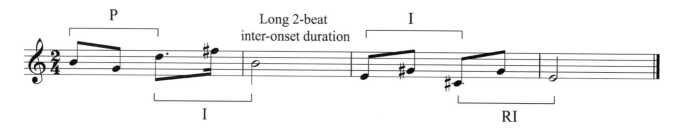

. . . and/or because the units are rhythmically parallel . . .

**EX. S.16**—Sample Exercise with Rhythmically Parallel Units

. . . or distinct.

**EX. S.17**—Sample Exercise with Rhythmically Distinct Units

Regardless of how they are broken down, each grouping contains two motives imbricated by pitch.

## Sets 3.7a–3.8b

The exercises in Sets 3.7a–3.8b consist of melodies with two isolated motives as illustrated in Example S.18. The second motive in Sets 3.8a and b is a transposed version of the first.

**EX. S.18**—Set 3.7a Sample Exercise

Intervals:       M3    m2                                    M3   m2

Prime Form:  (0 1 4)

Although these exercises continue to distinguish between jagged and smooth shapes, the intervals are mixed.

**TABLE S.11** Criteria for Sets 3.7a–3.8b

| Set | Interval Size | $T_n^p$ | Shape |
|-----|---------------|---------|-------|
| 3.7a | Mixed | No | Jagged |
| 3.7b | Mixed | No | Smooth |
| 3.8a | Mixed | Yes | Jagged |
| 3.8b | Mixed | Yes | Smooth |

The instructions are to . . .

> 1) Identify the two unordered pitch intervals of the repeated motive in the order they occur, and
> 2) Identify the matching prime form of the trichords in the exercise.

## Listening strategies for sets 3.7a–3.8b

The exercises in Sets 3.7a–3.8b take into account the fact that while melodies spring from a germinal motivic idea, the melody itself may not always be saturated by the motive. The untransposed motives in Sets 3.7a and b may be recognized by their pitch content as well as their shapes and intervals. Because the second motive in Sets 3.8a and b is transposed, the student will need to rely primarily on shape/interval criteria to identify motives. As in the other STREAM 3 exercises, the motives in these exercises are metrically and rhythmically highlighted.

## Sets 3.9a–3.10b

The exercises in Sets 3.9a–3.10b are similar to those in Sets 3.7a–3.8b with the exception that the second motive is either a transposed or untransposed P, I, R, or RI. (See Example S.19.)

**EX. S.19**—Set 3.9a Sample Exercise

Operation:                P                                                    I

Intervals:        P4        M2

Prime Form:     (0 2 5)

The shape and interval criteria is the same as for Sets 3.7a–3.8b.

**TABLE S.12** Criteria for Sets 3.10a–3.10b

| Set | Interval Size | $T_n^p$ | Shape |
| --- | --- | --- | --- |
| 3.9a | Mixed | No | Jagged |
| 3.9b | Mixed | No | Smooth |
| 3.10a | Mixed | Yes | Jagged |
| 3.10b | Mixed | Yes | Smooth |

The instructions are to . . .

> 1) Identify the two unordered pitch intervals of the repeated motive in the order they occur,
> 2) Identify the operation, P, I, R, or RI, of the second motive, and
> 3) Identify the matching prime form of the trichords in the exercise.

## Listening strategies for sets 3.9a–3.10b

The exercises in Sets 3.9a–3.10b require close attention to both interval and shape. Here, shape can be extremely helpful for extracting motives. In exercises with jagged motives, for example, much of the remaining content of the melody will consist of smooth ascending or descending motion. The opposite will be true in exercises with smooth motives.

Inversion, retrogression, and retrograde inversion are not the only processes used to generate melodic material. As the student gains facility listening to music using the concepts described in this supplement, other processes, including intervallic expansions and contractions, may also begin to surface. In addition, the skills used to complete these exercises may be extended to motives consisting of four or more pitches. Approached in this way, motivic analysis can provide a strong foundation for the aural interpretation of a broad array of works written since 1890 and even before.

# Appendix A

## Modes of Limited Transposition

Mode 1 (Whole-tone)—1 mode, 1 transposition

Mode 2 (Octatonic)—2 modes, 3 transpositions

Mode 3—3 modes, 4 transpositions

Mode 4—4 modes, 6 transpositions

Mode 5—3 modes, 6 transpositions

Mode 6—4 modes, 6 transpositions

Mode 7—5 modes, 6 transpositions

Olivier Messiaen (1956 [1944]) provides examples of all but the first mode of limited transposition in *The Technique of My Musical Language*, Vol. 2, Paris: Alphonse Leduc (50–61, Examples 312–82).

# Appendix B

## Set-Classes*

|  | PF | IC Vector | $T_n/T_nI$ Mappings |  | PF | IC Vector |
|---|---|---|---|---|---|---|
| 2–1 | (0 1) | [100000] | 1/1 | 10–1 | (0 1 2 3 4 5 6 7 8 9) | [988884] |
| 2–2 | (0 2) | [010000] | 1/1 | 10–2 | (0 1 2 3 4 5 6 7 8 T) | [898884] |
| 2–3 | (0 3) | [001000] | 1/1 | 10–3 | (0 1 2 3 4 5 6 7 9 T) | [889884] |
| 2–4 | (0 4) | [000100] | 1/1 | 10–4 | (0 1 2 3 4 5 6 8 9 T) | [888984] |
| 2–5 | (0 5) | [000010] | 1/1 | 10–5 | (0 1 2 3 4 5 7 8 9 T) | [888894] |
| 2–6 | (0 6) | [000001] | 2/2 | 10–6 | (0 1 2 3 4 6 7 8 9 T) | [888885] |
|  |  |  |  |  |  |  |
| 3–1 | (0 1 2) | [210000] | 1/1 | 9–1 | (0 1 2 3 4 5 6 7 8) | [876663] |
| 3–2 | (0 1 3) | [111000] | 1/0 | 9–2 | (0 1 2 3 4 5 6 7 9) | [777663] |
| 3–3 | (0 1 4) | [101100] | 1/0 | 9–3 | (0 1 2 3 4 5 6 8 9) | [767763] |
| 3–4 | (0 1 5) | [100110] | 1/0 | 9–4 | (0 1 2 3 4 5 7 8 9) | [766773] |
| 3–5 | (0 1 6) | [100011] | 1/0 | 9–5 | (0 1 2 3 4 6 7 8 9) | [766674] |
| 3–6 | (0 2 4) | [020100] | 1/1 | 9–6 | (0 1 2 3 4 5 6 8 T) | [686763] |
| 3–7 | (0 2 5) | [011010] | 1/0 | 9–7 | (0 1 2 3 4 5 7 8 T) | [677673] |
| 3–8 | (0 2 6) | [010101] | 1/0 | 9–8 | (0 1 2 3 4 6 7 8 T) | [676764] |
| 3–9 | (0 2 7) | [010020] | 1/1 | 9–9 | (0 1 2 3 5 6 7 8 T) | [676683] |
| 3–10 | (0 3 6) | [002001] | 1/1 | 9–10 | (0 1 2 3 4 6 7 9 T) | [668664] |
| 3–11 | (0 3 7) | [001110] | 1/0 | 9–11 | (0 1 2 3 5 6 7 9 T) | [667773] |
| 3–12 | (0 4 8) | [000300] | 3/3 | 9–12 | (0 1 2 4 5 6 8 9 T) | [666963] |
|  |  |  |  |  |  |  |
| 4–1 | (0 1 2 3) | [321000] | 1/1 | 8–1 | (0 1 2 3 4 5 6 7) | [765442] |
| 4–2 | (0 1 2 4) | [221100] | 1/0 | 8–2 | (0 1 2 3 4 5 6 8) | [665542] |
| 4–3 | (0 1 3 4} | [212100] | 1/1 | 8–3 | (0 1 2 3 4 5 6 9) | [656542] |
| 4–4 | (0 1 2 5) | [211110] | 1/0 | 8–4 | (0 1 2 3 4 5 7 8) | [655552] |
| 4–5 | (0 1 2 6) | [210111] | 1/0 | 8–5 | (0 1 2 3 4 6 7 8) | [654553] |
| 4–6 | (0 1 2 7) | [210021] | 1/1 | 8–6 | (0 1 2 3 5 6 7 8) | [654463] |
| 4–7 | (0 1 4 5) | [201210] | 1/1 | 8–7 | (0 1 2 3 4 5 8 9) | [645652] |
| 4–8 | (0 1 5 6) | [200121] | 1/1 | 8–8 | (0 1 2 3 4 7 8 9) | [644563] |
| 4–9 | (0 1 6 7) | [200022] | 2/2 | 8–9 | (0 1 2 3 6 7 8 9) | [644464] |
| 4–10 | (0 2 3 5) | [122010] | 1/1 | 8–10 | (0 2 3 4 5 6 7 9) | [566452] |
| 4–11 | (0 1 3 5) | [121110] | 1/0 | 8–11 | (0 1 2 3 4 5 7 9) | [565552] |
| 4–12 | (0 2 3 6) | [112101] | 1/0 | 8–12 | (0 1 3 4 5 6 7 9) | [556543] |
| 4–13 | (0 1 3 6) | [112011] | 1/0 | 8–13 | (0 1 2 3 4 6 7 9) | [556453] |
| 4–14 | (0 2 3 7) | [111120] | 1/0 | 8–14 | (0 1 2 4 5 6 7 9) | [555562] |
| 4–Z15 | (0 1 4 6) | [111111] | 1/0 | 8–Z15 | (0 1 2 3 4 6 8 9) | [555553] |
| 4–16 | (0 1 5 7) | [110121] | 1/0 | 8–16 | (0 1 2 3 5 7 8 9) | [554563] |

| | PF | IC Vector | $T_n/T_nI$ Mappings | | PF | IC Vector |
|---|---|---|---|---|---|---|
| 4–17 | (0 3 4 7) | [102210] | 1/1 | 8–17 | (0 1 3 4 5 6 8 9) | [546652] |
| 4–18 | (0 1 4 7) | [102111] | 1/0 | 8–18 | (0 1 2 3 5 6 8 9) | [546553] |
| 4–19 | (0 1 4 8) | [101310] | 1/0 | 8–19 | (0 1 2 4 5 6 8 9) | [545752] |
| 4–20 | (0 1 5 8) | [101220] | 1/1 | 8–20 | (0 1 2 4 5 7 8 9) | [545662] |
| 4–21 | (0 2 4 6) | [030201] | 1/1 | 8–21 | (0 1 2 3 4 6 8 T) | [474643] |
| 4–22 | (0 2 4 7) | [021120] | 1/0 | 8–22 | (0 1 2 3 5 6 8 T) | [465562] |
| 4–23 | (0 2 5 7) | [021030] | 1/1 | 8–23 | (0 1 2 3 5 7 8 T) | [465472] |
| 4–24 | (0 2 4 8) | [020301] | 1/1 | 8–24 | (0 1 2 4 5 6 8 T) | [464743] |
| 4–25 | (0 2 6 8) | [020202] | 2/2 | 8–25 | (0 1 2 4 6 7 8 T) | [464644] |
| 4–26 | (0 3 5 8) | [012120] | 1/1 | 8–26 | (0 1 3 4 5 7 8 T) | [456562] |
| 4–27 | (0 2 5 8) | [012111] | 1/0 | 8–27 | (0 1 2 4 5 7 8 T) | [456553] |
| 4–28 | (0 3 6 9) | [004002] | 4/4 | 8–28 | (0 1 3 4 6 7 9 T) | [448444] |
| 4–Z29 | (0 1 3 7) | [111111] | 1/0 | 8–Z29 | (0 1 2 3 5 6 7 9) | [555553] |
| | | | | | | |
| 5–1 | (0 1 2 3 4) | [432100] | 1/1 | 7–1 | (0 1 2 3 4 5 6) | [654321] |
| 5–2 | (0 1 2 3 5) | [332110] | 1/0 | 7–2 | (0 1 2 3 4 5 7) | [554331] |
| 5–3 | (0 1 2 4 5) | [322210] | 1/0 | 7–3 | (0 1 2 3 4 5 8) | [544431] |
| 5–4 | (0 1 2 3 6) | [322111] | 1/0 | 7–4 | (0 1 2 3 4 6 7) | [544332] |
| 5–5 | (0 1 2 3 7) | [321121] | 1/0 | 7–5 | (0 1 2 3 5 6 7) | [543342] |
| 5–6 | (0 1 2 5 6) | [311211] | 1/0 | 7–6 | (0 1 2 3 4 7 8) | [533442] |
| 5–7 | (0 1 2 6 7) | [310132] | 1/0 | 7–7 | (0 1 2 3 6 7 8) | [532353] |
| 5–8 | (0 2 3 4 6) | [232201] | 1/1 | 7–8 | (0 2 3 4 5 6 8) | [454422] |
| 5–9 | (0 1 2 4 6) | [231211] | 1/0 | 7–9 | (0 1 2 3 4 6 8) | [453432] |
| 5–10 | (0 1 3 4 6) | [223111] | 1/0 | 7–10 | (0 1 2 3 4 6 9) | [445332] |
| 5–11 | (0 2 3 4 7) | [222220] | 1/0 | 7–11 | (0 1 3 4 5 6 8) | [444441] |
| 5–Z12 | (0 1 3 5 6) | [222121] | 1/1 | 7–12 | (0 1 2 3 4 7 9) | [444342] |
| 5–13 | (0 1 2 4 8) | [221311] | 1/0 | 7–13 | (0 1 2 4 5 6 8) | [443532] |
| 5–14 | (0 1 2 5 7) | [221131] | 1/0 | 7–14 | (0 1 2 3 5 7 8) | [443352] |
| 5–15 | (0 1 2 6 8) | [220222] | 1/1 | 7–15 | (0 1 2 4 6 7 8) | [442443] |
| 5–16 | (0 1 3 4 7) | [213211] | 1/0 | 7–16 | (0 1 2 3 5 6 9) | [435432] |
| 5–Z17 | (0 1 3 4 8) | [212320] | 1/1 | 7–Z17 | (0 1 2 4 5 6 9) | [434541] |
| 5–Z18 | (0 1 4 5 7) | [212221] | 1/0 | 7–Z18 | (0 1 4 5 6 7 9) | [434442] |
| 5–19 | (0 1 3 6 7) | [212122] | 1/0 | 7–19 | (0 1 2 3 6 7 9) | [434343] |
| 5–20 | (0 1 5 6 8) | [211231] | 1/0 | 7–20 | (0 1 2 5 6 7 9) | [433452] |
| 5–21 | (0 1 4 5 8) | [202420] | 1/0 | 7–21 | (0 1 2 4 5 8 9) | [424641] |
| 5–22 | (0 1 4 7 8) | [202321] | 1/1 | 7–22 | (0 1 2 5 6 8 9) | [424542] |
| 5–23 | (0 2 3 5 7) | [132130] | 1/0 | 7–23 | (0 2 3 4 5 7 9) | [354351] |
| 5–24 | (0 1 3 5 7) | [131221] | 1/0 | 7–24 | (0 1 2 3 5 7 9) | [353442] |
| 5–25 | (0 2 3 5 8) | [123121] | 1/0 | 7–25 | (0 2 3 4 6 7 9) | [345342] |
| 5–26 | (0 2 4 5 8) | [122311] | 1/0 | 7–26 | (0 1 3 4 5 7 9) | [344532] |
| 5–27 | (0 1 3 5 8) | [122230] | 1/0 | 7–27 | (0 1 2 4 5 7 9) | [344451] |
| 5–28 | (0 2 3 6 8) | [122212] | 1/0 | 7–28 | (0 1 3 5 6 7 9) | [344433] |
| 5–29 | (0 1 3 6 8) | [122131] | 1/0 | 7–29 | (0 1 2 4 6 7 9) | [344352] |
| 5–30 | (0 1 4 6 8) | [121321] | 1/0 | 7–30 | (0 1 2 4 6 8 9) | [343542] |
| 5–31 | (0 1 3 6 9) | [114112] | 1/0 | 7–31 | (0 1 3 4 6 7 9) | [336333] |
| 5–32 | (0 1 4 6 9) | [113221] | 1/0 | 7–32 | (0 1 3 4 6 8 9) | [335442] |
| 5–33 | (0 2 4 6 8) | [040402] | 1/1 | 7–33 | (0 1 2 4 6 8 T) | [262623] |
| 5–34 | (0 2 4 6 9) | [032221] | 1/1 | 7–34 | (0 1 3 4 6 8 T) | [254442] |
| 5–35 | (0 2 4 7 9) | [032140] | 1/1 | 7–35 | (0 1 3 5 6 8 T) | [254361] |
| 5–Z36 | (0 1 2 4 7) | [222121] | 1/0 | 7–Z36 | (0 1 2 3 5 6 8) | [444342] |
| 5–Z37 | (0 3 4 5 8) | [212320] | 1/1 | 7–Z37 | (0 1 3 4 5 7 8) | [434541] |
| 5–Z38 | (0 1 2 5 8) | [212221] | 1/0 | 7–Z38 | (0 1 2 4 5 7 8) | [434442] |

|        | PF          | IC Vector  | $T_n/T_nI$ Mappings |         | PF          |
|--------|-------------|------------|---------------------|---------|-------------|
| 6–1    | (0 1 2 3 4 5) | [433221] | 1/1 |         |             |
| 6–2    | (0 1 2 3 4 6) | [443211] | 1/0 |         |             |
| 6–Z3   | (0 1 2 3 5 6) | [433221] | 1/0 | 6–Z36 | (0 1 2 3 4 7) |
| 6–Z4   | (0 1 2 4 5 6) | [432321] | 1/1 | 6–Z37 | (0 1 2 3 4 8) |
| 6–5    | (0 1 2 3 6 7) | [422232] | 1/0 |         |             |
| 6–Z6   | (0 1 2 5 6 7) | [421242] | 1/1 | 6–Z38 | (0 1 2 3 7 8) |
| 6–7    | (0 1 2 6 7 8) | [420243] | 2/2 |         |             |
| 6–8    | (0 2 3 4 5 7) | [343230] | 1/1 |         |             |
| 6–9    | (0 1 2 3 5 7) | [342231] | 1/0 |         |             |
| 6–Z10  | (0 1 3 4 5 7) | [333321] | 1/0 | 6–Z39 | (0 2 3 4 5 8) |
| 6–Z11  | (0 1 2 4 5 7) | [333231] | 1/0 | 6–Z40 | (0 1 2 3 5 8) |
| 6–Z12  | (0 1 2 4 6 7) | [332232] | 1/0 | 6–Z41 | (0 1 2 3 6 8) |
| 6–Z13  | (0 1 3 4 6 7) | [324222] | 1/1 | 6–Z42 | (0 1 2 3 6 9) |
| 6–14   | (0 1 3 4 5 8) | [323430] | 1/0 |         |             |
| 6–15   | (0 1 2 4 5 8) | [323421] | 1/0 |         |             |
| 6–16   | (0 1 4 5 6 8) | [322431] | 1/0 |         |             |
| 6–Z17  | (0 1 2 4 7 8) | [322332] | 1/0 | 6–Z43 | (0 1 2 5 6 8) |
| 6–18   | (0 1 2 5 7 8) | [322242] | 1/0 |         |             |
| 6–Z19  | (0 1 3 4 7 8) | [313431] | 1/0 | 6–Z44 | (0 1 2 5 6 9) |
| 6–20   | (0 1 4 5 8 9) | [303630] | 3/3 |         |             |
| 6–21   | (0 2 3 4 6 8) | [242412] | 1/0 |         |             |
| 6–22   | (0 1 2 4 6 8) | [241422] | 1/0 |         |             |
| 6–Z23  | (0 2 3 5 6 8) | [234222] | 1/1 | 6–Z45 | (0 2 3 4 6 9) |
| 6–Z24  | (0 1 3 4 6 8) | [233331] | 1/0 | 6–Z46 | (0 1 2 4 6 9) |
| 6–Z25  | (0 1 3 5 6 8) | [233241] | 1/0 | 6–Z47 | (0 1 2 4 7 9) |
| 6–Z26  | (0 1 3 5 7 8) | [232341] | 1/1 | 6–Z48 | (0 1 2 5 7 9) |
| 6–27   | (0 1 3 4 6 9) | [225222] | 1/0 |         |             |
| 6–Z28  | (0 1 3 5 6 9) | [224322] | 1/1 | 6–Z49 | (0 1 3 4 7 9) |
| 6–Z29  | (0 2 3 6 7 9) | [224232] | 1/1 | 6–Z50 | (0 1 4 6 7 9) |
| 6–30   | (0 1 3 6 7 9) | [224223] | 2/0 |         |             |
| 6–31   | (0 1 4 5 7 9) | [223431] | 1/0 |         |             |
| 6–32   | (0 2 4 5 7 9) | [143250] | 1/1 |         |             |
| 6–33   | (0 2 3 5 7 9) | [143241] | 1/0 |         |             |
| 6–34   | (0 1 3 5 7 9) | [142422] | 1/0 |         |             |
| 6–35   | (0 2 4 6 8 T) | [060603] | 6/6 |         |             |

*Hexachords in the right column have the same interval-class vector as their complements. If no complementary hexachord appears in the right column the hexachord is its own complement.

# Appendix C

## Familiar Sets

Diatonic Collection 7–35 (0 1 3 5 6 8 T)

| | | |
|---|---|---|
| 2–1 (0 1) | 3–10 (0 3 6) | 4–Z29 (0 1 3 7)* |
| 2–2 (0 2) | 3–11 (0 3 7) | 5–Z12 (0 1 3 5 6) |
| 2–3 (0 3) | 4–8 (0 1 5 6) | 5–20 (0 1 5 6 8) |
| 2–4 (0 4) | 4–11 (0 1 3 5) | 5–23 (0 2 3 5 7) |
| 2–5 (0 5) | 4–13 (0 1 3 6) | 5–24 (0 1 3 5 7) |
| 2–6 (0 6) | 4–14 (0 2 3 7) | 5–25 (0 2 3 5 8) |
| 3–2 (0 1 3) | 4–16 (0 1 5 7) | 5–27 (0 1 3 5 8) |
| 3–4 (0 1 5) | 4–20 (0 1 5 8) | 5–35 (0 2 4 7 9)** |
| 3–5 (0 1 6) | 4–21 (0 2 4 6) | 6–Z25 (0 1 3 5 6 8) |
| 3–6 (0 2 4) | 4–22 (0 2 4 7) | 6–Z26 (0 1 3 5 7 8) |
| 3–7 (0 2 5) | 4–23 (0 2 5 7) | 6–32 (0 2 4 5 7 9) |
| 3–8 (0 2 6) | 4–26 (0 3 5 8) | 6–33 (0 2 3 5 7 9) |
| 3–9 (0 2 7) | 4–27 (0 2 5 8) | |

*All-interval tetrachord
** Pentatonic scale

Octatonic Collection 8–28 (0 1 3 4 6 7 9 T)

| | | |
|---|---|---|
| 2–1 (0 1) | 4–3 (0 1 3 4) | 5–16 (0 1 3 4 7) |
| 2–2 (0 2) | 4–9 (0 1 6 7) | 5–19 (0 1 3 6 7) |
| 2–3 (0 3) | 4–10 (0 2 3 5) | 5–25 (0 2 3 5 8) |
| 2–4 (0 4) | 4–12 (0 2 3 6) | 5–28 (0 2 3 6 8) |
| 2–5 (0 5) | 4–13 (0 1 3 6) | 5–31 (0 1 3 6 9) |
| 2–6 (0 6) | 4–Z15 (0 1 4 6)* | 5–32 (0 1 4 6 9) |
| 3–2 (0 1 3) | 4–18 (0 1 4 7) | 6–Z13 (0 1 3 4 6 7) |
| 3–3 (0 1 4) | 4–25 (0 2 6 8) | 6–Z23 (0 2 3 5 6 8) |
| 3–5 (0 1 6) | 4–26 (0 3 5 8) | 6–27 (0 1 3 4 6 9) |
| 3–7 (0 2 5) | 4–27 (0 2 5 8) | 6–30 (0 1 3 6 7 9) |
| 3–8 (0 2 6) | 4–28 (0 3 6 9) | 6–Z49 (0 1 3 4 7 9) |
| 3–10 (0 3 6) | 4–Z29 (0 1 3 7)* | 6–Z50 (0 1 4 6 7 9) |
| 3–11 (0 3 7) | 5–10 (0 1 3 4 6) | 7–31 (0 1 3 4 6 7 9) |

*All-interval tetrachord

Pentatonic Collection 5–35 (0 2 4 7 9)

| | | |
|---|---|---|
| 2–2 (0 2) | 3–6 (0 2 4) | 4–22 (0 2 4 7) |
| 2–3 (0 3) | 3–7 (0 2 5) | 4–23 (0 2 5 7) |
| 2–4 (0 4) | 3–9 (0 2 7) | 4–26 (0 3 5 8) |
| 2–5 (0 5) | 3–11 (0 3 7) | |

Whole-tone Scale 6–35 (0 2 4 6 8 T)

| | | |
|---|---|---|
| 2–2 (0 2) | 3–8 (0 2 6) | 4–25 (0 2 6 8) |
| 2–4 (0 4) | 3–12 (0 4 8) | 5–33 (0 2 4 6 8) |
| 2–6 (0 6) | 4–21 (0 2 4 6) | |
| 3–6 (0 2 4) | 4–24 (0 2 4 8) | |

Circle-of-Fifths (no subsets given)

| | |
|---|---|
| 2–5 (0 5) | 7–35 (0 1 3 5 6 8 T)* |
| 3–9 (0 2 7) | 8–23 (0 1 2 3 5 7 8 T) |
| 4–23 (0 2 5 7) | 9–9 (0 1 2 3 5 6 7 8 T) |
| 5–35 (0 2 4 7 9) | 10–5 (0 1 2 3 4 6 7 8 9 E) |
| 6–32 (0 2 4 5 7 9) | |

*Diatonic collection

All-interval Tetrachord 4–Z15 (0 1 3 7)

| | |
|---|---|
| 2–1 (0 1) | 2–6 (0 6) |
| 2–2 (0 2) | 3–2 (0 1 3) |
| 2–3 (0 3) | 3–5 (0 1 6) |
| 2–4 (0 4) | 3–8 (0 2 6) |
| 2–5 (0 5) | 3–11 (0 3 7) |

All-interval Tetrachord 4–Z29 (0 1 4 6)

| | |
|---|---|
| 2–1 (0 1) | 2–6 (0 6) |
| 2–2 (0 2) | 3–3 (0 1 4) |
| 2–3 (0 3) | 3–5 (0 1 6) |
| 2–4 (0 4) | 3–7 (0 2 5) |
| 2–5 (0 5) | 3–8 (0 2 6) |

Other Familiar Chords

| | |
|---|---|
| 3–8 (0 2 6) Italian Sixth | 4–25 (0 2 6 8) French sixth |
| 3–10 (0 3 6) Diminished triad | 4–26 (0 3 5 8) Minor 7th |
| 3–11 (0 3 7) Major and minor triads | 4–27 (0 2 5 8) Dom. 7th/German sixth |
| 3–12 (0 4 8) Augmented triad | 4–28 (0 3 6 9) Fully diminished 7th |
| 4–14 (0 2 3 7) Half diminished 7th | |

# Notes

## Introduction

1 Paul Childs, *Modernism* (London: Routledge, 2000), 16–17.

2 Arnold Schoenberg, *Style and Idea* (New York: Philosophical Library, 1950), 39.

3 Arnold Schoenberg, *Style and Idea*, 47.

4 Arnold Schoenberg, *Style and Idea*, 104–5.

5 See Arnold Schoenberg, *Theory of Harmony* [*Harmonielehre*, 3rd ed.], Roy E. Carter trans. (Berkeley: University of California Press, 1978 [1922]), 432.

6 Twelve-tone compositions are based on a row derived from all twelve tones of the chromatic octave.

7 In tonal responses, intervals are adjusted to fit the key. Real responses preserve the precise interval content of the original theme.

8 Claude Debussy, *Claude Debussy on Music*, Richard Langham Smith trans. (New York: Alfred A. Knopff, 1977), 112. Debussy's dissatisfaction with German practice was apparently limited to the nineteenth century. He had great respect for J. S. Bach, who he acknowledged as the "one great master" (233).

9 See *A Ravel Reader*, Arbie Orenstein ed. (New York: Columbia University Press), 43–44.

10 The Spanish rhythms and themes used by Debussy (e.g., "*Iberia*" from *Image pour orchestre*, No. 2) and Ravel (e.g., *La Valse*, *Bolero*) are not necessarily examples of cultural appropriation. The Basque region of Europe, for example, extends from Spain to Southwestern France. Ravel was raised in the Basque region of France and Debussy spent time there.

11 Seeger himself recognized the negative connotations of his theory, having noted that "by definition the procedure was on the whole one of negation and contrariness." See Charles Seeger, "On Dissonant Counterpoint," *Modern Music* 7/4 (1930): 25–26.

12 See Pierre Boulez, "Schoenberg is Dead," in *Stocktakings from an Apprenticeship* (Oxford: Oxford University Press, 1991 [1966]), 212. This article was first published in 1952 in *The Score* 6 (1952): 18–22. Schoenberg's tendency to merge unfamiliar pitch structures with familiar forms and contrapuntal techniques has already been discussed in conjunction with Example 1. These are precisely the practices Boulez finds most offensive about Schoenberg's approach.

13 Pierre Boulez, "Schoenberg is Dead," 212. The term *serialism* is used to describe the practice of composing according to a predetermined series of musical elements such as pitches, dynamics, articulations, and durations.

14 See Pierre Boulez, "Incipit," in *Stocktakings from an Apprenticeship* (Oxford: Oxford University Press, 1991 [1966]), 215. See also Pierre Boulez, "Note to Tonight's Concert: Webern's Work Analysed" [sic], *New York Herald Tribune* (December 28, 1952).

15 See Pierre Boulez, *Stocktakings from an Apprenticeship* (Oxford: Oxford University Press, 1991 [1966]), 135. Boulez would later come to reject John Cage's methods. For more on Cage's complicated relationship with Boulez see Michael Hicks, "John Cage's Studies with Schoenberg," *American Music* 8/2 (1990): 125–40 and *The Boulez–Cage Correspondence*, Jean-Jacques Nattiez and Robert Samuels eds. (Cambridge: Cambridge University Press, 1995).

16  Joseph N. Straus provides an interesting perspective on this subject in *Remaking the Past: Musical Modernism and the Influence of the Tonal Tradition* (Cambridge: Harvard University Press, 1990), 185. Straus argues that twentieth-century composers sometimes recomposed the music of their predecessors in order to "push their precursors aside and clear creative space for themselves."

17  Socialist realism was the official stylistic paradigm advocated, and in some cases enforced, by leaders of the communist party in the Soviet Union beginning in 1917 and continuing until the 1980s.

18  Like modernism, postmodernism too is a contested term. In addition, there is disagreement about which artists, designers, and composers fit the category. Linda Hutcheon, for example, includes Stockhausen, a serialist composer and member of the Darmstadt school, among the ranks of the postmodernists. See Linda Hutcheon, *The Poetics of Postmodernism: History, Theory, Fiction* (London: Routledge, 1988), 24. Jonathan D. Kramer argues that many musical works cannot be accurately categorized as either modern or postmodern. See Jonathan D. Kramer, "Can Modernism Survive George Rochberg?" *Critical Inquiry* 11/2 (1984): 341–54. (See also George Rochberg, "Can the Arts Survive Modernism? (A Discussion of the Characteristics, History, and Legacy of Modernism)," *Critical Inquiry* 11/2 (1984): 317–40.) If works do not always fall into one or the other of these camps, their individual features often do. Here, we will take the position that postmodernism can be a useful designation as long as we differentiate between the characteristics it shares with modernism and those it does not.

19  See Charles Jencks, *What is Post-Modernism?* 4th ed. (Great Britain: Academy Editions, 1996), 29.

20  Charles Jencks, *What is Post-Modernism?*, 29.

21  Crumb explains his views on postmodernism in an interview with Anna Sale on "Outlook," *West Virginia Public Broadcasting* (December 21, 2007). This interview may be found online at www.YouTube.com.watch?v= 5xo86H;Txpc. Accessed June 25, 2010, 8:47 am central time.

22  Twentieth-century musicians and composers, including those in the Jazz and popular fields, continuously mediate between the eighteenth- and nineteenth-century musical traditions of Western Europe and those of folk, indigenous, and African descent. The inescapable historical and social legacies of colonialism and slavery generate artistic processes of reaction, hybridization, adaptation, appropriation, and even rejection, all processes that continue to engage with various aspects of the European canon.

## 1   Scales, Harmony, and Referential Collections

1  Webern borrowed this idea from Arnold Schoenberg, who took a similar stance in his *Harmonielehre*, first published in 1911. See Arnold Schoenberg, *Theory of Harmony* [*Harmonielehre*, 3rd ed.], Roy E. Carter trans. (Berkeley: University of California Press, 1978 [1922]), 20–21.

2  A lawyer in attendance wrote down the lectures in shorthand and they were subsequently published under the title *The Path to the New Music*. See Anton Webern, *The Path to the New Music*, Willi Reich ed. (Bryn Mawr: Theodore Presser, 1960 [1932–33]), 16. The harmonic series is a naturally occurring acoustical phenomenon and will be discussed more fully in Chapter 9.

3  Ancient theorists privileged these intervals, not because of their position in the harmonic series, but because of their simple proportional relations, 1:2 (the octave), 2:3 (the perfect fifth), and 3:4 (the perfect fourth).

4  The first of these chords incorporates an interesting technique. The performer is instructed to hold the keys down without playing them. The notes of the chord resonate sympathetically when the left-hand part is played because they are members of the same harmonic series.

5  A more thorough explanation of inversion may be found in Chapters 2 and 3.

6  Olivier Messiaen covers a broad array of added note chords in *The Technique of My Musical Language, Vol. 1*, John Satterfield trans. (Paris: A. Leduc, 1956 [1944]), 47–49.

7  Alban Berg's Op. 2 No. 3, *Nun ich der Riesen Stürksten überwand*, m. 6, contains another example of this same added note chord.

8  These transformations are known as neo-Riemannian transformations because they are derived from Hugo Riemann's model of tonal relations in pitch-space. See Brian Hyer, "Reimag(in)ing Riemann," *Journal of Music Theory* 39/1 (1995): 101–38. Riemann's original work appears in *Musikalische Syntaxis: Grundriss einer harmonischen Satzbildungslehre* (Leipzig: Breitkopf & Härtel, 1877, Repr. Wiesbaden: Martin Sändig, 1971). See also Richard Cohn, "Introduction to Neo-Riemannian Theory: A Survey and a Historical Perspective," *Journal of Music Theory* 42/2 (1998): 167–80.

9  The German term *Leittonwechsel* is sometimes substituted for the term leading-tone exchange.

10  This approach reflects two important voice-leading rules often taught in conjunction with part-writing: 1) keep the common tone and 2) move to the nearest chord tone.

11  Daniel Harrison adopts a similar approach to this passage based on augmented sixths. See Daniel Harrison, "Supplement to the Theory of Augmented-Sixth Chords," *Music Theory Spectrum* 17/2 (1995): 170–95.

12  The octatonic collection is an eight-note collection consisting of alternating major and minor seconds and will be covered in the discussion of synthetic scales later in the chapter.

13  See Richard Taruskin, "Chernomor to Kashchei: Harmonic Sorcery; Or, Stravinsky's 'Angle,'" *Journal of the American Musicological Society* 38/1 (1985): 93 and 134–35. Discussions of the octatonic collection in Stravinsky's work may be found in Arthur Berger, "Problems of Pitch Organization in Stravinsky," *Perspectives of New Music* 2/1 (1963): 11–42 and Peter Van den Toorn, *The Music of Igor Stravinsky* (New Haven: Yale University Press, 1983).

14  Primary heptatonic scales contain two semitones, each of which is separated by two or three whole-tones. These correspond to the diatonic modes already introduced. Secondary heptatonic scales contain two semitones separated by one or four whole-tones.

15  The term anhemitonic means "without semitones."

16  The octatonic scale is also known as a *diminished scale* because there are a number of diminished triads and seventh chords embedded within it. As Richard Taruskin observes, moreover, "melodically embellished diminished and diminished seventh chords" often surface in the octatonic regions of common-practice music. See Richard Taruskin, "Chernomor to Kashchei: Harmonic Sorcery; Or, Stravinsky's 'Angle,'" 95.

17  See Olivier Messiaen, *The Technique of My Musical Language*, John Satterfield trans. (Paris: Leduc, 1956 [1944]), 59–62.


## 2  Pitch and Interval

1  "A" and "B" are also sometimes used to denote the integers 10 and 11. See Robert D. Morris, *Composition with Pitch-Classes* (New Haven: Yale University Press, 1987), 8.

2  Although it is often assigned to middle C, 0 can also be assigned to other pitches.

3  The mod 12 congruence between pitches may be verified by applying modulo arithmetic; e.g., 13 (C♯5) − 1 (C♯4) = 12, which is exactly divisible by 12 (12 ÷ 12 = 1). Congruent numbers larger than the modulo generate the same remainder when divided by the modulo. This remainder corresponds to the number's mod 12 form. Both 13 and 25, for example, generate a remainder of 1 when divided by 12. The mod 12 form of both numbers is, therefore, 1.

4  John Roeder uses the term "total interval content" to refer to the intervals (1–11) of pc sets in "A Geometric Representation of Pitch-class Series," *Perspectives of New Music* 25/1–2 (1987): 364.

5  Interval cycles have been discussed by numerous authors, including Elliot Antokoletz, "Organic Development and the Interval Cycles in Bartók's Three Studies, Op. 18," *Studia Musicologica* 36/3–4 (1995): 249–61 and *The Music of Béla Bartók: A Study of Tonality and Progression in Twentieth-Century Music* (Berkeley: University of California Press, 1984); George Perle, *The Listening Composer* (Berkeley: University of California Press, 1990), "Berg's Master Array of the Interval Cycles," *Musical Quarterly* 63/1 (1977): 1–30, and "Symmetrical Formations in the String Quartets of Béla Bartók," *The Music Review* 16 (1955): 300–12; and Philip Lambert, "Interval Cycles as Compositional Resources in the Music of Charles Ives," *Music Theory Spectrum* 12/1 (1990): 43–82.

6  See Edward Gollin, "Multi-Aggregate Cycles and Multi-Aggregate Serial Techniques in the Music of Béla Bartók," *Music Theory Spectrum* 29/2 (2007): 146.

7  For more in-depth discussions of cells and their relevance to Bartók's music see George Perle, "Symmetrical Formations in the String Quartets of Béla Bartók," *The Music Review* 16 (1955): 300–12; Leo Treitler, "Harmonic Procedure in the Fourth Quartet of Bartók," *Journal of Music Theory* 3/2 (1959): 292–97; and Elliot Antokoletz, *The Music of Béla Bartók: A Study of Tonality and Progression in Twentieth-Century Music*, 67–137 and *Twentieth-Century Music* (Englewood Cliffs, NJ: Prentice Hall, 1992), 119–36.

8  The concept of transpositional combination was first introduced by Richard Cohn in "Inversional Symmetry and Transpositional Combination in Bartók," *Music Theory Spectrum* 10 (1988): 19–42.

## 3  Sets and Segmentation

1  When the designation ordered or unordered is not specified, pc sets are understood to be unordered. Unordered pitch and pc sets are sometimes denoted with curly brackets ( { } ).

2  In music, the term retrograde means to reverse the order of the elements in a set. Here, reversing the adjacency interval series has no effect on the ordering of the intervals. As we shall see in the following chapters, other elements, including strings of pitches, pcs, and durations, may also be subjected to retrogression.

3  There is some disagreement about where the inversional axis of ordered pitch sets should be located. Like unordered pitch sets, ordered pitch sets are sometimes inverted about 0. See, for example, John Rahn, *Basic Atonal Theory* (New York: Schirmer, 1980), 45–46. Another common method is to invert about the median or midpoint in pitch-space. This may be a pitch (if both pitches are even or odd) or midway between two pitches (if only one pitch is even or odd). To find the midpoint, divide the index in half. If the index is 11, the midpoint is 5.5, that is, between F4 and F♯4. See Robert Morris, *Composition with Pitch-Classes: A Theory of Compositional Design* (New Haven: Yale University Press, 1987), 44–45, for a more thorough description of this process. Michael Cherlin acknowledges multiple inversional centers using descriptive designations such as "I$^{firstnote}$" and "I$^{center}$." See Michael Cherlin, "Dramaturgy and Mirror Imagery in Schoenberg's Moses und Aron: Two Paradigmatic Interval Palindromes," *Perspectives of New Music* 29/2 (1990): 51–54. Here, we will maintain consistency by inverting about the first note of both ordered pc and ordered pitch sets.

4  Twelve-tone composition will be discussed in Chapter 8.

5  Robert D. Morris, *Composition with Pitch-Classes* (New Haven: Yale University Press, 1987), 51 and 64, shortens these terms to "pcyc" and "pccyc."

6  The piece continues by cycling through all seven rotations of the set as well as its retrograde, inversion, and retrograde inversion transposed.

7  Dora Hanninen supplies formal criteria for measuring the relative salience of these and other factors in "Orientation, Criteria, Segments: A General Theory of Segmentation for Music Analysis," *Journal of Music Theory* 45/2 (2001): 345–433. See also Yayoi Uno, "Temporal–Gestalt Segmentation: Polyphonic Extensions and Applications to Works by Boulez, Cage, Xenakis, Ligeti, and Babbitt," *Computers in Music Research* 5 (1995): 1–38, Christopher Hasty, "Segmentation and Process in Post-Tonal Music," *Music Theory Spectrum* 3 (1981): 54–73, James Tennery and Larry Polansky, "Temporal Gestalt Perception in Music," *Journal of Music Theory* 24/2 (1980): 205–41, and David Lewin, "A Theory of Segmental Association in Twelve-Tone Music," *Perspectives of New Music* 1/1 (1962): 89–116.


## 4  Unordered Sets and Their Operations

1  Because they are among the most commonly used operations in music, transposition and inversion are sometimes referred to as *canonical*—i.e., standard—*operations*.

2  The rhythms in the piece ( ♪♪ ⁊, ♪♪ ⁊, ♪♪ ⁊, etc.) reinforce this idea by incorporating a pause between the "landing" and "leaping" dyads.

3  Note that in this case, the term chord inversion is used to loosely specify the process by which a chord is rearranged to begin on each of its members one by one. Inverted chords in tonal music are identified as such by the note that occurs in the bass. The other notes of the chord do not necessarily occur in order as they do in rotations.

4  Pc sets are abstractions based on the actual pitches that occur on the musical surface. Figures like this one and those that follow represent only one of many possible versions of such sets.

5  In this chapter, the term "interval" is used in the broadest sense and includes ics.

6  Another method for deriving prime forms is given on p. 108. If the instructor indicates a preference for this alternative, the discussion below may be skipped.

7  Miguel A. Roig-Francoli uses a similar method for calculating prime forms based on normal orders. Unlike the method presented here, Roig-Francoli's method is effective in most, but not all instances. See Miguel A. Roig-Francoli, *Understanding Post-tonal Music* (New York: McGraw-Hill, 2008), 83.

8  When stating prime forms aloud, zero is often replaced with the easier to pronounce "oh." Hence, we sometimes say "oh, one, four" instead of "zero, one, four."

## 5  Set-Class Analysis

1   The index numbers for sets of cardinality 3 through 9 correspond to those identified by Allen Forte, who was the first to codify set classes in this way. See Allan Forte, *The Structure of Atonal Music* (New Haven: Yale University Press, 1973), 179–81. Forte uses a different method for determining prime forms than the one used in this text. In Forte's method, intervals are compared starting with the interval between the first and second pitches, rather than the interval between the first and next-to-last pitches. This leads to different results in six instances. These six set classes, identified by their Forte names, are 5–20 (0 1 3 7 8), 6Z–29 (0 1 3 6 8 9), 6–31 (0 1 3 5 8 9), 7Z–18 (0 1 2 3 5 8 9), 7–20 (0 1 2 4 7 8 9), and 8–26 (0 1 2 4 5 7 9 T). Regardless of the method used, the hyphenated set class names remain the same.

2   The term trichord refers to three-note sets. Other sets have similar names and include *dyads* (two-note sets), *tetrachords* (four-note sets), *pentachords* (five-note sets), *hexachords* (six-note sets), *septachords* (seven-note sets), *octachords* (eight-note sets), and *nonachords* (nine-note sets).

3   The term complement was introduced in Chapter 2 as a property of pcs and their intervals.

4   See, for example, Eric J. Isaacson, "Similarity of Interval-class Content Between Pitch-class Sets: The IcVSIM Relation," *Journal of Music Theory* 34 (1990): 1–28 and Ian Quinn, "Listening to Similarity Relations," *Perspectives of New Music* 39 (2001): 108–58.

5   Joseph Straus, *Introduction to Post-Tonal Theory*, 3rd ed. (Upper Saddle River: Prentice Hall), 126–27, notes that the return of pc set [2, 4, 8, T] on the downbeat of m. 4 also "captures the idea expressed in the text of returning to a homeland."

6   Although analysts often concern themselves with the similarities between pitch structures, there are instances, such as this one, in which disparity too can play a strong structural as well as expressive role. David Lewin's "dispersive transformations" engage a similar concept in that they entail "minimal" connections between sets. See David Lewin, *Generalized Musical Intervals and Transformations* (New Haven: Yale University Press, 1987), 142.

7   All three of these chords may thus be thought of as added note chords. (See Chapter 1, p. 9.)

8   Bernstein himself described *Chichester Psalms* as a "tonal piece." See Leonard Bernstein, *Findings* (New York: Simon and Schuster, 1982), 237. While the work has a number of tonal features, however, there are few functional harmonies. It may be the term *tonal* itself that is the source of confusion here. Diatonic collections, triads, and pitch centricity are all characteristics of tonal music. Defining music solely in terms of these features, however, does not take into account the important role consonance and dissonance play in tonal music. We can, of course, understand and respect Bernstein's wish to distance himself from German modernism. But it is also important to remember that he had just emerged from an intensive two-year study of atonal techniques prior to beginning his work on the *Chichester Psalms*. While at its core this music may in fact lean toward tonality, then, it is also true that it incorporates rich non-triadic harmony as well as unordered and inversionally equivalent pitch structures. These "non-tonal" features are certainly worthy of our attention. Fortunately, it is not necessary to renounce either the tonal or non-tonal aspects of the piece to recognize that it builds on a broad range of styles, producing an altogether fresh sound, one that is in many ways unique to Bernstein himself.

9   Set class 6–30, (0 1 3 6 7 9), has two degrees of transpositional symmetry, but does not map onto itself under $T_nI$.

10  For a more thorough investigation of atonal voice leading, see David Lewin, "Transformational Techniques in Atonal and Other Music Theories," *Perspectives of New Music* 21 (1982–83): 312–71 and "Some Ideas about Voice leading Between Pcsets," *Journal of Music Theory* 42/1 (1998): 15–72.

11  Transposition is an example of an operation that is not its own inverse; that is, it does not undo itself when repeated. Instead, we must use the complement of $T_n$. Pc set [0, 1], for example, maps onto [3, 4] at $T_3$ while [3, 4] maps onto [0, 1] at $T_9$, the complement of $T_3$.

12  David Lewin published a landmark article on Klumpenhouwer networks in 1990, naming them for his doctoral student, Henry Klumpenhouwer, who first identified them. See David Lewin, "Klumpenhouwer Networks and some Isographies that Involve Them," *Music Theory Spectrum* 12 (1990): 83–120. Further explorations on the subject have been undertaken by a number of authors, including Henry Klumpenhouwer, "A General Model of Voice-Leading for Atonal Music," Ph.D. dissertation, Harvard University (1991), Philip Lambert, "Isographies and some Klumpenhouwer Networks They Involve," *Music Theory Spectrum* 24/2 (2002): 165–95, David Lewin, "Thoughts on Klumpenhouwer Networks and Perle-Lansky Cycles," *Music Theory Spectrum* 24/2 (2002): 196–230, and David Headlam, "Perle's Cyclic Sets and Klumpenhouwer Networks: A Response," *Music Theory Spectrum* 24/2 (2002): 246–56. Wedge or "axial" progressions like those in Hindemith's *Mathis*

*der maler* are discussed by Philip Stoecker in "Klumpenhouwer Networks, Trichords, and Axial Isography," *Music Theory Spectrum* 24/2 (2002): 231–45.

13  This repetitive figure occurs in multiple scenes, including No. 6 (*Flight*), No. 7 (*Patrol Car*), and No. 10 (*The Rainstorm*).

## 6  Ordered Pitch Sets and Their Operations

1  Shape/Interval motives were first pioneered by John Wm. Schaffer at the University of Wisconsin in the mid 1990s. Subsequent modifications were introduced by John Schaffer in collaboration with the author. For a more in-depth discussion of this topic see Edward Pearsall and John Wm. Schaffer, "Shape/Interval Contours and Their Ordered Transformations: A Motivic Approach to the Aural Analysis of Twentieth-Century Music," *College Music Symposium* 45 (2005): 57–80.

2  Motive analysis does not necessarily reflect either the intentions of the composer or the absolute structure of music. Rather, it is a tool for interpreting music that takes into account our human penchant for coherence and order. The fact that a passage can be parsed into motives at all, on the other hand, suggests that motives of one kind or another may have at least some bearing on its compositional origins.

3  The final motive in this excerpt is imbricated, but not interpolated.

4  In fact, all reorderings of a trichord can be accounted for through retrogression and/or rotation.

5  See Julian Hook, "Signature Transformations," In *Music Theory and Mathematics: Chords, Collections, and Transformations,* Jack Douthett, Martha M. Hyde, and Charles J. Smith eds. (Rochester: University of Rochester Press, 2008), 137–60.

6  The practice of representing words with pitches has a long history. One early example is Josquin des Prez's *Missa Hercules dux Ferrariae,* composed in honor of Ercole I d'Este, Duke of Ferrara, who ruled from 1471 to 1505. To derive the theme for this mass, des Prez matched the vowels in the duke's name with Guido de Arezzo's solmization syllables, *ut, re, mi, fa, sol, la.*

7  The use of two different symbols for B-flat and B-natural dates from the eleventh century. During this period, soft b (*b molle*) was represented by a rounded letter b while hard b (*b durum*) was represented by a square letter b. These shapes are the basis for the accidentals we use today, rounded b for flats and square b for naturals and sharps. Flat or soft b was required in early music to avoid the dissonant tritone with F.

## 7  Rhythm and Contour

1  See Michael Friedman, "A Methodology for the Discussion of Contour: Its Application to Schoenberg's Music," *Journal of Music Theory* 29/2 (1985): 226, for the original discussion of this term.

2  The term contour class is adapted from Michael Friedman, "A Methodology for the Discussion of Contour" and Robert D. Morris, *Composition with Pitch-Classes* (New Haven: Yale University Press, 1987), 29. Elizabeth West Marvin and Paul A. Laprade refer to contour classes as c-segments or csegs. See Elizabeth West Marvin and Paul A. Laprade, "Relating Musical Contours: Extensions of a Theory for Contour," *Journal of Music Theory* 31/2 (1987): 225–67. For a discussion of the similarities and differences in terminology relating to contour see Michael Friedman, "A Response: My Contour, Their Contour," *Journal of Music Theory* 31/2 (1987): 268–74. More recent explorations of contour have been undertaken by Robert D. Morris, "New Directions in the Theory and Analysis of Musical Contour," *Music Theory Spectrum* 15/2 (1993): 205–28; and Ian Quinn, "The Combinatorial Model of Pitch Contour," *Music Perception* 16/4 (1999): 439–56 and "Fuzzy Extensions to the Theory of Contour," *Music Theory Spectrum* 30/1 (1997): 232–63.

3  Elizabeth West Marvin and Paul A. LaPrade, "Relating Musical Contours," 228, refer to the contour class of a contour subset (or "c-subsegment") as its "normal form."

4  Using this approach, the proportional equivalence among equivalent durations remains the same regardless of meter. Durations can also be expressed in more familiar terms by assigning the number 1 to the whole note. Under these conditions, proportions and note names match: 1/4 for the quarter note, 1/2 for the half note, and so on. Triplet names are less self-evident. There are 12 triplet eighths in a whole note, for example, so the proportional value of a triplet eighth in this approach is 1/12. That the student learns to recognize the proportional relations among durations is more important here than the nomenclature.

5  See Joseph Straus, *The Music of Ruth Crawford Seeger* (New York: Cambridge University Press, 1995), 125, for a discussion of rhythmic contours in Ruth Crawford's *Diaphonic Suite.*

6 The circled numbers indicate that the string should be stopped with the fingernail of the first finger of the left hand.

7 David Lewin discusses a similar passage from Elliot Carter's String Quartet No. 1 in *Generalized Musical Intervals and Transformations* (New Haven: Yale University Press, 1987), 62–75. All four instruments play at different "tempi" in the passage and, thus, incorporate different time-span intervals between beats. To account for these differences, Lewin constructs a non-commutative GIS (Generalized Interval System) modified by units of augmentation or diminution.

8 A performance of the piece with the rhythms of the theme performed as shown in Example 7.15 may be found on the album *Beneath the Mask*, Chick Corea Elektric Band, Grp Records, Released August 13, 1991.

9 The notion of nonlinearity in music will be explored more fully in Chapter 9.

# 8 Ordered Pc Sets and Rows

1 Notice too that Stravinsky here includes pitch imbrication as an integral part of the compositional design.

2 This piece was written by Dallapiccola for his daughter, Annalibera, and presented to her as a gift on her eighth birthday. The piece has other associations as well. The English translation of the work's title is *Musical Notebook for Annalibera*, which conjures a similarly titled work, *Musical Notebook for Anna Magdalena*, either of two sets of pieces J. S. Bach gave to his second wife, Anna Magdalena Bach.

3 It is this interval duplication feature of ordered sets in general (including ordered pitch sets) that allows them to be imbricated by interval.

4 Ordered and unordered duration classes are covered in Chapter 7.

5 The twelve-tone matrix is also known by several other names, including the "Babbitt square" (named for Milton Babbitt who is credited with having invented it) and the "magic square."

6 This is not to say that Schoenberg did not use sketches of any kind. If not matrices per se, these sketches did keep track of the transpositions and inversions of rows. See Ethan Haimo, "Atonality, Analysis, and the Intentional Fallacy," *Music Theory Spectrum* 18/2 (1996): 169–70. Igor Stravinsky, too, is known to have created elaborate charts containing "pre-compositional" ideas for his twelve-tone works. Stravinsky was aware of Milton Babbitt's "magic squares" and apparently "took great delight in these [and other] little acrostics." See Charles M. Joseph, *Stravinsky Inside out* (New Haven: Yale University Press), 184–85 and 249.

7 Roger Sessions, for example, once remarked that "neither the performer nor the listener need be expected to 'follow' the series [row] through all its adventures; it is the sense, and not the *rationale* behind this, that is of primary and overwhelming importance. The series governs the composer's choice of materials; only the composer's ear and his conception determine the manner or the effect of their usage." See Roger Sessions, "To the Editor," *The Score* 23 (1958): 63.

8 All-interval rows (or "series") and their properties are discussed by Daniel Starr and Robert D. Morris in "The Structure of All-Interval Series," *Journal of Music Theory* 18/2 (1974): 364–89. Note that unisons and octaves are excluded when identifying all-interval and all-ic rows.

9 The **H** symbol stands for *Hauptstimme* or head voice. In this context, the *Hauptstimme* is the principal row form or theme in the phrase. In contrast, the *Nebenstimme* ( **N** ) is an adjacent or subordinate voice and plays an accompaniment role.

10 The discussion of invariant hexachords originates with Milton Babbitt. See Milton Babbitt, "Twelve-tone Invariants as Compositional Determinants," *The Musical Quarterly* 46/2 (1960): 246–59. Donald Martino extends Babbitt's ideas to include dyads, trichords, and tetrachords in "The Source Set and Its Aggregate Formations," *Journal of Music Theory* 5/2 (1961): 224–73. The multiplicative relations between invariant subsets (in particular those that produce cycles of fourths and fifths) have been explored by Daniel Starr, "Sets, Invariance, and Partitions," *Journal of Music Theory* 22/1 (1978): 1–42. Symmetrical as well as asymmetrical partitions of rows are discussed by Robert Morris and Brian Alegant in "The Even Partitions in Twelve-tone Music," *Music Theory Spectrum* 10 (1988): 74–101.

11 Reginald Smith Brindle, *Serial Composition* (Oxford: Oxford University Press, 1966), 21–22, counts R, I, and RI among the derived forms of a row.

12 See Milton Babbitt, "Some Aspects of Twelve-tone Composition," *The Score and IMA Magazine* 12 (1955): 53–61. Extensions of Babbitt's ideas on this subject may be found in Daniel Starr and Robert D. Morris, "A General Theory of Combinatoriality and the Aggregate (Part 1)," *Perspectives of New Music* 16/1 (1977): 3–35 and "A General Theory of Combinatoriality and the Aggregate (Part 2)," *Perspectives of New Music* 16/2

(1978): 50–84. Catherine Nolan explores the origins of combinatorial approaches to music in the theoretical writings of nineteenth-century mathematicians and musicians in "Combinatorial Space in Nineteenth- and Early Twentieth-Century Music Theory," *Music Theory Spectrum* 25/2 (2003): 205–41.

13 Each of these trichords belongs to set class 3–3 (0 1 4). The hexachords are hexatonic scales and were discussed in Chapter 1, p. 37.

14 Aggregate composition is discussed by Richard Swift, "Some Aspects of Aggregate Composition," *Perspective of New Music* 14/2 (1966): 236–48 and Reginald Smith Brindle, *Serial Composition*, 178–94.

15 Pointillism along with a number of other important textural features will be discussed more fully in Chapter 9.

16 See Reginald Smith Brindle, *Serial Composition*, 161–77 for a discussion of "integral serialism" and its analytical applications. See also Arnold Whittall, *The Cambridge Introduction to Serialism* in Cambridge Introductions to Music (New York: Cambridge University Press, 2008).

17 Robert P. Morgan's analysis of the first movement of Stockhausen's *Kreuzspiel* appears in *Anthology of Twentieth-century Music* (New York: W. W. Norton, 1992), 381–85.

18 Richard Swift provides an analysis of Babbitt's *Composition for Four Instruments* in "Some Aspects of Aggregate Composition," 239–41.

# 9 Texture and Sound Color

1 Leon Dallin makes a similar observation in *Twentieth Century Composition: A Guide to the Materials of Modern Music*, 3rd ed. (Dubuque: Wm C. Brown, 1974), 138.

2 For discussions of stratification in both tonal and non-tonal music see Philip Rupprecht, "Tonal Stratification and Uncertainty in Britten's Music," *Journal of Music Theory* 40/2 (1996): 311–46, Maury Yeston, *The Stratification of Musical Rhythm* (New Haven: Yale University Press, 1976), Edward T. Cone, "Stravinsky: The Progress of a Method," *Perspectives of New Music* 1/1 (1989): 293–301, and Wallace Berry, "On Structural Levels in Music," *Music Theory Spectrum* 2 (1980): 19–45.

3 The "parade effect" is probably derived, at least in part, from acoustical experiments Ives's father, George Ives, conducted in Danbury, Connecticut while Charles was growing up. Frank R. Rossiter describes one of these experiments in which George Ives, to the chagrin of the community, instructed two bands to march past each other while playing different pieces "so that the separate keys and rhythms were brought together in cacophonous conflict." See Frank R. Rossiter, *Charles Ives and His America* (New York: Liveright, 1975), 16.

4 Like many of the devices described in this text, collage has a long history dating from the Renaissance.

5 For an in-depth discussion of quotation and other related techniques see J. Peter Burkholder, *All Made of Tunes: Charles Ives and the Uses of Musical Borrowing* (New Haven & London: Yale University Press, 1995).

6 Igor Stravinsky's description of Webern's compositions—many of which have pointillistic textures—as "dazzling diamonds" reinforces this imagery. See Igor Stravinsky, "Foreword," *Die Riehe* 2 (1959), vii.

7 For a more extensive discussion of Penderecki's views on materials and their uses, see Danuto Mirka, "To Cut the Gordian Knot: The Timbre System of Krzysztof Penderecki," *Journal of Music Theory* 45/2 (2001): 435–56.

8 The techniques of tape composition are explored by David Keane in *Tape Music Composition* (London: Oxford University Press, 1997).

9 This institute was called the *Groupe de Recherche de Musique Concrète*.

10 These and other techniques are discussed by Charles Dodge and Thomas A. Jerse in *Computer Music: Synthesis, Composition and Performance* (New York: Schirmer Books, 1997). Synthesizer sounds are produced by means of oscillating electronic signals. Low frequency oscillators, used to modulate sounds in FM synthesis, are generally referred to as *LFOs*.

11 This term is introduced near the end of Schoenberg's prolific treatise on harmony. Schoenberg speculates that "if it is possible to create patterns out of tone colors that are differentiated according to pitch [*höhe*], patterns we call 'melodies' . . . then it must also be possible to make such progressions out of the tone colors [*Klangfarben*] of the other dimension, out of that which we call simply 'tone color', progressions whose relations with one another work with a kind of logic entirely equivalent to that logic which satisfies us in the melody of pitches [*Klanghöhen*]." See Arnold Schoenberg. *Theory of Harmony*, Roy E. Carter trans. (Berkeley: University of California Press, 1978 [1922]), 421.

12 See Alfred Cramer, "Schoenberg's 'Klangfarbenmelodie': A Principal of Early Atonal Harmony," *Music Theory Spectrum* 24/1 (2002): 2. Since the time of Pythagoras, acousticians have understood that instrumental timbre stems from the number and strength of the overtones present in a sound.

13   Quoted in Marina Lobanova, *György Ligeti: Style, Ideas, Poetics* (Berlin: Kuhn, 2002), 126. (Emphasis mine.)

14   This quote, attributed to Christian Wolfe, is cited by John Cage in *Silence: Lectures and Writings by John Cage* (Middletown: Wesleyan University Press, 1961), 54 and Leonard B. Meyer, "The End of the Renaissance?" in *Music, the Arts, and Ideas: Patterns and Predictions in Twentieth-Century Culture* (Chicago: The University of Chicago Press, 1967), 72.

15   See, for example, Jonathan D. Kramer, *The Time of Music: New Meanings, New Temporalities, New Listening Strategies* (New York: Schirmer Books, 1978), 178 and Leonard B. Meyer, "The End of the Renaissance?," 72.

16   Both Leonard Meyer, "The End of the Renaissance?," 72–73, and Jonathan D. Kramer, *The Time of New Music*, 23–25, have suggested that linearity in music reflects the Western emphasis on progress and causality while nonlinearity is more compatible with Eastern conceptions of time, which tend to be more conceptually cyclical in nature.

17   For a more detailed description of performative silence see the author's "Anti-Teleological Art: Articulating Meaning through Silence" in *Approaches to Meaning in Music*, Byron Almén and Edward Pearsall eds. (Bloomington: Indiana University Press, 2006), 41–61.

18   John Tavener, *The Music of Silence: A Composer's Testament*, Brian Keeble ed. (London: Faber and Faber, 1999), 157–58. Interestingly, other composers too make references to religious subjects when describing the silent aspects of their music. These include Olivier Messiaen, who associates silence with the "mysteries of Jesus-Christ" in his *"Regard du silence"* from *Vingt Regards sur l'Enfant-Jésus* (See Example 9.21), Ernest Bloch, who describes the first movement of his Judeo inspired *Avodath Ha-Kodesh* (Sacred Service) by saying that "first there is a Silent Meditation which comes in before you to take your soul out and look at what it contains," and Charles Ives, who stipulates that the offstage strings in his *The Unanswered Question* are meant to "represent 'The Silences of the Druids—Who Know, See and Hear Nothing.'"

19   This reading of the passage reflects my own way of hearing it. The concept of silence is a slippery one. Hence, the perception of structural silence may vary from listener to listener.

20   For a more in–depth exploration of silence in this movement see Matthew Hill, "Faith, Silence and Darkness Entwined in Messiaen's '*Regard du silence*,'" In *Silence, Music, Silent Music*, Nicky Losseff and Jenny Doctor eds. (Burlington: Ashgate, 2007), 37–52.

21   See John Cage, *Silence*, 7–8.

22   John Cage, 4′33″ (1960).

23   See Joanna Demers, *Listening Through the Noise: The Aesthetics of Experimental Electronic Music* (Oxford: Oxford University Press, 2010), 171.

24   See Kim Cascone, "The Aesthetics of Failure: 'Post-Digital' Tendencies in Contemporary Computer Music," *Computer Music Journal* 24/4 (2000): 12.

25   See Pauline Oliveros, *Sonic Meditations*, V (Baltimore: Smith Publications, 1974).

26   Dora Hanninen makes a similar observation in "Orientation, Criteria, Segments: A General Theory of Segmentation for Music Analysis," *Journal of Music Theory* 45/2 (2001): 345.

## Aural Skills Supplement

1   Edward Pearsall and John Wm. Schaffer, "Shape/Interval Contours and Their Ordered Transformations: A Motivic Approach to Twentieth-Century Music Analysis and Aural Skills," *College Music Symposium* 45 (2005): 58.

2   Edward Pearsall and John Wm. Schaffer, "Shape/Interval Contours and Their Ordered Transformations," 57.

3   John Wm. Schaffer, Unpublished Manuscript, University of Wisconsin (*ca.* 1993), v.

4   Similar intervals are those that belong to the same step class. (A step class includes all scale steps with the same ordinal number regardless of size: seconds, thirds, fourths, fifths, etc.) An exercise with dissimilar intervals, then, might contain a second and a fourth, but not a minor second and a major second. We will also assume that fourths and fifths are similar even though they do not belong to the same step class because they are inversionally equivalent and near each other in size. Intervals in twentieth-century music are not always grouped according to step class, of course. To the extent that students are familiar with intervals in tonal music, however, these distinctions may still play a role in their perception of twentieth-century music.

5   The contour adjacency series keeps track of the ascents and descents of a series of pitches, expressed as (+)s and (–)s. (See Chapter 7, p. 164.)

# Acknowledgment of Sources

Many institutions and individuals have kindly granted permission to reproduce a generous number of musical examples in this textbook. Every effort has been made to obtain permission for use of previously published material. Any permission holder who feels that he or she has not been properly acknowledged is invited to contact Routledge, who will endeavor to correct any omissions in future editions of this work.

*Elegy for Anne Frank* by Lukas Foss. Copyright © 1991 by Carl Fischer LLC. International copyright secured. All rights reserved. Used by permission.

*Thirteen Ways of Looking at a Blackbird* by Lukas Foss. Used by permission.

*Prologue*, measures 1–2. Composer: Gérard Grisey. © Universal Music Publishing Ricordi.

*Quatuor pour la fin du temps*; VII, measures 1–2, 62–65; VI, measures 1–4. Composer: Olivier Messiaen. © Editions Durand.

*Vingt regards sur l'enfant Jesus*, measures 87–92. Composer: Olivier Messiaen. © Editions Durand.

*Napoli*, measures 128–132. Composer: Francis Poulenc. © Editions Salabert.

*Valse*, Measures 1–9. Composer: Francis Poulenc. © Editions Durand.

Luigi Dallapiccola, "Contrapunctus Primus" from *Quaderno musicale di Annalibera* for piano.

© Sugarmusic S.p.A.—Edizioni Suvini Zerboni, Milan (Italy).

"Little Things that Count" written by John Patitucci/Dave Weckl. Copyright © published by Iccutitap/Dave Weckl Music. All rights reserved. Used by permission.

# Subject and Author Index

# Index of Musical Examples